CP lot 209

FOLIES DE PARIS

The Rise and Fall of French Operetta

FOLIES DE PARIS

The Rise and Fall of French Operetta

James Harding

CHAPPELL AND COMPANY / ELM TREE BOOKS · LONDON

Chappell & Company Limited
50 New Bond Street, London, W1A 2BR

London   Amsterdam   Brussels   Hamburg
Johannesburg   Madrid   Milan   Paris
Stockholm   Sydney   Toronto   Wellington
Zurich   New York

in association with
Elm Tree Books Limited
Garden House, 57-59 Long Acre, London WC2E 9JL

ISBN 0 903443 28 7

Printed by Clarke, Doble & Brendon Ltd.,
Plymouth and London

CONTENTS

Acknowledgements
Introduction

Overture and Beginners
   i.   And in the beginning was Adam   11
   ii.   A daughter gone to the bad   17
   iii.   Jeannette and her long-running marriage   20
   iv.   A loony   22

Act I The Age of Gold
   i.   'The little Jew'   37
   ii.   The conquest of Paris   43
   iii.   'The Mozart of the Champs-Elysées'   46
   iv.   Orpheus goes down to the Underworld   48
   v.   Friday nights with Jacques   52
   vi.   From Helen of Troy to native bitch   57
   vii.   'Very nice, Liverpool!'   67
   viii.   The last illusion   72

Act II The Age of Respectability
   i.   The cripple and Dr Miracle   78
   ii.   The father of Madame Angot's daughter   83
   iii.   A little Duke   86
   iv.   Old friends and a parrot   90
   v.   To end with Ali Baba   92

Entr'acte
   Higher fliers   97

Act III A Late Flowering
   i.   Miss Eliot's bottom   105
   ii.   Gallimaufry   110
   iii.   Success in blue stockings   121
   iv.   A second marriage   128

v. Véronique and the battle of Pelléas   132
vi. Some very Parisian talents   140

Act IV Decline and Fall
   i. Reynaldo from Venezuela   151
   ii. The boobs of Tirésias   166

Bibliography   174
Index   177

For

Alan Ridout

creator, life-enhancer, musician

Acknowledgements

As usual my gratitude is due to Mlle Martine Kahane and her colleagues at the Bibliothèque de l'Opéra, Paris; to Mrs D. L. Mackay of Duns; and to Mrs Stella Mayes-Reed for her photographic skill. I must also acknowledge the sympathetic co-operation of Mr David Holmes and his colleagues, Chappell & Co. Ltd, and of Monsieur Behar of Chappell France. Mr Vivian Liff and Mr George Stuart kindly enabled me to draw on the resources of the celebrated Stuart-Liff Collection. Quotations from the operettas *Phi-Phi* and *Trois jeunes filles nues* are made by permission of the publishers, Editions Francis Salabert, Paris.

Illustrations

ADOLPHE ADAM
HERVE
OFFENBACH
Caricature of OFFENBACH
HORTENSE SCHNEIDER
ZULMA BOUFFAR
ANNA JUDIC
A scene from OFFENBACH's *Le Voyage à la Lune*
DESIRE
LEONCE
JEANNE GRANIER
ROBERT PLANQUETTE
CHARLES LECOCQ
EDMOND AUDRAN
ANDRE MESSAGER
JEAN PERIER
JEAN PERIER and MARIETTE SULLY
MAX DEARLY
REYNALDO HAHN
HENRI CHRISTINE
SACHA GUITRY
YVONNE PRINTEMPS
ALBERT WILLEMETZ
A Scene from *Mozart* with SACHA GUITRY
    and YVONNE PRINTEMPS

Introduction

Fred Barlow, despite his name, was a Frenchman. He wrote operettas and could dash off a pop song as easily as a requiem mass. Somewhere, I have no doubt, there exists a scholar who has dedicated a lifetime to the study of Barlow's work. Why, this scholar will demand, have I not paid tribute to the neglected master?

Perhaps, in the remoter Hebrides, or in a quiet corner of Lostwithiel, there dwells another learned man who devotes himself to the music of that Parisianised Hungarian, Joseph Kosma. He will be annoyed that I do not so much as refer to that prolific musician. Some will be shocked to find no mention of Tiarko Richepin, the instigator of *Rapatipatoum*. Where, still others will ask, is the long overdue appraisal of Louis Beydts and Moïse Simon? What, they will clamour, has become of Vincent Scotto, whose output of over four thousand songs and seventy operettas includes the immortal *Gangsters du Château d'If?*

Such are the hazards of writing a book on French operetta. There is no composer, however obscure, however specialized, who does not have his champion. Reasons of space alone prevent me from distinguishing more than a small number among the hundreds of musicians who have attempted the genre. And we should remember that for every Offenbach and every Messager there are dozens of camp-followers like Louis Varney and Edouard Legouix who stumble along, way behind, at the rear.

In France the operetta as we know it today was born with Adolphe Adam. It peeps forth, somewhat untidily, from the lighter works of Auber and Halévy. The 'loony composer' Hervé gained his nickname by developing the form and endowing it with the crazed irreverence that was his hallmark. Offenbach presided over the golden age and won immortality by forever linking the genre to his name. Middle-aged respectability set in with Lecocq. Then came the autumn flowering of Messager and Reynaldo Hahn.

Even earlier than this, by the nineteen-hundreds at least, the mainstream of French operetta had begun to lose its Gallic flavour.

The initiative passed elsewhere. Viennese and Americans made up for a late start by exporting their own very successful creations. The Paris theatre was invaded by the cake-walk and fox-trot. *Oklahoma!* and *Annie du Far-West* cast their obliterating shadows. *Comment réussir dans les affaires sans vraiment se fatiguer* proved but a camouflage for *How to Succeed in Business Without Really Trying*. A hint of the native genius managed to flicker again in *Irma la douce*, which in its London version enabled Elizabeth Seal to display her charming talent. But the lamp had gone out.

I hope, in chronicling the rise and fall of French operetta, that I have done justice to the quantity of skilful, attractive and accomplished music which its best exponents left behind. In their day they had some brief moments of glory amid the inevitable disappointments that are the lot of anyone who writes for the theatre. They were hard-working craftsmen who sometimes hit on excellence. Now they are mostly forgotten — not least in France.

While charting the paths followed by Offenbach and others, I have also turned aside occasionally to map some pleasing by-ways. Here may be found such 'classical' composers as Saint-Saëns, Chabrier, Honegger and Poulenc, all of whom amused themselves from time to time with composing operetta. It is a fallacy to imagine that perfection can only be achieved in the larger forms. Fragonard, in his way, is as successful as Titian, and Messager, no less than Mozart, is lord of his particular domain. Artistic snobbery takes no heed of relative values.

OVERTURE AND BEGINNERS

i.

And in the beginning was Adam . . .

Monsieur Adolphe Adam was feeling decidedly unwell. He neither spoke nor understood English. The streets of London confused him. He found Englishmen haughty, their women unresponsive. And his wife had chosen this very moment to become pregnant. Of course, he had to agree it was not entirely her fault.

The twenty-nine year old composer was lucky enough to find a doctor who knew his language and could diagnose his ailment. Fortified with a prescription, Adam hastened to the chemist. The man of science had no French, his customer no English. They jabbered at each other uncomprehendingly. Then, rummaging in his memory, Adam produced a few shreds of Latin. The chemist responded. At last they found themselves able to carry on a form of conversation by translating literally into the ancient tongue. A box of pills was proffered. Later, when Adam read the instructions, he was horrified: *'capiendum totâ nocte'* could only mean "Spend the whole night taking pills"! His doctor enlightened him. The chemist had transposed the English idiom bodily into Latin. What he really meant was that the pills should be taken each night.

Why had Adam come to this damp island and plunged into such a strange and unsettling existence? The theatre business in Paris, where he had been struggling to make his name, was still disrupted by the events of 1830, when insurrection forced Charles X from the throne and replaced him with Louise-Philippe. (It was also the year of Victor Hugo's *Hernani* which was to revolutionize French drama with the same effectiveness as the insurgents who smashed the old political régime.) Two years later cholera broke out. All in all, Paris, at that time, was not a favourable place for a young composer with theatrical ambitions. So, with his wife, who happened to be the sister of the manager of Covent Garden, a

Frenchman called Laporte, Adam thought he would try his luck in England. Laporte invited the couple to stay with him at his house in London and also at his cottage in a place Adam transcribes as "Whamley". The exact name of that typical English village may be left to the reader's imagination.

England was an odd country, with musical customs that were even odder. One Thursday evening Adam heard an opera at Covent Garden and was so impressed by the excellent performance that he later enthused about it to the conductor. "If," said the latter, "you decide to hear it again, above all avoid a Saturday evening." He smiled meaningly and left Adam perplexed. His curiosity aroused, Adam came back on the Saturday. At first the overture went quite well. Then the oboist fluffed his solo. The clarinet quacked disgracefully. The brass rumbled dyspeptically. The violins went horribly out of tune. Worse still, the players sprawled about all over the place. One of them stuck the slide of his trombone into the pocket of a neighbour. Another, a double-bass player, put aside his instrument and gravely drew his bow back and forth over a stool placed between his legs. Afterwards, to Adam's increasing surprise, he learned that the singers were in no way put out by the antics of the orchestra. At last he asked the stage-manager why the playing was always so bad on a Saturday. "Because," came the reply, "Saturday is pay-day in the English theatre, and the musicians never fail to go straight from the cashier to the pub."

In London, thanks to the support of his brother-in-law, Adam had two operas produced at Covent Garden. *The First Campaign* was well received. *The Dark Diamond* ran for only three performances. The ever-thrifty composer utilized the music of both these operas for later works given in Paris. He did the same again with his three-act ballet, *Faust*, which appeared at the King's Theatre. This was to give the economical Adam some of the material he used in his best-known work, the ballet *Giselle*. London was not, he decided, proving to be such a bad place.

Social triumph came when Adam was received by Lady Blessington. She gave him her poem "The Aeolian Harp" which he set and respectfully had engraved by a London publisher. His command of English was now equal to the inspirations of nobility.

When Adam returned to Paris in the mid-eighteen-thirties, he was an experienced musician. His father had been a piano teacher who counted Gounod's mother as one of his pupils. Perhaps because Adam *père* knew how fragile a musical career could be, he tried to discourage his son from taking up the art. During the hours when he thought the boy to be at school, the doubly precocious Adolphe was teaching himself harmony in the attic of a dressmaker who was also his mistress. Later he was permitted to enter the Conservatoire. There he studied composition under Boieldieu, a composer of many operas, among which *La Dame blanche* was not the least notable.

As soon as Adam left the Conservatoire he was drawn into theatrical life. His father, still disapproving, continued to provide him with board and lodge but would allow him no money. Adam gave a few lessons and wrote potboilers. These became even more necessary because of a novel arrangement he had made with the drummer in a theatre orchestra. This enabled him to join the band as triangle player on condition that he paid the drummer the forty sous he received at each performance. For the privilege of at least being admitted behind the scenes, Adam avowed, he gladly paid. This first professional engagement is, in a way, symbolic, for the melodies Adam was later to write are as frail as the sound of that tinkling instrument.

So keen was his enthusiasm that he offered to supply music free of charge to songwriters. He even went so far, in the early days of struggle, as to write curtain-raisers and refuse all payment: it was reward enough for him to see his work played in a theatre. Such persistence made him known at least as a ready collaborator. It endeared him to the famous Eugène Scribe, at that time a powerful figure in the world of opera.

There was nothing Scribe did not know about the stage. His eye for theatrical effect was unerring. The action of the plays he wrote developed with immaculate precision. It did not matter that the characters were stock symbols or that the things they said were expressed in the dullest of platitudes. What counted was the speed of events and the shrewd pacing of climax. Scribe was such a brilliant producer that he could make a kitchen chair play a vital part in a drama merely by positioning it in a certain way.

Having gained Scribe's favour by not insisting on payment for one of the early trifles, Adam next worked with him on a one-act piece called *Le Chalet*. This time he was paid — which is just as well, for *Le Chalet* was a success and often came up for revival after its initial run. It is a light-hearted work with three characters. The overture, which contains a perky march that Offenbach might not have disdained to write, sets the tone immediately: one of good-humoured indulgence, the mood that is created by a good dinner and a healthy digestion. The tunes are bright and often strangely innocent. None of them is very long, for Adam knew that his audience wanted melody that was easy to grasp and would settle in the mind just long enough to stay there on the way home after a pleasant evening in the theatre. A duet, in which the bass demands the return of his mistress from the tenor, is one of the most charming things in the score. It is all very agreeable and very neatly tailored.

Adam and his contemporaries described this sort of thing as "opéra-comique". Another such was *Le Toréador*, a delightfully amoral two-acter in which Don Belflor, an elderly husband, resolves at last to live in peace with his beautiful young wife and her lover. It is a practical arrangement that brings credit to all concerned for their good sense. The trio in the first act is based on the traditional tune of "Ah vous dirai-je, maman!", better known here as "Baa-Baa Black Sheep", and flowers into variations that Mozart might have written but did not. Adam composed the whole piece in less than a week.

On a slightly higher plane was *Le Postillon de Longjumeau*, perhaps the greatest success he knew in his lifetime. It was so popular that one of its refrains became a well-known catch phrase:

Oh! oh! oh! qu'il était beau
Le postillon de Longjumeau.

This opera gave to the town of Longjumeau a fame that had never come its way before. Grateful citizens built a statue to Adam which is still there. Not so, however, the inn-sign which had been put up earlier on. Invading Germans took that away as a souvenir during the Franco-Prussian War. The opera and its joyous hero were dangerously well known beyond the Rhine.

Si j'étais roi was another big hit. One of Adam's librettists for this work, a writer who often collaborated with him, was Adolphe Dennery, the author of some two hundred plays, who could adapt *Uncle Tom's Cabin* for the stage with as much aplomb as Jules Verne's *Around the World in Eighty Days*. He was, in private life, a witty man. Why, enquired a friend, did he not put some of this wit into his plays? Because, replied he, if he did so his public would become worried and suspect he had not written the play they were watching. Dennery was cursed with a shrewish wife who often went out on her own in the evening. A ritual dialogue ensued each time.

'Where are you going?' Dennery would ask.
'Wherever I like,' she would snap in reply.
'Very well — but when are you coming back?'
'Whenever I like.'
'All right then — but mind, no later!'

In old age one night they both sallied forth together on a rare expedition to the theatre. During the interval they had a terrible quarrel. His wife, having run out of arguments, finally hissed at him: "Cuckold!"

Dennery was silent for a short while. Then, staring at her grey hair, her raddled cheeks, her sagging figure, he made the reply: "Not any longer!"

For Adam, as for Dennery, Paris and the theatre were all that really mattered. Adam had no use for the country except as a place where he could write music free of interruption. There, at a little table placed in a flowery grove, he composed, within two months, the whole of *Si j'étais roi*, the sheets of manuscript being rushed to the theatre where rehearsals had already begun. As soon as it was finished he started on another opera.

Inevitably he was tempted into theatrical management. By 1847 he had fallen out of favour with the director of the Opéra-Comique, that established institution where, until then, his work had regularly been performed. He decided, with a partner, to set up what was to be called the Théâtre National where he would produce not only his own operas, but those of young composers who showed promise. Having assembled many hundred thousands of francs by way of promissory notes, mortgages and loans, he bought up the premises of a well-known circus in the boulevard du Temple. It was a good situation, for the boulevard du Temple, since demolished to emerge as the Place de la République, contained many theatres. They specialized in colourful melodramas — of gentle maidens betrayed, villains foiled, and young heroes triumphant — which gave the thoroughfare its nickname the "boulevard du Crime". It has been vividly re-created in the film *Les Enfants du Paradis*.

Adam opened his Théâtre National with an opera for which Dennery wrote the libretto and a thirty year-old Aimé Maillart provided the music. A few years later Maillart was to compose *Les Dragons de Villars*, a famous operetta of its time that went through many revivals. That Adam had a flair for discerning young talent was also proved by his selection of an aspiring 'cello player called Offenbach to write a new work for his theatre. Before Offenbach's *L'Alcôve* could be produced, however, Adam was out of business.

Once again political events blighted his career. In 1848 Louis-Philippe's cosy reign came to an abrupt end. The Second Republic was proclaimed and Louis-Napoleon took his first step towards absolute power. From the roof of his theatre Adam could see fighting in the streets. Cries of *'Vive le roi!'* were drowned by shouts of *'Vive la réforme!'* Shops were shut and barricades thrown up.

Adam struggled on. He was losing over a thousand francs a night, and soon there was no money left at all. In the attempt to meet enormous debts he sold all his possessions. Those of his belongings which he cherished most he lodged with a pawnbroker. Of them all, he was able to redeem only a diamond snuff box, a gift from the Prussian king, and that after a long wait of three years.

He did not complain. Scribe came to the rescue with a new libretto and soon he was composing again. As a member of the Académie des Beaux Arts, to which he had lately been elected, he drew a small but regular fee that helped to mollify his creditors. A teaching post at the Conservatoire also brought in useful revenue. He found that he could earn money by writing music criticism. Here his sense of humour did not desert him. Once he warmly praised a composer and declared his work to be "almost a masterpiece". The composer wrote to him declaring that the article contined one word too much: that word was 'almost'.

On the whole Adam was a happy man. He adored the world of the theatre and asked for nothing more than to be involved in it. In 1850, on the death of his first wife from whom he was separated for many years, he married the companion who had given him all her money and seen it swallowed up in the disaster of the Théâtre National. She continued to love him. On his fiftieth birthday he wrote: "Thanks be to Heaven, there is only my birth certificate to remind me of it." He enjoyed life. The singer Marie Grenier, who first played the part of Venus in Offenbach's *Orphée aux enfers*, was a beautiful blonde nicknamed "Eve" because of her initimate links with . . . Adam.

In 1856, by a graceful turn of events, Offenbach commissioned Adam to write a little opera for him. It was Offenbach, now, who was the rising man, with a theatre of his own. Adam obliged with *Les Pantins de Violette*, an airy trifle involving pierrots and Colombines, magicians and Punchinellos. Never had his brittle melodies sounded so appealing.

Four days after the first performance of *Les Pantins de Violette*, he spent an evening at the Opéra. Then he called on a friend at the Théâtre Lyrique before going home. He wrote some letters and went to bed. Next morning he was found dead. He was fifty-three. Yet within that short life he had contrived to keep his name well known in the theatre for over a quarter of a century.

It was by his grand operas that Adam hoped to be remembered. But such cold and unmoving productions as *Richard en Palestine* had no hope of survival. Where he excelled was in the simple tunes of his comic operas and ballets. *Giselle* remains his most substantial monument as the greatest of Romantic ballets. He deserves tribute, also, as a pioneer of French operetta.

ii

A daughter gone to the bad

Saint-Saëns once remarked that operetta was a daughter of the opéra-comique who had gone to the bad. Although, he added thoughtfully, girls who go to the bad are not always bereft of charm. We can experience her charm in the works of Adolphe Adam, where ease and grace are the essentials. He acknowledged as much when he wrote that ideas came quickly to him, smiling and bustling and 'at risk of disarranging their pretty dresses'. With *Le Toréador*, *Les Pantins de Violette* and so many other genial *oeuvrettes*, he aspired to produce nothing more than an evening's amusement.

It will not do to translate 'opéra-comique' as 'comic-opera'. *Carmen* and *Pelléas et Melisande* have been, on the face of it, unlikely members of the repertory at the old Opéra-Comique in Paris. At one time it was possible to distinguish *opéra* ('grand opera' in English) from *opéra-comique* by the latter's use of spoken dialogue. History has blurred the difference. The originals of operetta lie buried in the ancient fairs of Paris where the showmen of booths and open-air stages invited the crowd to witness comic turns tricked out with songs and dances. Jugglers, dancers and tightrope-walkers combined to provide entertainment for the mob.

As early as the opening years of the eighteenth century there were parodies of operas like *Alceste* and *Télémaque*. Such parody was known as 'opéra comique'. So operetta, having sprung from mockery and the ridicule of exalted sentiment, is doubly rakish in its descent.

Such works of Adam as *Le Toréador* and *Les Pantins de Violette* show clearly how operetta derives from the old opéra-comique and returns to a simpler form of music. The plot is generally light-hearted or comic. The treatment is airy and avoids moral judgements. These qualities appear in not a few of the opéras-comiques being written at that time by the distinguished head of the Conservatoire, Daniel François Esprit Auber, an elegant Parisian figure who composed many stage-works. Indeed, his very first piece, *L'Erreur d'un moment*, has a distinct flavour of operetta.

Auber used to say that as a young man he loved music so much that it had become his mistress — but, he would add wryly, 'since then it has become my wife'. He wrote at great speed, partly out of habit, partly because the old urge to conquer audiences was not yet stilled. His industrious routine was aided by an ability to catch up on his sleep anywhere and at any given moment: in his box at the Opéra, in the drearier moments of committee meetings at the Académie des Beaux Arts, or during auditions at the Conservatoire.

Adam, for whom there was no relaxation from music, used to envy Auber the pursuits that enabled him to enjoy a change of subject from time to time. Auber loved women and horses. He relished both with untiring vigour until the end of his life at the age of close on ninety. His idea of Heaven was to trot through the Bois de Boulogne with a pretty woman at his side. The dinner parties he gave were noted for the lavish fare and the number of women present, far exceeding that of the men, who strove to outshine each other with their jewels and toilettes while the host feasted his little black eyes on them. Music, by an unwritten law, was never mentioned at these grand receptions. The dapper, small-featured Auber preferred to talk theatrical gossip. Or he might take aside one of the guests who happened to be a singer and grant her an audition in a more intimate chamber.

Equally prone to the spirit of operetta was Auber's colleague, Fromenthal Halévy. Today no one ever revives any of that chain of operas which brought Halévy fame during his lifetime. He was the uncle of Ludovic, Offenbach's librettist, and the father of

Geneviève, Bizet's wife, who was to be a source for Proust's Duchesse de Guermantes. Himself a precocious student who knew everything from an early age, he became a teacher at the Conservatoire and actually wrote a substantial treatise on counterpoint which was supposed to be the work of his master Cherubini. He was nearly always too busy to teach his own students and would often set them exercises while he frenziedly completed his latest opera, or would get the brightest of them to conduct a lesson so that he could use the time to finish off a scene or three.

The grandest of the grand operas this amiable man wrote is perhaps *La Juive* which persisted into this century as a vehicle for Caruso. Against this must be set works such as *L'Eclair*, which is operetta in all but name. It has, in the manner of Adam, a small cast of four. The story tells of a naval officer struck blind by lightning and nursed back to health by one of two sisters. When his sight is restored, he falls gratefully in love with the wrong sister — though in time the mistake of his eyes is corrected by the prompting of his heart. The style is a pleasant change from the Meyerbeerian pomps that Halévy went in for too often.

On a lower level than Halévy or Auber came the now entirely forgotten Antoine-Louis Clapisson. With them, however, he shared extreme facility. Commissioned to write a one-act opéra-comique with the proviso that it must be delivered within a fortnight, he produced the goods on the dot. Such are the ways of the theatre that it was not actually put on for another year. And when eventually it did appear, *Le Pendu* ran for only thirteen nights. Clapisson persisted until he had written his biggest success, a work with the barely grammatical title of *Gibby ia cornemuse*, which, more correctly, should have been 'Gibby the Bagpipe Player'. The fortunate Clapisson could now buy himself comforts up to then denied him. He laid carpets on his bare floor and installed a heater in the dining-room. *La Fanchonnette*, another of his many opuscules, confirmed his popularity and earned him enough to extend his valuable collection of old musical instruments, a hobby which, like Auber's horses and women, gave him a rest from music.

As he grew older he sought refuge from the uncertainties of theatre life. By arrangement with the authorities he made over to the Conservatoire his rich assortment of musical instsruments. In return he was paid a lump sum and a pension. He was also given the post of curator, with his own rooms, at the Conservatoire. The

instruments may still be seen there, a little dusty, but piously
preserved. Here, his existence undisturbed, save by the irreverent
jeers of Bizet, he lived a pleasant life surrounded by his own viols
and rebecs and lutes. It did not last long. One day, feeling a trifle
indisposed, he took a purge of an imprudently volcanic nature.
The result finished the poor man off completely. With him died
Gibby la cornemuse and La Fanchonnette.

iii

Jeannette and her long-running marriage

Music could be heard everywhere in Paris during the eighteen-
fifties. There was music in the churches, where, before long, the
reforms initiated by Gounod and others were to bring back the
purer styles of Bach and Palestrina. There was music — a great
deal of it — in the drawing-rooms. The popular tone was one of
romantic wistfulness. Young ladies sang of unrequited love and of
heroines rewarded for their devotion. The sentiments expressed
were impeccable, if a trifle dull. Publishers who would not dream
of putting out quartets or symphonies were delighted to pay a
fashionable composer anything up to seven hundred pounds for an
album of half a dozen songs.

Singers were admired and their careers followed as if they had
been twentieth-century pop stars. Packed houses waited anxiously
for the moment when the prima donna reached her famous note or
embroidered the music with the dazzling roulades expected of her.
Tenors were cherished for their heroic battles to dominate the
orchestra. Basses were prized for their ability to produce the lowest
note possible to mankind.

At the Opéra, assisted by Rossini, Auber and Halévy, the
powerful Meyerbeer held audiences in fee. The Théâtre des
Italiens was the home of those singers whose flashy vocal antics
delighted the sporting instincts of their admirers: Cruvelli of the
thrilling voice; Alboni with her easy span of more than two octaves;
Tamburini with his dramatic baritone. Things were cosier at the
Opéra-Comique, where, with occasional help from eighteenth-
century light-heartedness in the shape of Grétry, undemanding
fare was provided by Hérold, Boieldieu, and those two prolific
workmen Adam and Auber. Their opéras-comiques were favoured

by middle-class audiences who, not keen on the modish and glittering clientèle at the Opéra and the Théâtre des Italiens, were more interested in patronising light but decent entertainment to which they could safely escort their marriageable daughters.

In 1852 a new name was added to the repertory of the Opéra-Comique. Victor Massé was an ambitious Breton who early made his mark as a reliable composer of drawing-room songs. *Galathée* signalled his first success on the stage with an amusing version of the tale used by Bernard Shaw for *Pygmalion*. His librettists were Jules Barbier and Michel Carré, who later worked on Gounod's *Faust* and provided verse for many other composers to set. The tunes, like Adam's, are brief and immediately attractive, and they have a touch that betrays the influence of Halévy.

Next year brought even greater luck to Massé with *Les Noces de Jeannette*. This one-act piece, detailing the quarrels between a country girl and her unpolished fiancé before they get married, won immense popularity. The rôle of Jeannette was sung by Madame Miolan, a tyrannical prima donna who, as the first Marguerite in *Faust* and as the earliest Mireille, drove Gounod quite crazy. At the time of *Jeannette* she was not yet so unmanageable, and her portrayal of the simple-hearted but shrewd heroine much appealed to audiences. There is a scene where Jeannette vocalizes a duet with solo flute in imitation of the nightingale: it is not difficult to imagine the "brilliant" effects with which La Miolan gilded it.

Success and failure chequered Massé's life in a recurring pattern. While *Galathée* and *Les Noces de Jeannette* came up again and again for revival during his lifetime and long afterwards, his dozen or so other works never really established themselves. Though he held important posts at the Opéra and the Conservatoire, and succeeded Auber at the Académie des Beaux Arts, he was later forced to resign through ill-health towards the end of his life.

He had to bear with many irritations, not the least of them the well-meant but annoying remarks of people who went to his first nights. 'Very good, my dear Massé,' they would say, all unconsciously turning the dagger in the wound, 'and when are you going to give us a successor to that lovely *Noces de Jeannette*?'

Galathée contains a very pretty entr'acte where horn and flute carry on a pleasing dialogue. Massé was, understandably, fond of it. One evening at the Opéra-Comique the flautist, having had two teeth extracted earlier, was not at all sure of his *embouchure* and

asked for the entr'acte to be left out. His request was granted. Now
Massé had chosen that very evening to come to hear it. The details
were a little dim in his memory and he was anxious to renew
acquaintance with this favourite passage. Suddenly the curtain rose
on the second act without the interval music having been heard.
Massé, already embittered by his disappointments, fell into a rage
of frustration. Somehow the anecdote is typical of his career.

iv

A loony

In the fatal year of 1848 Adam revived his own opéra-comique, *Le
Brasseur de Preston*, and was able to put on a new work before ruin
and bankruptcy overcame him and his Théâtre Lyrique. His saga
of the North-Country brewer did as well as it ever had. The new
piece, a farrago entitled *Don Quichotte et Sancho Pança*, had
been written by a twenty-three year old composer and was
discovered by Adam at a performance in a little Montmatre
theatre. The composer's name was Hervé. He was tall and
handsome, with fair hair and a fine moustache, blue eyes, and a
determined chin. Offstage he dressed so elegantly that he might
have been taken for a cavalry officer. Onstage — for he acted and
sang as well as writing music — he was unrecognizable under
grotesque make-up. His speciality was zany, knockabout humour.
With a cold impassiveness which underlined the comic effect, he
delivered absurdity after absurdity that eventually overcame the
most difficult audiences.

Hervé had written *Don Quichotte et Sancho Pança* at the
request of the well-known comedian Désiré. The latter, whose real
name was funnier than the pseudonym he chose (Courtecuisse,
meaning short thigh), was plump and squat. Hervé was tall and
thin. They made perfect foils to each other as Don Quixote and
Sancho Panza. When Adam saw them performing together, he
immediately signed them up for his own theatre. It was virtually
the last production he sponsored at the Théâtre Lyrique.

According to some historians the first night of *Don Quichotte
et Sancho Pança*, on 5 March 1848, marks the introduction of
operetta into France. The word itself was not to be used until 1856
when it was coined to describe an obscure one-acter called

Madame Mascarille by the even obscurer Jules Bovery. Certainly nothing quite like Hervé's work had been seen before. Beside it, even the lightest of opéras-comiques appeared sedate in the extreme. One of the songs was taken up and featured in vaudeville and revues. Long after Adam's Théâtre Lyrique had collapsed, *Don Quichotte* went on popping up again and again in various Parisian theatres.

The young man whose first success this was had been born as Florimond Ronger at Houdain, a mining town in that unlovely region known as the Pas de Calais. His father was a policeman, his mother a young and pretty Spaniard. The marriage between the staid representative of public order and the passionate girl from Madrid resembled a promising situation in one of those operettas which the son was later to turn out by the dozen. Florimond was six years old when his father died suddenly. What was there to do in the bleak and grimy surroundings of Houdain? Widow and child emigrated to Paris.

There Madame Ronger found work in the church of Saint-Roch. Her son became a member of the choir. Already he had a good voice and a feeling for music. He went on to learn basic harmony and the organ. His mother, sensing a gift, arranged lessons for him with a teacher at the Conservatoire. Impressed by his talent, the teacher introduced him to Auber who gave him lessons in competition.

One day Florimond went for a walk in the country outside Paris. As he wandered along, he heard the sound of an organ. It was coming from the church of Bicêtre, that roomy hospice which, built by Louis XIII to accommodate his wounded soldiers, has since been used as a centre for chaining prisoners on the way to the galleys and at last as a home for the insane. Eagerly Florimond went in.

By that time service was over and everyone had left the church. Urged by a sudden whim, he clambered up the dark little stairway that led to the organ and came face to face with the startled organ blower. After some argument he persuaded the man to carry on. Then, his short legs dangling from the seat, he improvised and sang an *'O Salutaris'*.

'Who is taking the liberty of playing the organ now?' came an astonished demand from the vestry. The priest appeared. Explanations followed. The Abbé Paradis, for such was his reassuring name, ended by offering Florimond a job as organist.

His mother also, added the benevolent cleric, could join him and work in the laundry. A week later mother and son were installed.

The boy was still only fourteen years old. Between playing the organ he had to complete his general education. His day began at six o'clock in the morning and, after music had alternated with sessions of French, history, philosophy and reading, it ended at midnight. By careful saving from the proceeds of lessons given at neighbouring schools he was able to buy a small harmonium and install it in the apartment he shared with his mother.

From his windows he could observe the patients in the yard below. Usually docile and quiet, they would sometimes break out, for no reason at all, into violent argument and even fights, and nurses would have to intervene to separate them. On one occasion, when a sudden dispute flared up, he started playing the harmonium. As if by magic, the warring patients quietened down and listened with pleasure. Similar experiments showed that their moods could be changed by music.

The excitement of his discovery inspired Florimond to ask if he could arrange music classes for the patients. He taught them singing and the rudiments of music. Then he started writing songs and choruses for them. They loved it. Next he was encouraged to compose a little one-act piece for them to perform. When he first outlined his idea to the medical staff they feared that he, too, had lost his senses. In the end his enthusiasm convinced them.

With patience, with tact, with great diplomacy, he coached and rehearsed his unusual cast in *L'Ours et le Pacha*. Sometimes an actor would break into somersaults, believing he was an acrobat. Others would embroider their rôles with mad private fantasies. Nonetheless, the young musician persevered.

An orchestra of ten or so doctors accompanied the first performance, with Hervé directing from the piano. The cast, dressed in costumes provided by the linen supervisor, spoke and sang their rôles perfectly. At curtain-fall, delighted by the warm applause, they shook hands with each other and hopped about for joy. Florimond, quick to seize a favourable opportunity, struck up a lively polka which the actors straightaway danced with brio. There were many curtain calls.

From then onwards music classes became a regular feature of life in the asylum. Doctors began to study more closely the effect that music could have on the minds of their charges. Besides producing and acting in home-grown entertainments at Bicêtre,

Florimond started working at spare moments in suburban theatres. His income benefited. By 1844, when he was nineteen years old, he decided he was in a position to marry. His bride was Eugénie, daughter of Madame Groseille, the linen supervisor at Bicêtre. Eugénie too, thanks to his training, was a good musician. When he slipped off to act in a theatre it was she who discreetly took his place in church. She cannot with much regret have exchanged her maiden name for Ronger, which in French means to gnaw or nibble. For Mademoiselle Groseille would in English have been known as Miss Gooseberry.

Florimond himself did not feel that his name was the sort that would look well on theatre posters. He said as much to one of his pupils, the youthful Marquis d'Hervé.

'Never mind,' said the latter. 'Take my name. You can be Ronger at Bicêtre, and Hervé in the theatre.'

By now, a year after his marriage, Hervé had won, against strong competition, the post of organist at the church of Saint-Eustache. It was one of the most important jobs of its kind and he held it for another eight years. Had the church authorities known of his work in the theatre, he would doubtless have been sacked. And, had his theatrical colleagues been aware of his post as organist, there would have been many dubious jokes. Hervé loved church music and the religious atmosphere. He also loved the theatre. So he reconciled the two aspects of his personality by calling himself Ronger in the organ loft and Hervé on the stage. It was a situation he later treated amusingly in one of his better operettas, *Mam'zelle Nitouche*.

When the obliging Adam produced *Don Quichotte et Sancho Pança* he was, all unawares, opening the gates to a flood of over a hundred operettas, a score of ballets and countless popular songs. Once launched, Hervé never stopped composing. For a time he conducted the orchestra at the Odéon. It paid well and gave him a ready-made outlet for his own productions. Then theatrical jealousies intervened and he lost the job. There were times when he was profoundly thankful for the small but regular income that came from Saint-Eustache and Bicêtre.

An engagement at the Palais-Royal was offered to him. Hervé was already showing his gifts as an all-round man of the theatre. The geniality which made him so popular among the people he worked with did not prevent him from keeping a ready eye and ear for all that was going on during a performance. He took account of

every detail, every entrance and exit, every change of scene, and
every move on stage, though few could have realized that his
amiability concealed a razor-sharp vigilance. On many occasions
when crisis threatened, his unshakeable resource and calm saved
the day.

In 1853 *Les Folies dramatiques* brought him recognition in
high places. The spectacle was a parody of every type of theatrical
fare then available in Paris. Comedy, tragedy, ballet, opera,
drama and vaudeville were mocked in turn by Hervé and his
collaborators. In particular they laughed at the extravagancy of
Italian music which at that time was very popular. The singers
were shown as uniquely preoccupied with vocal effects and quite
oblivious of acting, so that at the most dramatic moments soloist
and chorus remained blank-faced and unmoving. The libretto was
written in dog Italo-French. The hero, a *basso cantante*, at one
point orders a tenor to be thrown into a prison cell with the
words:

Soldati, presto!
Qu'il soit saisito,
Qu'il soit plongeato
Précipitato
Dans un cachoto!

Audiences were even more amused by the Italian pronunciation of
the French words.

Advance news of *Les Folies dramatiques* filtered through. An
early visitor was the Comte, later Duc, de Morny, the influential
politician who had played a vital part in the success of Louis-
Napoleon's coup d'état a year before. Morny himself was a
dramatist *manqué* whose interest in the theatre was only slightly
less than his absorption in politics and in speculating (with huge
success) on the stock exchange. Later, as we shall see, he was to
help Offenbach's career also. He reported back glowingly to the
Emperor Louis-Napoleon on the new spectacle that was all the talk
of Parisian clubs and cafés.

A command performance was ordered at the Tuileries.
Escorted by their family and retinue of ministers, the Emperor and
his Empress made a royal progress backstage. The Emperor
graciously told the company not to make any change in the text for
fear of causing offence to anyone.

'Blimey, he's a good sort, that guy!' exclaimed one of the comedians who, in his rusty voice, was notorious for irreverent remarks. A deathly silence fell. The Emperor paused. He laughed heartily. The rest of the company breathed again.

Inaugurated under the sign of Imperial favour, *Les Folies dramatiques* convulsed packed houses for many months. Morny even offered Hervé a post as secretary in his department. The latter prudently refused. He did, though, seize the chance to ask for a theatre licence.

The Paris theatres in those days were officially restricted in number and governed by ordinance as to the sort of entertainment they purveyed. The regulations dated back, as so very much else inevitably does, to the first Napoleon. Within the hierarchy the Comédie-Française and its annex, the Odéon, were permitted tragedy and comedy. The Opéra alone had the right to perform spectacles entirely in music, and ballets 'of a noble and graceful nature'. Comedies or dramas mingled with music, ariettas and concerted numbers were reserved for the Opéra-Comique. Among the remaining 'théâtres secondaires' was distributed the right to play vaudeville, melodrama, pantomimes and harlequinades. Apart from the four State-subsidized institutions, the number of theatres to be allowed 'in our good town of Paris' was a maximum of eight.

In order to set up a new theatre it was necessary to apply for a *'privilège'*. This is what Hervé asked of de Morny. He did not get it, but as a consolation prize was awarded a licence to open a *'spectacle-concert'*. Immediately he started looking for premises. In the boulevard du Temple, where Adam had established his Théâtre National, Hervé found what he needed. Inhabited successively by a comic singer and a conjuror who had both failed to attract an audience, No 41 passed into the hands of one who could.

Newly painted, decorated and renamed the Folies-Concertantes, the theatre opened at the beginning of 1854. Hervé produced, wrote the words and music, and played leading parts, as well as directing. Quickly he gathered round him a troupe of singers and comedians well adapted to his brand of knockabout humour. All season they played to capacity audiences. In July they closed down for repairs and renovations. Opened again in October, transformed, embellished, and with a seating capacity of over eight hundred, the house was baptized the Folies-Nouvelles. A row of flickering gas-lights illuminated the name outside.

A prologue by the poet Théodore de Banville introduced the first night:

C'est ici qu'on oublie
La pâle mélancolie . . .

And the spectators were entertained by a 'Spanish' farce in which one of the characters announced, 'We've crossed the seas and we only stopped at Nanterre. And since my sister is enormously fat we were obliged to make her do the journey twice.'

By the end of the year Hervé had written the music for eighteen one-act operettas and pantomimes. (In French a pantomime is not, as in English, a Christmas entertainment but is simply a show in mime.) He found, besides the limitations imposed by his resources, that he was subject to other restrictions. According to the terms of his licence the plays he presented were to be of one act only and with a cast of no more than two. In pantomimes three actors were allowed. Police informers often joined the audience to ensure that these and other regulations were observed.

For a man of such ingenuity as Hervé, the rules were so many challenges to inventiveness. When he was refused permission to include a chorus of Greek soldiers in *Agamemnon; or The Camel with Two Humps*, he had a picture of the forbidden choristers painted on a piece of scenery. This he displayed while a choir sang in the wings. As soon as they had finished, the scenery was switched round and showed its other side: a line of rose trees. Another device to elude officialdom was the stage camel. Two actors were concealed within. The front legs started a quarrel with the back legs. The cardboard creature disintegrated . . . and once again the decree about the number of spoken rôles was evaded.

One of his most sprightly inventions was a farcical drama set in revolutionary times. It contained six rôles. One of them was sung by a bass from the prompter's cubby-hole. Three were played by Hervé. First he appeared as a knight, then as the knight's wife's lover, and finally as a servant. Provided none of these characters were on stage at the same time there was no end to the quantity of parts a determined actor could play. In this particular masterpiece a nobleman, who has had the misfortune to be decapitated, takes part in a trio while holding his head in his hand, the voice coming from the bass lurking in the cubby-hole.

It is no wonder that, in 1856, Hervé fell ill and was ordered to rest. In the previous year he had written twenty pieces and, at the time of his illness, had completed another eleven. He left the Folies-Nouvelles enough productions to keep going whil he led a slightly less strenuous life touring the provinces. Even here he could not resist novelty. In Montpellier he sang tenor, comedy-tenor and light baritone rôles in standard repertory operas by Auber, Boieldieu and Donizetti.

Back in Paris he took an appointment as conductor at a little theatre where, from time to time, the proprietor staged revues in which amateurs were invited to try their luck. The place was noted for riotous evenings. By tradition young men-about-town made a point of ironically applauding the inept performance of the would-be actors and singers, and of urging them to do even worse. Sometimes the police had to clear the boxes whence the noisiest encouragement proceeded.

A disagreement with the impresario who had engaged him as conductor eventually inspired Hervé to look further afield. He heard that a new theatre had just been built in Cairo. With a company that included his son as violinist, Hervé set off gaily for Egypt. Their season began well. Then receipts started to drop. One day the manager suddenly vanished, having meanwhile overlooked the matter of paying wages. And finally the theatre went up in flames.

Hervé decided to ask for help from the Viceroy, Ismail Pasha. He wrote a cantata in honour of the potentate and threw in an Egyptian March as well. The idea was to perform these works in his presence. An unusual procession set off on the way to the royal palace. It was led by two huge dromedaries, the first carrying on its hump a battery of drums, the other bearing cymbals that flashed and glistened in the sun. Behind came Hervé driving the donkey cart followed by his son, and, in a variety of carriages, by the rest of the company and their instruments.

When they arrived at the palace they learned that His Highness had left for another of his residences. The procession clanked off once more. At the end of a broad avenue they glimpsed the Viceroy and his suite trotting along. Hervé gave the signal to put on speed. No sooner had he done this than the viceregal party also began to quicken its pace. An officer galloped back to Hervé and demanded the reason for this bizarre pursuit.

Hervé, most gracefully, explained that they wished to serenade His Highness and to solicit his goodwill. The officer glanced suspiciously at the strange objects that glittered on the humps of the dromedaries. 'What are those devices for?'

'Why, they're only rather large musical instruments.'

The officer, who had suspected them to be infernal machines intended for the assassination of his master, burst out laughing. He went back and enlightened the Viceroy, who, once he had recovered from the shock and suspicion of an attempted murder plot, invited Hervé and his company to play to him next day. The cantata and the march were heard with approval and a grant of twenty thousand francs brought the adventure to a pleasant end.

Soon afterwards Hervé was offered a tempting post: that of permanent conductor at the Eldorado, the most famous café-concert in all Paris. The salary was to be the same as that of the conductor at the Opéra. Hervé made no bones about accepting. He had had enough of the uncertainties and risks that a composer's career entailed.

The 'Eldo', as it was known, had been taken over by a new and energetic manager. The same sort of hampering regulations applied to the café-concert as to theatres. A performer was not allowed to wear costume which might 'tend to encroach upon the domain of the theatre'. Anyone who carried a stick or wore a fancy collar at the Eldo was liable to be fined forty francs. The new manager sought to evade the rules by engaging a tragic actress who had left the Comédie-Française. Every night, wearing evening dress, she declaimed, among the cigar smoke and fumes of drink, choice extracts from Racine. In these unlikely surroundings she was warmly applauded each night. The Press reported her triumph and started a campaign to allow café-concert performers to wear what they liked. In the end authority gave way and permission was granted.

Hervé was no less original in his contribution. Of course, he wrote hundreds of songs for the Eldo stars to sing, together with marches, polkas, quadrilles and dances of every sort. Most unusually, he also persuaded the manager to let him give classical concerts. Not content just with playing the symphonies of Beethoven, he added commentaries, delivered with all the humour and art which he commanded as an experience actor.

Deliberately vulgar in his approach, he would remark: 'What a bore! Here's that theme coming back again. It's too much!' The audience loved it. They even took a fancy to Beethoven as a result. At the Eldorado they never quite knew what an evening would bring forth, whether it was Racine, the composer of the *Eroica*, or the impish Thérésa singing 'There's something tickling me up my nose' (words and music by Hervé).

Until now he had specialized in short works, mostly one-acters, featuring a basic situation. With *L'Oeil crevé* ('One in the Eye'), in 1867, he assumed a more ambitious style. This was a full-length piece for which he himself wrote both words and music. Apart, however, from noting that it is in three acts, there is little that can be said about the plot. This is a wild and incoherent affair involving a well-born young lady who becomes a carpenter and falls in love with a cabinetmaker.

One of the characters chirrups:

Ronflez, tambours, en avant la pastourelle!
Latorilla! Latorilla! Good morning, sir!

It is useless to try to identify the topical allusions. The humour and the puns are as impenetrable to the modern mind as will be those of current television shows to people a hundred years from now.

L'Oeil crevé ran for six months, a good figure at the time, and was often revived. The last act, where an archer whose shot was so badly aimed is put in prison, supplied the music of a popular quadrille to which several generations danced with enjoyment. It was scores like this which, bearing in mind Hervé's life in the asylum at Bicêtre, won him the distinctive nickname of *'le compositeur toqué'*, or 'the loony composer'.

So great was the success of *L'Oeil crevé* that, a year later, Hervé's next full-length operetta, *Chilpéric*, was accepted for production. Chilpéric, so history records, was the son of that sixth-century monarch, Clotaire, who ruled over the Franks. At Clotaire's death, his kingdom was shared out among his four sons. To Chilpéric fell the area of Soissons. He died some twenty years later, murdered by order of his queen, Frédégonde, who took power and governed until their son came of age.

What Hervé made of this venerable piece of history it is not difficult to imagine. He himself took the rôle of the king. His version includes a 'Légende de Chilpéric' which runs:

Tout est plaisir
Pourquoi s'enfuir
Voilà le chic
De Monsieur Chilpéric.

When the king visits the druids to discover what fate holds in store for him, a sudden rainstorm breaks out and he smartly unfolds his umbrella: 'Quick, to horse, we must go, for the sky is heavy with a-a-a-a-anger.' The Franks march off to the accompaniment of a war song that dissolves into a yodel.

The Prince of Wales saw *Chilpéric*, as he did everything else, on one of his many trips to Paris. One of the attractions of the operetta which doubtless encouraged his approval was the statuesque Blanche d'Antigny, who played the part of Frédégonde in a wispy sheepskin that failed delightfully to conceal her opulent form. What a pity, mused His Royal Highness, that Hervé had no English. If he played *Chilpéric* in London it would be immensely successful.

The remark came to Hervé's ears. He remembered an approach he had lately received from a London impresario. Why not repeat in London the rôle he had created? In English! 'I'll learn English,' he announced. 'Come back and see me in three months.' By the end of that period he was speaking a language which, though strictly neither French nor English, combined features of both in a novel manner.

Chilpéric and his creator opened at the Lyceum. A fashionable audience, which included the Prince of Wales in his royal box, applauded enthusiastically. They were amused by Hervé's original English. When he could not remember an idiom he said it in French, mixing up the two tongues with such wit that few people realized he was extemporizing.

During the interval the Prince came to his dressing-room and presented him with a diamond ring. How, marvelled the Prince, did he manage to learn English so quickly, not having known a word of it before?

Hervé replied, the perfect courtier,: 'Your Highness, the miracle wasn't my doing. Your Highness had said: "What a pity Hervé can't come and play *Chilpéric* in English!" That was enough for me. I began instantly to learn English.'

The visit to London prepared the way for later expeditions that were to be equally rewarding. In the meantime, Hervé came back to Paris for the production of *Le Petit Faust*. This was an exercise in the sort of parody he had already ventured on with *Roméo et Mariette* (Gounod's *Roméo et Juliette*) and *Les Troyens en Champagne* (*Les Troyens à Carthage* of Berlioz).

There is a story that on the first night of *Le Petit Faust*, while the overture was being played, the audience burst into spontaneous applause at the sudden and unexpected return of the pretty waltz theme halfway through. The orchestra could not be heard for the noise of clapping. Hervé, standing behind the curtain, experienced one of the greatest moments of his career. He ran backstage to hide his emotion. Before he could appear in the title rôle he quickly had to repair the damage done to his make-up.

This moment of sentimentality was followed by the more customary joking, for the raucous strains of 'The Carnival of Venice' then took over and brought the overture to a lively close. Most of the well-known numbers in Gounod's masterpiece were duly parodied. The 'Soldiers' Chorus' developed into the rhythm of a scottische. 'When a soldier goes to war,' sings Valentine, 'he embraces his father.'

'And what if he hasn't got a father?' enquires the chorus.

'He embraces his mother,' replies Valentine.

'And if he hasn't a mother?'

'He embraces his brother.'

'And if he hasn't a brother?'

'He contents himself with embracing a career.' And so on.

Marguerite makes herself known with a yodelling song and adds in a Teutonic accent, quite correctly, 'The Gerbans call be Gretchen.' Where Gounod supplied her with a touchingly medieval 'Chanson du Roi de Thulé', Hervé provides a 'Chanson du Roi de Thune', thune being nineteenth-century slang for the five-franc piece. She recounts the misadventure of this grand old king who received the gift of a handsome pair of elastic braces from his queen. But one day they snapped, and an astonished populace saw revealed ' . . . what I'll call quite frankly government secrets'.

In a similar vein, with 'Le Satrape et la puce', Mephisto tells of the prince who conceived an affection for a flea and treated it so well that all its relatives came up from the provinces — after which no one ever dared scratch himself for fear of annoying these royal favourites. Mephisto, one should add, was sung en travesti by a woman.

For all the broad parody, there are things of genuine charm in Le Petit Faust. Such a one is Mephisto's ballade 'Les Quatre Saisons'. Others occur in Marguerite's 'Chanson du Roi de Thune', which, though comic, is set in a minor key, gentle and nostalgic. Its effect in the original production was enhanced by the ripe loveliness of Blanche d'Antigny.

Soon after this Hervé fell silent. Between the end of 1869 and the closing months of 1871 his name did not appear on any theatrical poster. Only an overwhelming catastrophe could have stemmed his exuberant fertility, and it came in the shape of the Franco-Prussian War. Duped by the clever manoeuvring of Bismarck, Napoleon III led France into a conflict that neither he nor his country was in a condition to sustain. The result was humiliating defeat.

During those tortured years which saw the collapse of France, the siege of Paris and the bloody episode of the Commune, Hervé came to London and took up an engagement already offered him. At the old Gaiety Theatre he put on his *Aladdin the Second* for the Christmas season of 1870. Later, after the war, he staged it in Paris. The cast then included his son, who also wrote a curtain-raiser for his father's production.

Hervé made many useful connections in London. He was back again in 1874 to conduct at the Promenade Concerts where he gave the first performance — and probably the last — of a rare work entitled *The Ashantee War,* a 'heroic symphony' for solo voices and orchestra to words and music by himself. More in his line were the programmes at the Empire Theatre which became increasingly his London headquarters.

The France which emerged from the tumultuous months of 1871 was a republic, the third in order of time. Hervé wooed it with his first post-war production, *Le Trône d'Ecosse,* an extravaganza featuring a commercial traveller who, mistaken for a descendant of Robert Bruce, is bundled into a marriage with the Queen of Scotland. One of the characters is a dashing fellow called Buckingham, a dandy noted for his superb, highly varnished Wellington boots. One of the ladies, who falls in love with him, declares: "In my maddest dreams I'd like — and you'd laugh at this — to be the varnish on his boots so as to spend my life at his feet.'

Certain refinements in the score, which Hervé composed while in London, suggest that he was able to write better than usual when free of the intense pressures to which he had been exposed for the whole of his theatrical life. Soon, though, he went back to his old habits, turning out music by the yard and revelling in the crises that arose to test his resourcefulness. Once he left a sketch for an operetta with a manager who kept it for two years. Suddenly the manager was in touch again. He wanted to stage the piece and begin rehearsals the day after tomorrow. Within just over three weeks the rest of the music was written by Hervé and the operetta prepared and given its first night. He enjoyed such challenges.

One of the new café-concert stars to arouse his attention was a plump little girl called Anna Judic. As the daughter of a cashier at one of the big Paris theatres, she had spent her childhood backstage. After studying at the Conservatoire she played in comedy and married an actor called Israël who had changed his name to Judic. Then she gravitated to the café-concert and pleased audiences with her delicacy and charm. She had the pouting, dimpled prettiness of a Boucher nymph. For this exquisite singer Hervé wrote a series of vaudevilles and operettas. Among the last of them was to be *Mam'zelle Nitouche*

It was also the best and the only one of Hervé's works that stands a chance of revival today. One reason for this is the workmanlike libretto for which Henri Meilhac, who collaborated with Offenbach, Massenet and Bizet among others, was partly responsible. The idea came from Hervé's own early years when he doubled as church organist by day and composer of raffish operetta by night. The heroine of *Mam'zelle Nitouche* (from *'sainte nitouche'*, a demure young person in whose mouth butter would not melt), is an outwardly devout girl who secretly cherishes a passion for the theatre. She discovers the hidden life of the organist at the convent where she is immured: he is a composer of operettas. How, on the first night of his latest production, she steals away to sing the leading rôle; how she and the composer are subsequently arrested by the night patrol; how, disguised as dragoons, they slip into the convent in the early hours of the morning; and how, in the end, she marries a dashing young viscount, is recounted with skill and a practised ingenuity at tying up loose ends.

The music has a military flavour that had become popular at the time. There is nothing like a stirring march rhythm and the crashing roll of timpani to liven an audience. The 'Legend of the Big Drum' is a good example. A charming interlude is the *'Alleluia'* sung by the heroine to a solo harp accompaniment. It shows that Hervé's religious music owed a lot to the style of Gounod.

After *Fla-Fla*, which closed ignominiously in 1886 with only five performances, Hervé seems to have tired of his feverish life in Paris. A tempting prospect again awaited him across the Channel: a regular post as conductor at the Empire Theatre, with security and a salary paid like clockwork each month, come what may. He grasped the chance with both hands. One report says that he took

English nationality. This is unlikely. It is true, however, that Paris was to see little of him in the remaining years of his life. At the Empire he led a happy and assured existence. Naturally, the old urge to compose never deserted him. He wrote over half a dozen ballets for the Empire and saw them produced. Drury Lane also welcomed his music. Things were less hectic, more easy-going, among the phlegmatic Anglo-Saxons.

Hervé had many deficiencies as a composer. His musical education was scanty and he lacked the technical equipment of a Lecocq, a Messager or even an Offenbach. The occasional felicity in his scores results from happy chance. He was dogged by poor libretti and the sheer physical strain of writing non-stop to keep up with the demands of managers and audiences. Yet it was he who took over from Adam and prepared the way for modern French operetta.

His knowledge of the theatre and his stage-sense were impeccable. There was no job which he could not do. He must be unique among composers in that he was equally adept as producer, actor, singer and even as stage-hand. The rough and unscrupulous world of the theatre failed to blunt either his essential kindliness or his optimistic character.

There was one occasion, though, when his stoicism faltered. In 1892 one of his operettas was very roughly handled by the music critic of *Figaro*. As the professional of professionals he had learned to shrug his shoulders at the critics. This time, however, aged and wracked by the asthma which had plagued him for so long, he was caught on the raw. He wrote indignantly that he had cancelled his subscription, '*Figaro* having no more cause to cross the threshold of a French composer who has honoured his country.' Nine days later he died during a fit of asthma. He was sixty-seven years old.

ACT I

THE AGE OF GOLD

I

'The little Jew'

It was 1855. The second Empire of Louis-Napoleon had reached its third anniversary. In that year, the birth of a Prince Imperial seemed to assure the future of the dynasty.

Despite the grandiose Column in the Place Vendôme and the triumphal arches and the bridges which the Emperor's uncle, the first Napoleon, had built, Paris remained what it was under Louis-Philippe, that is to say a city of the eighteenth century, and even earlier. Apart from the central boulevards, where activity was intense, it was still a place of narrow streets and houses huddled together amid dark, crooked alleyways.

At the Tuileries a rich and fashionable court glittered around the Emperor and his red-haired Empress, Eugénie de Montijo, the Spanish beauty. The great noble families spent the summer on their country estates. In Paris they entertained lavishly and kept up expensive mansions. They were envied and imitated by a lesser society of financiers and lawyers, merchants and businessmen. Sometimes the two classes met and commingled through marriage or professional relationships.

The middle range of doctors, solicitors, army officers and civil servants worked and prospered. So did those who came a little beneath them on the social ladder: the artisans, the commercial travellers, the shopkeepers, the craftsmen who travelled the country in guilds, and the shop assistants, a few degrees lower down, who dreamed one day of opening up on their own account and thriftily put by every sou, every franc they could spare.

At the bottom were the labourers, the chimney-sweeps, the

dustmen and the porters. As industrialization grew they were to
form the nucleus of a depressed protelariat. They were forced to
work even harder and live in conditions that became worse instead
of better. For the moment, though, everyone seemed content to
stay within his own class. The Revolution of 1789 might never have
happened.

Towards the middle of the year Hervé was busy rehearsing one
of the twenty operettas he put on during 1855. The arrival of an
importunate young man interrupted him. The apparition was
short and painfully thin. He had a large nose, all bone and beak,
with pince-nez carelessly perched upon it. His eye was lively, his
thin lips wore an ironic but amusing twist.

"Bonchour!" he said in a throaty German accent. From his
pocket he drew the manuscript of an operetta which he offered to
Hervé. The piece was called *Oyayaye*, or 'The Queen of the
Islands'. Hervé read it with an interest whetted by the sub-title,
'Cannibalism set to music'. The hero was a double-bass player who,
sacked for having fallen asleep over his instrument, decides to seek
his fortune in America, but ends up by mistake on a desert island
inhabited by cannibals. Their queen, Oyayaye ('Oh oh oh!'), casts
an appreciative look at his well-covered limbs. He tries vainly to
distract her with serenades and variations on her laundry bill which
he sets to music. The greedy light in her eye only deepens. Finally
he makes his escape by sailing away in his double-bass, converted
into a canoe for the occasion and powered by a handkerchief as a
sail.

Hervé liked it. He needed something to fill a vacant date. The
wild humour of *Oyayaye* appealed to him. Here was a man after his
own heart. Moreover, he himself would play the part of the
cannibal queen.

Oyayaye at the Folies-Nouvelles was the first important success
of Jacques Offenbach, otherwise Jakob, from Cologne. He had just
reached his twenty-sixth birthday and was, in fact, six years older
than Hervé. It had, though, taken him much, much longer than
the composer of *Chilpéric* to establish himself.

He could look back on a youth of struggle and poverty. As the
seventh child of a penurious Jewish cantor, he had few expectations.
His father, Isaac Juda Eberst, hailed from the town of Offenbach-
am-Main. Known as 'the man from Offenbach', he eventually
adopted the name for himself. He played the violin at dances, gave
lessons and chanted in the synagogue. Very little money came his

way, but he was a happy man, content with his large family and rooted in a faith that supported him alike against the buffets and rewards of life.

Most of Isaac's ten children showed a gift for music. Jakob was clearly the most talented. At the age of six he was playing the violin. Soon afterwards took up the 'cello. He started composing when he was eight. Very soon he had learned all that local teachers could impart to him. Only in Paris, decided his father, could he find tuition equal to his gifts.

Having saved with much difficulty the money needed for this long and wearing voyage, Isaac took Jakob and his brother, who also had talent, on the coach trip to Paris. An interview with Cherubini, then head of the Conservatoire, seemed unpromising at first. Forgetting that he had once himself been a foreigner, Cherubini declared that Jakob's nationality prevented his acceptance as a pupil.

Isaac did not give way. He argued politely but with a tenaciousness learned from hard experience. The peppery old musician at last agreed. Jakob could be admitted. He stayed there for about a year. Lessons bored him and he was impatient to get out into the world.

Already his ambition was intense. Jakob turned into Jacques, a Jacques who quickly picked up French and spoke it with excitable fluency though with a gurgling German accent that he never lost. Parisians chuckled at the way he murdered their language. They were amused by his gangling figure, by the threadbare clothes that were never quite big enough even for his scarecrow form, by the spluttering eloquence with which he spoke.

His brother Julius, who Gallicized himself into Jules, was quieter, more easy-going. Jules looked on music as a way of earning his living. For Jacques it was something much more important. He saw in it the key to success, a means that would assure him, he was convinced, a glorious reputation. In the squalid little garret which he shared with his brother, he thought incessantly of the day when his name would be famous and his music played throughout Europe. The dream sustained him through the often unkind mockery of his classmates and the snubs and humiliations he met with in this strange foreign country. The future was all.

The impetuous 'little Jew', as he was nicknamed, burst out of the Conservatoire with relief. 'Left of his own free will', a clerkly hand added to the official record of his departure. No more fugues!

No more dull cramping exercises! The fifteen year old musician took a job as cellist in the orchestra at the Opéra-Comique. At last he found himself in the atmosphere he loved, amid the footlights and the smell of greasepaint, before a curtain that promised every sort of pleasurable mystery.

It was good experience and he learned quickly. From the orchestra pit he could observe how the job was done. Night after night he saw the standard repertory played on the stage and could size up the techniques of composers and singers. But he was easily bored. The tedium of playing the same thing over and over again drove him to desperation. And desperation impelled him to practical jokes in the hope of lightening the monotony. As a result the disapproving conductor often imposed fines which reduced his salary to a lamentable figure.

The great operatic success at that time was Halévy's *La Juive*. The young cellist admired it. He esteemed the composer even more, for here was a famous man, a personality whose name was on everyone's lips. One evening, with immense nerve, he waylaid Halévy outside the Opéra and introduced himself. Perhaps amused by the impudence of the voluble youth, Halévy took him under his wing. He gave him lessons, and Jules also. Soon Halévy was writing to a delighted Isaac in Cologne that Jacques seemed destined for 'genuine success' as a composer.

What else could he do but write music? Songs, mazurkas, galops and waltzes gushed from his pen in frenzied profusion. A waltz called 'Rebecca' was taken up by that flamboyant purveyor of light music, Louis Antoine Jullien. It was played at the Jardin Turc, a much-frequented pleasure garden where Jullien staged his ornate programmes. The tunes included melodies which Offenbach remembered hearing in the synagogue as a boy. People who recognized them were not amused and charged him with irreverence. The accusation was to become a familiar one throughout his career.

Offenbach soon made a little reputation for himself in the fashionable houses of Paris. He found he had gifts as a society entertainer. From the lugubrious depths of his 'cello he could draw sounds like those of the trombone or bagpipe. His skittering fingers could make the instrument bleat like a sheep or moo like a cow. Audiences laughed in wonderment at the skill with which he reproduced these comic sounds.

In addition he would give little talks spiced with humour

and the latest jokes. His shiny black eyes darted restlessly as he chattered in his heavy accent. The bony hands flapped in the air. The thin body leaned forward confidentially as he delivered a witticism. He crouched back, bow at the ready, to produce from his 'cello the noises of the whole repertory of fowls and animals. His ready wit and quaint mannerisms put everyone in a good mood. His guttural eloquence was stimulated by the sight of pretty women, jewelled toilettes, costly perfume and all the show of good living. He flourished on light, laughter, and quicksilver repartee.

In one of the salons where he performed he made the acquaintance of a dramatist who asked him to write the music for his latest piece. The thing was done and put into rehearsal. Offenbach, for the first time, saw his name on a theatre poster. The experience did not last long. Within days the unlucky spectacle was swept off the stage.

Then, in Cologne, his youngest brother suddenly died. His mother took to her bed. A week later she, too, expired. So deep was his mourning that for a time he gave up all thought of his career in Paris. He wandered about the silent house and wrote melancholy verse in her honour.

Yet the magnet of the boulevards drew him back. Once more he did the rounds of the salons and organized concerts at which he played his own music. He was, in that small world, on the fringe of celebrity. His person, as much as his music, was responsible for that. Was it true, whispered impressionable young persons, that Monsieur Offenbach had the malign gift of the evil eye? He was, in fact, only long-sighted, though he did not discourage the legend that behind his pince-nez there gleamed an occult power.

From time to time he organized concerts of his music. 'Monsieur Offenbach', wrote a magazine, 'regularly composes three waltzes before his lunch, a mazurka after his dinner and four galops between the two meals.' He was inordinately quick. His pen flashed over the paper leaving behind it a trail of little dots almost microscopic in size. His hand was always outpaced by the teeming brain.

One evening in 1843 he met a girl called Herminie de Alcain. She was the stepdaughter of a Mr John Mitchell, proprietor of the French theatre in London. Her mother had previously been married to a Spaniard. Offenbach was instantly fascinated by Herminie. She, in turn, was captivated by his exuberance and his irrepressible chatter. Up to now his love affairs had been momentary things, the satisfaction of a passing whim. For Herminie he felt something different.

At the age of twenty-four he offered himself as a prospective husband. The family remained cautious. He had little money and his career had only just begun. Mr Mitchell put forward two counter-suggestions. Offenbach must get together some funds by going on a concert tour to London which was then, as Rossini and others had found, a rich field for the virtuoso. The aspiring bridegroom must also give up his Jewish faith and become a Catholic.

Of these two conditions, it was the first that seemed the harder to fulfil. Though he made money in London, where he was hailed as the 'Paganini of the 'cello', he grudged every day spent away from Paris. Though he played to the Queen and her consort at Windsor Castle, he longed for 'my beautiful Paris . . . my own dear town' and for the charms of Herminie.

From London he brought back enough money to convince her family of his prospects. There remained his conversion to Catholicism. This was easy enough. Though deeply emotional and much given to sentimentality, he had not an ounce of mysticism in him. It cost him little to renounce his Jewish beliefs. At the baptism his sponsor was one of the society ladies in whose homes he shone as entertainer.

In 1844, at the age of twenty-five, he married a bride who had yet to reach her eighteenth birthday. They took a small flat just behind what is now, appropriately, the Folies-Bergère. A year later their first daughter was born. Others were to follow with a speed almost rivalling that of Offenbach's own fertile parent.

How was this growing family to be kept on so little money? Herminie alone had the secret. Young though she was, instinct enabled her to handle the mercurial Jacques in all his moods ranging from the blackest anguish to the most sparkling gaiety. He was nervy, impetuous, excitable. She was calm and thoughtful, reassuring and systematic. His love for her was sincere. She knew that, however often he adventured outside the family, he would always come back to her.

ii

The conquest of Paris

By 1847 Offenbach thought he was on the verge of theatrical success. The benevolent Adam had agreed to stage his one-act operetta, *L'Alcôve*, at the Théâtre National. Whereupon, soon afterwards, the revolution of 1848 shattered the hopes of both Adam and his protégé. The comfortable reign of Louis-Philippe melted into the sterner régime of the Second Republic. The King fled in exile to England. Offenbach hastily made off for Cologne with his wife and family. There they lived for a while in near poverty but at least in a calm unruffled by noisy demonstrators whose Parisian habit of tearing up paving-stones and murdering each other across barricades dismayed the pacific musician.

One cannot but admire Offenbach's single-mindedness in the devotion he showed to his own cause. For a while he signed himself 'Jakob' instead of 'Jacques'. To meet a popular demand he turned out songs which glorified the purity of the typical German girl as compared with her crafty Latin sisters. In stirring marches and solemn ballads he exalted the virtues of the Fatherland. At a ceremony to mark the six-hundredth anniversary of Cologne cathedral he skipped onto the platform with his 'cello and twanged out a flashy fantasia on operatic melodies by Rossini. Offenbach, claimed an admiring newspaper report, was 'one of us.'.

But when, after a year or so, Louis-Napoleon became President of France and put a stop to the Republican drift — or so it seemed — Cologne lost its appeal. Was it not foolish to stay in that respectable though dreary town when, in a Paris reborn, all sorts of new opportunities must be springing up? The Offenbach household trundled hopefully over the border again.

Very soon a piece of luck came Offenbach's way. He was appointed musical director at the Comédie-Française. At that time music was provided, amid the babble of an unhearing audience, by a lackadaisical quartet. The new director changed all that by bringing in a proper orchestra. The music was carefully adapted and written to meet the demands of the stage. Offenbach himself added dignity to his post by appearing in formal dress and white gloves. Gaily he clashed with actors who disapproved of the new-found emphasis on music. Tenaciously he out-manoeuvred their intrigues.

All the while he continued to lay siege to the Opéra-Comique. His blandishments failed. The manuscripts of unperformed operettas cluttered his desk and grew into an ever-increasing pile. Frustration nagged and gnawed at him. The Opéra-Comique, he felt, was being false to its tradition. No one any longer wrote 'truly funny, gay and witty music'. No one, that is, except Offenbach.

Why should not he, like Hervé, set up his own theatre? Then, and only then, would he be able to give Paris a taste of genuine operetta. For a long time he had envied the composer of *Don Quichotte et Sancho Pança* and studied his methods with professional curiosity. Hervé, rather than the impregnable Opéra-Comique, must be his next objective. And so we find him, loquacious and optimistic on that summer day in 1855, persuading Hervé that *Oyayaye* must, quite definitely must, be his next production.

The success of *Oyayaye* encouraged Offenbach to persist with his search for premises where he would be his own master. At last he discovered them. The building he leased in the Champs-Elysées was cramped and ruinous. The wooden planks of which it was built hardly kept out wind and rain. It had once belonged to a failed conjuror and was just what Offenbach wanted. The situation, moreover, was excellent, for his new theatre stood not far from the centre of the 1855 Exhibition which was designed to show off the splendour of Imperial France. Crowds of visitors would be passing close by. His audiences were ready-made!

Carpenters and painters invaded the wooden building. A company was set up to run the Bouffes-Parisiens, as Offenbach decided to call it. One of the partners was Hippolyte de Ville-messant, a typical Second Empire figure, crude and Balzacian, the man who established the *Figaro* newspaper and built it into a powerful influence. His genius for publicity rivalled Offenbach's own. Another well-wisher was the Duc de Morny, the Emperor's illegitimate half-brother who occupied a very important position in the new régime. Yet, though he was perhaps the most formidable member of the Emperor's administration, and a skilled manipulator of the stock market, he had two weaknesses: the theatre and women. Like Richelieu, he was stagestruck and longed to make a name for himself in the theatre. It was Morny who, behind the scenes, arranged for Offenbach to be granted a theatre licence.

Three weeks before the scheduled opening of the Bouffes-

Parisiens, Offenbach started the work of composing and producing. The bill, he decided, would include four one-act pieces. He was well into three of them but had trouble finding a librettist for the fourth. Suddenly he remembered a young man who might be able to help. His name was Ludovic Halévy, nephew of the composer Fromenthal who had assisted Offenbach in his early career.

At that time, and for some years afterwards, Ludovic worked as a civil servant: His duties were not onerous, however, and left him ample leisure for writing dramas. On his own, and in partnership with Henri Meilhac, Halévy was to craft many successful comedies and libretti for various composers. He inspected, with friendly amusement, the breathless, excited Offenbach who now erupted into his office.

The composer was offering the twenty-one year old writer a chance he could not refuse. He thought of the mound of plays that lay unperformed in his drawer and agreed to collaborate. The prologue he wrote served as curtain-raiser to the programme that opened the Bouffes-Parisiens on 5 July 1855.

The tiny theatre established itself immediately. The novelty of the surroundings, with seats arranged so steeply that they looked like the rungs of a ladder, and boxes so small that it was necessary to open both door and window if you wanted to take your jacket off, caught the imagination of the Parisians. The music, too, was unusual. One of the items on the bill, *Les Deux aveugles*, an impudently cynical piece about two beggars who pretend to be blind, ran for at least a year and the comedians who played it became celebrities.

By the end of the first month the books showed a profit of eleven thousand francs. The Bouffes-Parisiens was now an institution. Anxious not to lose a single opportunity, Offenbach went on ceaselessly dreaming up new spectacles, new ideas, new music. He badgered his collaborator with demands for libretti and exhortations to keep up the flow. Almost as soon as he had received the words his greedy pen set them to music and he was clamouring for more.

Halévy grew used to the urgent appeals. 'I shall need it tomorrow at the latest, so try to make it this evening. If at all possible, we'd go into rehearsal the day after tomorrow . . . .' During the next twenty years he was to receive hundreds, if not thousands, of these hurried notes scribbled in the minute handwriting that galloped and twisted exuberantly across the page.

iii

'The Mozart of the Champs-Elysées

On the evening of 31 August, a trembling girl awaited her entry in the wings at the Bouffes-Parisiens. It was a very hot night and she sweated, though with fear. Her cue was given. She could not move, so intense was the stage fright that rooted her to the spot.

Ludovic Halévy came up behind her. 'You're on!' he hissed. Still she did not budge. Fear had immobilized her and locked every muscle. 'Get on and play your part!' whispered Halévy. He seized her shoulders and literally pushed her onto the stage. She stumbled blinking into the circle of light, dazzled by the flicker of gas and the misty figures beyond.

There was no need for her to speak or sing. In a moment the theatre fell silent. Then a spontaneous roar of applause surged up from the audience. It was not so much her beauty, though she was beautiful, nor her figure, though she was shapely, that cast a spell. What enthralled the spectators was the look in her eye, the magnetism that seemed to fill the stage with a mysterious and indefinable excitement.

Indeed, when you looked more closely at her it was easy to see flaws. Yet in the thrill of her presence you forgot about the rather narrow lips and the slightly misshapen hand. The girl had that rare gift of star quality which excuses every imperfection. Mademoiselle Hortense Schneider had made her Paris début.

She was half-German, the daughter of a shoemaker from Cologne who settled in Bordeaux. At the age of six she determined to go on the stage. Soon she was travelling the provinces and acting in every type of play and opera. In Paris she became the mistress of one of the comedians from *Les Deux aveugles*. He took her to see Offenbach.

Mademoiselle Schneider told the story of her twenty-two years. She sang for Offenbach. He abruptly shut the piano. 'Take no more lessons!' he admonished her. She would only succeed in spoiling her natural gift. He was engaging her at two hundred francs a month.

The Bouffes-Parisiens had discovered its first and most famous star, and Offenbach, for a time, had found a new and enchanting mistress. Of course, as soon as they tired of each other she graduated to other and more distinguished beds. Her lovers were to include millionaires, politicians and the Duc de Morny himself. Among foreign royalty she distributed her charm so liberally that she earned a ribald nickname taken from that much-frequented thoroughfare, the 'Passage des Princes'.

Everything was going so well for Offenbach that he left his ramshackle establishment in the Champs-Elysées and took another more permanent theatre which also was to be known as the Bouffes-Parisiens. This he renovated and upholstered with spendthrift luxury. His theatre, though tiny still, would be the most beautiful in the whole of Paris! He opened it with *Ba-ta-clan*, a '*chinoiserie musicale*' to words by Halévy.

This was the first time Halévy's name appeared in full on a theatre poster instead of being hidden under a pseudonym, for he had decided to make a secret no longer of his stage ambitions. *Ba-ta-clan*, which means something like 'the whole damned lot', contains the essence of everything Offenbach intended with his new concept of what operetta should be. It set the style for the dozens of sprightly entertainments which gave the Bouffes during the years to come its distinctive flavour.

Ba-ta-clan had wit and no reverence. It mingled parody with satire and high spirits with absurdity. The ruler of an obscure Chinese kingdom plans to decorate five of his subjects. Being Parisian-born he does not speak the language correctly and his orders are misunderstood, so that the unlucky quintet are agonisingly impaled. At the same time a plot is being hatched against this improbable monarch. He, in common with two other exiles, longs for his native Paris. By arrangement with an ambitious courtier, to whom he hands over power, the three of them make their way back, unhindered, to the city of their nostalgic dreams.

That, in outline, amounts to all there is of a story in *Ba-ta-clan*. What cannot be conveyed is the *élan* of the music and its inexhaustible rhythms. It has boundless vitality. The big drum booms imperiously, the brass blows magnificent raspberries, and, at the end, voices and trumpet dialogue with rapid wit in a mad helter-skelter. There is parody of Italian opera and, in particular, of Meyerbeer's *Les Huguenots*, all of it sung in a scatty mixture of French, Italian and 'Chinese'. Satire, though mild, is present in the mockery of dictatorship and its inevitable clumsiness.

Buoyant on a wave of success, Offenbach's mind teemed with exciting new ideas. He paid tribute to Mozart by putting on a version of *The Impresario*. Another novelty was Rossini's *Il Signor*

Bruschino, an opera which had not caught on at its first performance some years before in Venice. It did not do much better in Offenbach's production, though his hardihood earned the amused admiration of Rossini who nicknamed him 'the Mozart of the Champs-Elysées'.

One of his better ideas was a competition he launched in 1856 to publicize his own Bouffes-Parisiens and at the same time encourage new ideas in operetta. French light music, Offenbach declared, had drifted away from its earlier standards of grace and gaiety. He wanted to revive the true original style. So he invited young composers to set a libretto entitled *Le Docteur Miracle*. A committee of well-known musicians, among them Gounod and Fromenthal Halévy, decided that the best entries were by an eighteen year old prodigy called Georges Bizet and a crippled youth by the name of Charles Lecocq.

Since the two versions were deemed to be of equal merit — though Lecocq thought decidedly otherwise — they were played on alternate nights at the Bouffes-Parisiens. For the rest of his life Charles Lecocq nursed a grievance against Offenbach. The latter did not know at the time that he had earned the enmity of a composer who, in the years after 1870, was to become his most dangerous rival.

Money went on pouring in at the box-office. Offenbach and his troupe were gratified with signs of Imperial favour when, by command, they gave a special performance at the Tuileries. The Empress Eugénie had a notable dislike for symphonic music and preferred the lighter sort. Making polite conversation with Offenbach she enquired, knowing him to be of German birth, whether he came from Bonn?

No, he replied, Cologne was his birthplace. The name of the musician from Bonn was . . . He thought deeply. What *was* the fellow's name? He'd written an opera . . . one only. 'Ah, Your Majesty, he was a composer called Beethoven.'

iv

Orpheus goes down to the Underworld

Like Hervé, Offenbach had to contrive ingenious ways of evading the official rules which limited his productions to four characters.

When objection was made to the cast of five in *Croquefer*, a farce about the Crusades, he turned the fifth character into a mute. It was explained that Saracens had cut off the tongue of the unfortunate hero. What he would have said, had he possessed the power of speech, was displayed on sheets of cardboard. These remarks were of the most insane illogicality and drew the loudest laughs. Not long afterwards the embargo was removed, and eventually no limit was placed on the number of characters allowed.

Despite the ceaseless flow of cash that nightly passed into the box-office, the accounts made odd reading. This was because Offenbach conducted his affairs, as he conducted his orchestra, with heedless brio. He thought nothing of upholstering the entire theatre simply because he had spotted a small tear in one of the seats. His outlay on silk and velvet alone was prodigious, and the costumes and scenery he lavished on his productions were enormously expensive. He failed to understand why all the money that piled up in the safe could not be spent, every penny of it, on beautiful stage creations.

Financial crisis threatened to submerge the Bouffes. When Offenbach's harassed business manager at last succeeded in convincing him of the danger, the optimistic composer suggested an English tour. He had made a lot of money in England as a young man. How much more he would earn with his own troupe and a string of Bouffes successes!

They did a season at the St James's Theatre in London. The English proved to enjoy his music nearly as much as did Parisians. At Richmond the troupe had an emotional audience of the exiled Louis-Philippe's widow. Queen Victoria came to see them at the St James's one evening and gave an excellent fillip to business.

By the middle of 1858 even Offenbach had begun to flag. He was besieged on all sides by creditors. Life had become a devious game of hide-and-seek between him and those to whom he owed money. Besides, even more worryingly, he was dogged by attacks of the rheumatism which, from his forties onwards, darkened his existence with spasmodic agony. He slipped out of Paris and took a cure at Ems. Here the soothing waters and freedom from bailiffs enabled him to concentrate entirely on writing music.

Ems did not assuage the rheumatism. This was unimportant, for now he became obsessed with an idea that helped him to forget his bodily pains. The legend of Orpheus and Eurydice haunted his brain — or, rather, the humorous travesty cooked up for him by his

collaborators, Halévy and Hector Crémieux, yet another civil
servant with a passion for the theatre. As always he boiled with
impatience to complete the music and bullied the two writers
whom he accused, in reproachful comic tones, of failing to keep up
with his winged pen. He was convinced that *Orphée aux enfers*
would be his greatest triumph and would rescue his dear Bouffes-
Parisiens from disaster.

The affecting tale of Orpheus and his beloved wife had
already inspired one of Gluck's loveliest operas. In place of those
chaste melodies, the Offenbach version contained racy choruses,
patter songs and a riotous can-can. Impious librettists, not content
with an eternal triangle, contrived an elaborate situation in which
Eurydice had a retinue of lovers comprising Pluto, his servant, and
Jupiter himself. Political satire flavoured the mixture and
confirmed Offenbach's new rôle as court jester. A fleet quotation
from the 'Marseillaise', then a forbidden revolutionary song, is
heard when the gods sing out against tyranny. Louis-Napoleon
laughed as heartily as anyone else when he heard it.

Yet there are moments of quiet beauty in the score. Among
them are a dulcet humming chorus at the start of the second scene
and an idyllic clarinet solo which prefaces Act I. Another is the
song given to Pluto's manservant who laments his past life before
descending to Hades.

Naturally Offenbach wanted Schneider for the part of the
flirtatious Eurydice. She was not available. A catastrophic love
affair with the libertine Duc de Gramont-Caderousse had resulted
in her giving birth to a mongol child. She, moreover, asked
Offenbach for a ridiculously high salary. He refused and chose a
new singer called Lise Tautin, a ravishing discovery he had made
in Brussels. A pert-faced girl with an enchanting smile, she had
pretty legs that showed to advantage in the can-can. At one
moment she was coyly naïve, at another she startled with her
brazenness. Both as a stage personality and as a mistress she was,
Offenbach discovered, equally adroit.

With her in the strong cast he assembled for *Orphée* was the
comedian Bache. He had started life as a notary in the provinces
but soon turned to acting. His figure alone was enough to unleash a
roar of laughter when he appeared on stage. Thin, immensely tall,
he resembled nothing so much as a giraffe. He never smiled and
always delivered his speeches in a comically lugubrious tone. When
acting he alternated between a drawl and a quick staccato delivery

which captured the audience's attention. Yet as Pluto's servant he showed a gift for pathos as well as buffoonery.

No one fully shared Offenbach's conviction that *Orphée* would succeed on the grand scale. At the first night, and for some time afterwards, it did quite well, but not so brilliantly as the composer hoped. He cut, adjusted, revised. As with every production, he watched the audience carefully and noted weak spots that needed strengthening, scenes that would have to be revised, dialogue that failed to come off.

Several weeks after the show opened a well-known critic happened to attack *Orphée* on account of its disrespectful attitude toward the classics. Offenbach was delighted. One of Pluto's speeches was, in fact, a passage taken from the selfsame critic's own writings, and it had been deliberately chosen in a spirit of mischief because it was such a banal piece. Once the trick was revealed, the publicity did *Orphée* nothing but good. Receipts began to rise dramatically.

For two hundred and twenty-eight nights straight off, the gods and goddesses of Olympus danced the can-can, cuckolded each other, and made topical gags about life under the Second Empire. They only stopped in 1859 because the cast was tired out. *Orphée* was to be revived many times. When, in the future, business was looking bad, Offenbach had only to put on *Orphée* again to be sure of excellent houses. It was taken up abroad and produced everywhere in Europe. The one town where Offenbach never allowed it to be performed was Cologne, the place of his birth. Did he feel guilt? Or contempt? Or a wish to forget his early poverty? He himself was never quite sure.

In any case, by 1860 he was a Frenchman with naturalization papers to prove it. However much people laughed at the thick German accent which he never lost, and which caused him secret pain, he had now acquired, he felt, the unassailable right to consider himself a native of Paris. Had not the Emperor presented him with the gift of a bronze statuette after a command performance of *Orphée*?

V

Friday nights with Jacques

Offenbach had arrived. He took a large and handsome apartment in the expensive neighbourhood of the Opéra. Here he installed his wife and the quartet of daughters, soon to be enlarged, which then made up his family. The place was filled continually with noise and visitors. Amid the din Offenbach bustled around with unquenchable vivacity.

Early in the morning his barber came to arrange and curl the locks of which Offenbach was so vain. Then it was time to select the jacket, the trousers, the spats, the shirt for the day from wardrobes crammed with clothes in every style and cut. Shoes were the subject of much thought. He had dozens of pairs. Once the choice was made, his favourite daughter had the task of easing onto his gouty left foot the shoe of the day.

Impresarios, actors, singers, librettists and a throng of supplicants jostled in the outer rooms. He saw them all. Since he could never resist a hard-luck story few of them were disappointed. In between, he wrote vast numbers of letters. When the time for lunch arrived, he would eat little. His appetite was small: a few mouthfuls of boiled egg, a square inch of roast lamb, a scrap of potato and a bite of fruit were more than enough. He was in haste to light up his cigar, whose taste and fragrance he enjoyed much more than any food. He rarely weighed over six and a half stone. Although Herminie often ordered the choicest meals to be brought in from nearby restaurants, after a few half-hearted pecks he would reach gratefully for his cigar.

The afternoons were usually spent in rehearsal. Sometimes this meant visiting several theatres, for often he had up to three productions running simultaneously. Notes were taken, box-office receipts inspected. If the results were poor, instantly he would start planning a new operetta. To save time he composed on a desk set up in his carriage. The rumble of traffic stimulated him. At night a guttering candle enabled him to work on his manuscript as he travelled the raucous streets of Paris.

He was a tyrant at rehearsals. Nothing every satisfied him. He danced, acted and sang in his croaking voice every part in the show. With sweat streaming down his face, his lorgnette flying madly in the air, he urged on singers and players until they were exhausted. Then it was the turn of his business manager and the front-of-house people to be harried about posters, bookings, designs, repairs, cleaning. No detail of administration at the Bouffes-Parisiens escaped him.

When he reached home in the early evening he would go on composing, occasionally trying out a melody on the piano. Herminie would be called to give her opinion. Although he might disagree, after pondering for a moment, he would see the justice of her view. 'And do you know,' he would declare wonderingly afterwards, 'Herminie was right!'

He loved to have noise and bustle around him. If the children were silent he became uneasy. 'Is there a dead body in the house, then?' he enquired irritably. Their shouts and their laughter were an essential background to creation. Without them the flow of ideas dried up. As he wrote the music he also envisaged exactly what would be happening on stage. Each position, each exit and entrance was clear in his mind. At rehearsal he found that everything worked out as he had foreseen. Even so, once the piece had been unveiled to an audience, he was ruthless in the alterations he made. The audience was supreme. Its judgement was the only one that mattered.

In the evening he might drop in at theatres where his work figured on the bill. Hardly ever did he go to see operetta by other composers. Most nights he spent at home playing endless games of cards. Friday evenings were different. He had a superstitious respect for Friday and, if possible, preferred to do any important business on that day. 'Les vendredis de Jacques' became an institution in the social life of Paris. After a ceremonious family dinner, the house was thrown open to any and all of his friends who cared to arrive. And they came not as single spies but in battalions.

The tide of guests flowed up the stairs and into the welcoming rooms above. They were painters, musicians, actors, writers, journalists, wits, men about town. The photographer Nadar usually came on a Friday, and so did the artist Gustave Doré who designed sets for *Orphée aux enfers*. Léo Delibes was there, a young composer whom Offenbach was to help by staging some of his early operettas. Another musician of the future was Bizet. Offenbach's business partner Villemessant, editor of *Figaro*, threw his corpulent person with zest into charades organized by the popular novelist Edmond About. Fancy dress and impromptu burlesques were the order of the night.

Offenbach circulated gleefully among the crowd, champagne fizzing and slopping in his goblet. With Herminie and the girls safely at the other end of the room, he told risqué stories and exchanged the latest theatrical gossip. Only when grey dawn broke and the last friend had gone, when stale cigar smoke hung like a fog throughout the apartment and the ultimate champagne bottle had been emptied, did Offenbach reluctantly prepare for bed. And then, when he was finally asleep, one of his daughters would stealthily search through the pockets of his abandoned clothes. For he, prodigal in most things and wildly generous to those in bad luck, was extremely mean where house-keeping money was concerned. Only by gleaning coins and notes while he slept were the thrifty women of his family able to keep the home going.

With the royalties from *Orphée*, he built a seaside house in the little Norman fishing village of Etretat (he could never quite pronounce the name correctly) which was rapidly coming into fashion. The Villa Orphée, a riot of balconies, verandahs and chimney pots, contained a dozen bedrooms, each of them christened after one of his operettas. The garden gates were, like his writing paper, embellished with his monogram JO. From the window he could look out down the hill to the sea.

At about this time Offenbach made a solitary excursion into the realm of ballet with *Papillon*. It came out under distinguished auspices: the choreography was designed by the famous Marie Taglioni and the star was a superb young dancer called Emma Livry. Moreover, it was presented at the Opéra, a temple which the profane Offenbach had never yet been allowed to frequent. The auguries were good.

Yet *Papillon* was haunted by ill-luck. Critics did not like the innocent campery of the plot nor the airy balletic tunes. While they had nothing but praise for Emma Livry, they dismissed Offenbach's contribution. Very soon afterwards the exquisite ballerina was tragically and horribly burned to death. *Papillon*, which came at the end of the Romantic era in ballet, was never revived.

The only remedy Offenbach knew for unhappiness was work. In a week or so he had written *La Chanson de Fortunio*, a piece based on Alfred de Musset's tender comedy, *Le Chandelier*. This sentimental meditation on love and age was presented with a charming freshness. The song of the title is a slight but winning little air which became very popular. So did the rest of the music which fuelled polkas, waltzes and quadrilles for drawing-room consumption. The first night at the Bouffes was so successful that the whole thing had to be encored. Offenbach had returned to favour with his public.

The Légion d'Honneur, awarded to him in 1861, showed that he continued in the Emperor's favour as well. He was ever assiduous at cultivating friends in high places. That is why he flattered the Duc de Morny's theatrical longings. When that important personage revealed that he had an idea for a 'bouffonnerie', the composer and his friend Halévy knocked it into shape as *Monsieur Choufleury restera chez lui*. This was not the first time they had given such service to Morny. It was an open secret that the 'M. de Saint-Rémy' to whom programmes attributed the libretto was none other than the powerful duke. Curiosity attracted many of the famous and the fashionable to the Bouffes on nights when *M. Choufleury* was playing. Offenbach's diplomacy was good for business as well.

Unfortunately the patronage of the great did not save him from the dizzying reverses of fortune common in the theatre. Despite the success of *Orphée*, despite the reputation he had won as entertainer-extraordinary to the city of Paris, at the beginning of 1862 he decided to give up the Bouffes.

He had reached a point where he could no longer afford even to pay the salaries of his cast. Perhaps, had his health been good, he might have carried on the battle. But his rheumatism was growing worse. It gnarled his fingers and crippled his legs in a painful embrace. He must, for the time being, give up his jewel of a theatre. The lease went to a musician called Alphonse Varney whose son was to compose at least one famous operetta. As for Offenbach, crushed with debt and gout, he sadly withdrew to Etretat.

There, as the last tragedy of a disastrous year, a fire wrecked the Villa Orphée. With tears in his eyes Offenbach saw his wedding-cake folly dissolve into flame and smoke. He swore he would rebuild it and for years afterwards he was to use up the greater part of his earnings in the attempt until, eventually, he succeeded.

One bright spot lit up a year of otherwise unrelieved blackness. Herminie presented him with a son. Though he loved his daughters and cosseted them in whimsical affection, he had always longed for a son and heir. The Duc de Morny was recruited as godfather. The boy, to be known as Auguste (a name he later detested), grew up to show musical promise. Offenbach noted this with mingled feelings. Could he, with a clear conscience, let any child of his, especially a child so adored as this one, go through all the torments and disappointments which he knew from experience were an inescapable part of a musical career?

As if to prove the point his next production failed lamentably. By way of distraction he went to Ems. While there he composed an operetta called *Les Bavards*, in which a young suitor wages verbal war with the gossipy mother of the girl he wants to marry. He out-talks her so successfully that the delighted father agrees to the wedding. The 'gossip' duet between suitor and mother is the high point of the work. In Ems *Les Bavards* was very popular. It proved equally so in Paris and then throughout Europe.

Something about Ems made it a favourite with Offenbach. He adored his wife, he adored his family . . . but it was pleasant, once a year, to install them at Etretat and to make for Ems with its provincial charm and leisurely ways. The casino, in particular, he much frequented. The thrill of roulette never lost its potency. His heart always beat a little faster when he approached the gaming tables. He once told a friend: "I have two — no, three — passions. Cigars, women and gambling." He rolled his eyes significantly.

It was in Ems that he took up a famous wager. The challenge was to write and put on the stage an operetta, all within a week. He accepted, and before the time limit was out he had produced *Lischen et Fritzchen*. The libretto makes gentle fun of the Auvergnat character and accent which were favourite butts with Offenbach. The duet *'Je suis alsacienne, Je suis alsacien'* turned overnight into a hit song.

For the part of the comic little heroine Offenbach discovered a singer called Zulma Bouffar. He had seen her performing in a theatre and immediately went backstage to find out more about this attractive creature with her blonde hair and startlingly blue eyes. Though she was not a classic beauty, her mobile features and expressive gestures had a singular fascination.

In her dressing-room she told him her story. From her earliest days she had been a singer, continually wandering from town to town with her father, himself a musician. In Cologne (Offenbach pricked up his ears) she had sung at a restaurant he knew well. She was now twenty years old. Very soon Offenbach became her lover.

He remained so for an unusually long time, at least a decade or more. When he launched her in Paris, she quickly made a name for herself and was to star in many of his productions. On and off he was to stay faithful to her with, for him, remarkable persistence. He even paid Herminie the supreme compliment of taking elaborate precautions, which included the despatch of misleading newspaper reports, so that she would not know Zulma was on tour with him.

While in Ems he decided one summer to make a descent on Vienna. There he met Johann Strauss and imprudently advised him to write operetta. For his own peace of mind at the time, it was as well that he did not discern in his German colleague the rival of later years who, with others, was to overshadow his own work.

vi

From Helen of Troy to native bitch

It was high time, he decided, for another rock-bottomed, copper-plated success, a long-running show that would lift his fortunes in the way *Orphée aux enfers* had. *Orphée* had been suggested by Greek legend. Why shouldn't he use the same source again? He envisaged a sequel. The subject would be the capture of Troy, and Homer would appear as a war correspondent sending reports back from the front.

His collaborators were to be Ludovic Halévy and Henri Meilhac. The two men had been at school together, and a chance reunion inspired them to co-operate on plays and libretti. So was born a partnership that became famous in the theatre. They worked in perfect harmony: Meilhac sketched out the plots and general content, Halévy wrote the verse. They both took a hand with the dialogue. Instinctively they could tell whether an idea would work or not. Their collaborations went unclouded by disagreement.

By the time they finished writing *La Belle Hélène*, the Trojan War had been dropped. In its place emerged a farcical comedy about the beautiful Helen, daughter of Zeus and Leda, her cuckolded husband, Menelaus, and the handsome Paris. Other characters include Achilles, who is afflicted with a sore heel, and various goddesses. Once again the inhabitants of Olympus are treated with uproarious discourtesy.

It isn't surprising, we are told, that Helen should be a flirt. Is she not the daughter of a bird? (According to legend, Zeus had turned himself into a swan to seduce Leda.) She wins a beauty contest through having secretly promised her favours to Paris in return for his vote. Then follows a rigged competition in which Paris duly ends up as the victor. This has included a charade to which the solution is the word 'locomotive' — how clever, Paris exclaims, to have found the term four thousand years before the coming of railways! Throughout the scene there are mischievous references to *Tannhäuser* and an ugly, noisy fanfare. Someone asks who wrote it. Menelaus explains: 'It's some German music I commissioned for the ceremony.'

When Halévy called on Offenbach in the rue Laffitte to deliver instalments of the libretto, he never ceased to wonder at the composer's feverish industry as he wrote at the little desk in his study. From time to time, in search of harmony, Offenbach 'would strike a few chords on the piano with his left hand while his right hand still flew writing across the paper. His children came and went around him, shouting, playing, laughing and singing. Friends and collaborators arrived . . . . Entirely at ease, Offenbach chatted, talked, joked . . . and his right hand travelled on and on . . . ."

Schneider was the inevitable, the inescapable choice for the titie rôle. At that moment her private life was so desperate that she planned to leave the theatre. Her lover was on the point of death, she had no money, and she resolved to settle in her home town of Bordeaux. With some reluctance she opened her door to Halévy and Offenbach.

The composer dashed to the piano. He played and sang *'Amour divin'*, the plaintive aria where Helen sighs after love. Next he played the 'Invocation to Venus'. Finally, in his rusty voice he gargled *'Un mari sage est en voyage'*, which tells of the deceived husband who returns from his journeyings at a moment which, so far as the wife is concerned, is emphatically the wrong one.

La Schneider listened in silence. 'What a part, darling, what a part!' crowed Offenbach as he tried to persuade her. She let them go without saying that she would or would not play Helen. A little later she agreed — for two thousand francs a month.

At rehearsal she was terrifying. Well aware that she was the irreplaceable star of the show, Hortense demanded her own way in everything. She was opposed only by the girl who played Orestes, a pretty, boyish actress called Léa Silly. Between them a furious vendetta arose. Each loathed the other with a virulent hatred. Their battles raged tirelessly throughout all the preparations for *La Belle Hélène* and the run that followed.

As if rehearsals were not lively enough, there was always Offenbach to drive the cast into exhaustion with his tireless demands for perfection. Over and over again he made them run through a chorus, or act out a scene, until they were ready to drop. Sometimes he would decide a passage needed adjustment. Out came the red pencil. There and then, on the spot, he rewrote. After which, hobbling painfully among the players, he gave them new instructions. Off they went again. 'Very good, my dears! Charming!' they heard with relief, only to be told a few moments afterward: 'But do it once more — *it's not at all what I wanted!*'

La Belle Hélène did not, like *Orphée aux enfers*, have to wait for success. This came, dazzling and overwhelming, on the first night. The only flaw was a number sung by Paris, '*Au mont Ida trois déesses*'. It was heard, much to Offenbach's surprise, in disapproving silence. Overnight he wrote three different versions. Next morning he asked the singer to choose which one he preferred. They both decided on the tune with the lightest, lilting air. This became, and has remained, a popular item in the score, brightly nonchalant yet wistful.

La Schneider was confirmed as one of the town's most glamorous personalities. The combination of her particular brilliance with Offenbach's vivacious music conquered everyone. The box-office sold out for months in advance. Within the three hours' traffic of the stage on that tumultuous first night, Hortense made herself the queen of the Paris theatre. The most potent weapons in her armoury, said Meilhac, were 'her smile and her voice: that smile which, even when it said yes, did not prevent you from fearing, and which, when it said no, did not prevent you from hoping.'

Everywhere in France the tunes of *La Belle Hélène* could be heard. Soldiers marched to the brisk strain of the tune about the old kings of Greece, '*Ces rois remplis de vaillance, plis de vaillance, plis de vaillance*'. Dancers swirled round the ballroom to Helen's waltz, a luscious melody filled with remembrance of things past, and dry as the driest of champagne. Catch-phrases and slang words from *La Belle Hélène* were soon a part of daily speech.

Outwardly, the message of *La Belle Hélène* is youth, beauty, pleasure. Looked at more closely, it is a vigorous satire, one that is not aimed at the Second Empire in particular but at humanity in general. Men and women always have been, and always will be, frivolous. The types represented are eternal: Menelaus the comic cuckold; Calchas the pompous intellectual; Achilles the vulnerable hero; and Helen the spirit of gaiety and uncaring youth.

In the history of French operetta *La Belle Hélène* is an important landmark. It showed — or rather, Offenbach showed — that operetta was no longer a matter of curtain-raisers and modest one-act burlesques. The genre had flowered now into a full-length production with three acts. Those who played in it were not the talented clowns of former days who eked out their wispy voices with broad buffoonery. They were actors and actresses who could sing as well as they spoke dialogue, Characterization was deeper. The rôle of Paris, for example, had undertones of seriousness never heard in the work of Offenbach's predecessors. Instead of a scratch ensemble of bored musicians, there was an orchestra of some thirty players. The music had not been thrown together to accompany an arbitrary text but had been wedded to a carefully thought-out libretto. Although the themes of abduction and cuckoldry were hackneyed boulevard fare, they were here treated with a freshness that made for originality. Above all, the music, eternally inventive and theatrical in its very essence, carried *La Belle Hélène* to definitive triumph.

With this historica operetta Offenbach and his team became the most popular entertainers of the Second Empire. Money flowed into his coffers, and as quickly flowed out again. Much of it he spent on festivities in Etretat to celebrate the marriage of his eldest daughter, Berthe, to his business manager, Charles Comte. He even wrote a solemn mass for the church service.

In the theatre he followed up *La Belle Hélène* with another three-act work. *Les Bergers,* even though it featured a live ox on stage, failed to divert the audiences. More rewarding was the five-hundredth performance of *Orphée aux enfers* in which Cora Pearl, most notorious of courtesans, appeared as Cupid. *'Je suis Kioupi-donne!'* she crooned in her English accent. Rich lovers applauded the performance. Unruly students, who austerely deplored the event, did not. In reply to their noisy demonstration, the star of the evening cocked a snook at them.

Intensive harrying at last produced from Meilhac and Halévy the libretto of *Barbe-Bleue*. Here Bluebeard is shown as a comic figure whose wives are duly passed on to his chemist for disposal. The latter, who is a kindly man unwilling to murder these delightful girls, keeps them as his own private harem. What, in the third act, is to be done with them? A solution is provided by the Queen of Brittany. She has a band of discarded lovers who are now at a loose end. Bluebeard's surplus wives are conveniently married off to them.

Hortense Schneider played Boulotte, the simple peasant-girl who ridicules the elaborate pomp of courts and ends up by making Bluebeard her husband for life. (One very effective number satirizes the humiliating stances a good courtier must adopt to preserve his place.) She did not appear in Offenbach's next production, *La Vie Parisienne*, however, because the owner of the theatre insisted on its being cast mainly from his regular troupe. Offenbach did manage, though, to give his adored Zulma Bouffar an important rôle as the attractive little glovemaker.

No one save the composer really expected *La Vie Parisienne* to succeed. Halévy came to rehearsals in the gloomiest of moods and with 'very, very little confidence' in the new operetta. Offenbach, the eternal optimist, sent Schneider a light-hearted invitation to the first night. 'I hope you'll wear out more than one pair of gloves clapping the delightful things I've written in *La Vie Parisienne*,' he wrote, signing himself 'Your respectful father'.

He was right. On that evening of 31 October 1866, the audience cheered so enthusiastically that they drowned the singers' voices. Indeed, Hortense noted that one of her neighbours, the Princess Metternich, did just what Offenbach had facetiously proposed: she applauded with such vigour that her gloves split.

Well-timed to catch the visitors who were soon to pour into the capital for the Exposition Universelle, *La Vie Parisienne* was the talk of the town. It showed a glamorous, glittering Paris where a rich assortment of characters chase after their own idea of happiness. For the Swedish Baron de Gondremarck it is the theatre and pretty actresses. For his wife it consists of hearing great operatic singers. And for the Brazilian millionaire (*Je suis Brésilien et j'ai de l'or,*' he declares eagerly), it means, quite simply, the women of Paris.

Around them circulates a host of keenly observed types. They include the all-knowing but reticent headwaiter, the cynical woman of pleasure, the dubious adventurer, the social climber, the con-man, and the widow who, lately relieved of her husband, is out for a good time. *'Tout tourne, tout danse'*, they sing as they whirl in rhythm to Offenbach's pulsating measures.

Whereas in *Orphée* and *La Belle Hélène* Meilhac and Halévy veiled their social satire with classical drapes, in *La Vie Parisienne* they were able to comment openly. There is a scene where domestic servants rig themselves out in grand clothes and play the part of high society figures. The reversal of rôles may be taken as indirect comment on Louis-Napoleon's recent liberalisation measures. Amid all the exuberance, too, there is room for gentler emotion. When the courtesan Métella reads out a love letter, *'Vous souvient-il, ma belle?'*, Offenbach creates a moment of unforgettable tenderness.

Elsewhere in the score his music crackles in breathless patter-songs or surges into expansive melodies. An example of the latter is the waltz in the final act. The tune swells up on the dark notes of the 'cello — Offenbach always had an affection for his old instrument and gave it some of his best inspirations — to accompany verses that depict revelry and debauchery. The champagne flows, the songs get wilder and wilder, enjoyment mounts to a frenetic pitch. Then dawn breaks, and with it come leaden reality, hangovers and bills to be met. The effervescent gaiety of *La Vie Parisienne* melts fleetingly into disillusion. The combination of poignant words and beautiful melody offers a moral that needs no elaboration.

Even while *La Vie Parisienne* filled every seat in the house, Offenbach was at work on *La Grande Duchess de Gérolstein*. His collaborators 'Meil' and 'Hal' were, as usual, bombarded with exhortations, new ideas, afterthoughts. Though he apologized humorously for tearing their libretto to pieces and rewriting whole sections of it until he was satisfied, they could not take offence. He so obviously knew from instinct and experience what would work and what would not. When an audience proved him wrong, he was the first to throw out his own ideas and to replace them with something else.

In this operetta Offenbach and his writers sailed even closer to the wind of satire. They openly mocked war, scoffed at the military spirit and guyed power politics. Their Grand Duchess, a ruler of despotic power, falls in love with a ranker in her army, promotes him by the end of Act I to the supreme post of commander-in-chief, and, by the conclusion of the piece, has downgraded him to private again.

If promotion is a matter of whim and favouritism, the winning of battles is equally an affair of pure chance. Elaborate campaign plans are drawn up by the Grand Duchess's temporary commander-in-chief. 'Will they bring victory?' she enquires.

'Well,' he shrugs, 'they've as much chance of defeat as anyone else's.'

In the event, the war is won by strewing thousands of bottles of wine over the terrain (the *champ de bouteilles*' or bottlefield). These the enemy imbibe and, hopelessly drunk, give themselves up without a shot being fired.

The absurdity of war is embodied in the explosive General Boum (Boom!). He struts through the operetta with a fire-eating swagger, ever ready for a chance of battle. That he, the professional, is shown up by the humble private, an amateur, is only to be expected according to the logic proposed by *La Grande Duchesse de Gérolstein*.

For although the humour is farcical, although every convention of warfare and political intrigue is boisterously turned upside down, *La Grande Duchesse* formulates a view of things that is known within their cynical heart of hearts to every commander and to every politician. Why else should Bismarck roar with laughter when he saw it and exclaim: 'That's it! That's just how it is!' Why should Louis-Napoleon come to it twice and each time chuckle as loud and long?

They were only two of the many celebrities who, night after night, gathered to savour the pointed idiocies of *La Grande Duchesse*. In that year of the Exposition Universelle, when Paris acted as host to all the world, it was as important to have seen Offenbach's latest production as it was to have visited the splendid Exposition itself — indeed, many of the kings and princes and grand dukes and rulers of petty kingdoms probably enjoyed the *Grande Duchesse* more, since they booked seats for return visits over and over again. The King of Egypt had his favourite box. The first thing the Prince of Wales wanted, on arriving in Paris, was to see *La Grande Duchesse*.

One of the strongest attractions was Hortense in the name part. It brought her perhaps the greatest success of her career and a breathtaking fee of four and a half thousand francs a night. She designed for herself a gorgeous uniform, spangled with decorations across her magnificent bosom. Three dressing-rooms were knocked into one so that she might have a dignified setting in which to receive the visiting royalty who came to pay tribute. The rôle she played on stage overflowed into her private life. One day, arrived at the private entrance restricted to noble personages on their visit to the Exposition, she was infuriated to learn that it was closed to all plebeians. 'Open up,' she demanded. 'I am the Grand Duchess of Gérolstein!' The gate was duly opened.

The military flavour of *La Grande Duchesse de Gérolstein* gave excuse enough for Offenbach to fill his score with stirring march rhythms and galops. *'Oh! que j'aime les militaires!'* sang Hortense to a lively measure in which, stopping the show, the Grand Duchess explains how she adores soldiers and their uniforms and manly ways. Another comic masterpiece is her song *'Voici le sabre de mon père'*, in which she hands over the family sabre to her new commander-in-chief. The music everywhere abounds in foot-tapping *'rat-a-plan'* metres. Satire is not confined to words alone. In the scene where the discredited General Boum and his cronies plot against the favourite who has been promoted over their heads, Offenbach could not resist planting a barb in Meyerbeer's hide with a parody of *Les Huguenots*.

The vigorous humour of the operetta does not, however, forbid moods of emotion. In *'Dites-lui'*, when the Grand Duchess first notices the handsome soldier and gives her lady-in-waiting a message for him, she expresses the feelings of a woman whose love is frustrated by rank and age. Tell him, she says, that she finds him attractive. Tell him that, should he be agreeable, Heaven knows what she might do. Tell him that she loves him, that he is beautiful . . . The tune is a subtle mingling of the comic and the pathetic.

As an employee of the government administration — he had wisely kept on his salaried post in spite of success as a writer for the theatre — Halévy knew better than Offenbach how grave the European situation was becoming. He was deeply pessimistic about what the immediate future would bring. Offenbach, typically, cared little for international politics. If they provided useful material for *La Grande Duchess de Gérolstein*, all well and good, and he enquired no further.

In the autumn he brought out an ambitious work entitled *Robinson Crusoe*. It was produced at the Opéra-Comique and he took greater care than usual over the writing — did it not offer an admirable chance to show that a composer of operetta was not to be despised? — and composed for it recitatives and full-scale arias. With a mezzo-soprano in the part of Man Friday, and a libretto that had only the slimmest link with Defoe's original, *Robinson Crusoe* just managed to keep its head above water.

Equally disappointing was *Le Château à Toto*, a tilt at the old aristocracy which even the combined talents of 'Meil', 'Hal' and Zulma Bouffar were not enough to sustain. There were better auspices, though, for *La Périchole*. Meilhac and Halévy took their story from Prosper Mérimée's *La Carrosse du Saint-Sacrement*, which in its time has inspired an opera by Lord Berners and a film by Jean Renoir. The heroine is a fiery cocotte who enslaves the pompous old Viceroy of Peru. In the hands of Offenbach's team the story became a vehicle exclusively designed to show off every facet of Hortense Schneider's dominating talent.

At rehearsals, well aware of her power, she was unbearable. Tantrum followed tantrum. She even quarrelled with Offenbach over the exquisite letter song, which, like the similar number in *La Vie Parisienne*, must rank among his finest things. 'O mon cher amant, je te jure,' sings La Périchole, stressing the impossibility of love, however sincere, when there is no money for food.

There is another scene where La Périchole (the Gallicized nickname means 'native bitch') gets just a little bit tipsy when the Viceroy gives her dinner. *'Je suis un peu grise,'* she murmurs genteelly, and, despite some alarming lurches, manages to stay upright. Here, it is said, Hortense was superb, playing, with the utmost refinement, a number which a less assured actress might have ruined with vulgarity.

Helped by these two lovely songs and a generous mixture of seguedillas and boleros, *La Périchole* blazed its way to favour. Never was Hortense to enjoy such a resounding personal success again. She embodied with startling brilliance the cunning and the passion of the exotic heroine. 'How stupid men are!' she sang resignedly in one disenchanted number — and she put into it all the experience of life she had gained from a career which had taught her that moral above all others.

After *La Périchole* it seemed a reasonable idea to benefit from her renewed poppularity by starring her in the sort of thing Hollywood was later to term a 'bio-pic', in other words a thinly dramatised version of her own life, its excitement and its backstage romances. But in the theatre nothing is reasonable or even logical. *La Diva* withered as decidedly as *La Périchole* had flourished.

Failure did not restrain Offenbach, it only spurred him on more keenly than ever. He was full of new ideas clamouring to be tried out. The rheumatism that now contorted his limbs was so ardent that the often had to be carried on an improvised stretcher from his coach into the theatre. Even this failed to stop the crabbed fingers from holding a pen or jabbing frantically as he whipped up the orchestra to a frenzy of crescendoes.

By the end of 1869 he was rehearsing three new productions at the same time. One of them was *Les Brigands*. Its title hints at the fun Meilhac and Halévy made by including among their targets the newly-rich financiers of the Second Empire. There is also a policemen's chorus which, hymning a fine body of men who invariably arrive too late at the scene of the crime, acidly mocks those officials known with some contempt to the French as *'flics'*. W. S. Gilbert adapted the operetta for its London performance and, when he wrote *The Pirates of Penzance*, did not forget the idea behind *'Nous sommes les carabiniers'*.

Offenbach was a political innocent who judged life solely in terms of what it could provide in the way of ideas for operettas. That is a very sensible view, for what can any sane person do but shrug his shoulders at the behaviour of politicians? The antics which that breed perform often make *La Grande Duchesse de Gérolstein* appear to be a model of statesmanlike subtlety. Untroubled by events that seemed, in the thoughtful Halévy's opinion, to predict catastrophe, he continued his merry dance at the edge of the volcano.

On the eve of that terrible year of 1870 he organized a 'Grand Nautical, Aquatic and Rustic' celebration for his silver wedding. At Etretat a giant dinner party was ordained, to be followed by a masked ball, processions and theatricals. The programme included dances by 'the tottering toad' and 'the grasshopper that had missed its train'. In charge of the proceedings was 'the most illustrious, the most excellent, the most fantastic MAESTRO JACOBUS OFFENBACHUS MAGNUS.'

It was all very funny and very light-hearted. Yet underneath there ran a warm, solid love for his family and above all for Herminie. He knew how much he owed her. Despite his many infidelities, despite his meanness with money, she created the one still centre of his harebrained existence, the haven to which he knew he could always return for comfort when the outside world defeated him. He wrote for her a little rhyme, to be sung to the chorus in *Orphée*, where the goddesses tease Jupiter, otherwise and irreverently known as 'Jupin'. Offenbach, ran the verse, is unbearable and full of silly little fads. If at any moment he's at all congenial, it's only because he's thinking of Herminie.

In December that year he put the finishing touches to a little one-act piece called *La Romance de la Rose*. It was a trifle, the sort of programme-filler he could throw off in a day or so. *La Romance de la Rose* had, nonetheless, a mournful significance about it. This was to be the last new Offenbach production that appeared under the Second Empire. And his use in it of the traditional song 'The Last Rose of Summer' provided, with its air of sentimental regret, an involuntary requiem for the epoch through which he had lived and prospered.

At Ems — Ems! the resort so dear to Offenbach — the German Chancellor issued a statement deliberately designed to make the French government declare war. Patriots thronged through the streets shouting *'A Berlin!'* They did not get there. The last adventure of a sick and confused Emperor ended in defeat at Sedan. Paris was besieged and eventually taken by German troops. A republic was declared. Revolutionaries set up the Commune. Only after some twenty-five thousand Frenchmen had been killed by their fellow-countrymen did peace return. The glories of the Second Empire had vanished like tinsel buckling and twisting in the grip of an avenging fire.

vii

'Very nice, Liverpool!'

The Emperor Louis-Napoleon, who had been taken captive after the battle, was imprisoned on the night of Sedan in a small castle. The icy correctness with which Bismarck treated him only emphasised his humiliation. He sprawled in a chair, his look fixed vaguely in the distance. The room grew darker but he refused candles. Somewhere outside, a German regiment was going home. They marched, with a band at their head, to a selection of themes from *La Belle Hélène*. It is said that the Emperor put his head in his hands and wept.

The composer of those tunes was even then beside the sea at Etretat. His fiftieth birthday in June had coincided with the start of the crisis, and from then on he watched, in anguish, the struggles of his adopted country. For safety's sake he decided to take his family over the border into Spain and set up house in San Sebastian. War had silenced him.

In a land made ultra-sensitive by defeat, he became a target

for attacks not always free of spite or envy. His success and his
reputation as entertainer to a fallen régime emphasised his
vulnerability. He was caricatured as a Boche, as a countryman of
the nation which had despicably ruined France. His German
accent caused angry ridicule. There was no respite. Even German
newspapers campaigned against him as a symbol of all that was
corrupt.

He came back to Paris in the summer of 1871. At first glance
it had not really changed all that much. Although many of its
finest buildings lay in ruins, there still remained the grandiose
vistas and wide boulevards created by the Emperor's favourite town
planner, Haussmann. Fashionable women still preferred a mode
that recalled the crinoline. Gentlemen were as heavily moustached
as before, though they discreetly avoided the type of small beard
once known as 'imperial'.

There was, in general, less brilliance, less obvious flaunting
of luxury. The tone was set by the plain, quiet but shrewd lawyer
Adolphe Thiers. Under his presidency France paid her enormous
debts and was soon prosperous again. The middle classes who
with the Second Empire had flourished, now discovered that a
Republican régime was no less favourable to their ambitions. The
noble families, the old aristocracy of the Faubourg Saint-Germain,
did not snub the new order, but waited, curiously, to see how
things would develop and, in the meantime, flirted cautiously with
Republican politicians. Even the workers, their lot slightly
improved by the hesitant social measures introduced under Louis-
Napoleon, began to find life a shade easier.

In the theatre, however, all was uncertainty. Managers sensed
that the old pre-war frivolity would not do. Offenbach's Second
Empire gaiety sounded a hollow note in the altered atmosphere.
Revivals of *Les Brigands* and of *Les Bavards* fell flat. He was still
being vilified. Moralists saw in him a flagrant cause of the
irresponsibility and materialism that contributed to the downfall of
France.

Baffled though he was, and deeply hurt, by the vicious
enmities he aroused, Offenbach returned to work. He collaborated
with the dramatist Victorien Sardou, master of the 'well-made'
play, the Anouilh of his time. They produced *Le Roi Carotte*, an
allegory in pantomime form about the reign of Louis-Napoleon.
Offenbach had not lost his eye for young talent. With Zulma
Bouffar he cast Anna Judic, originally Hervé's discovery. He

admired her talent for conveying a double meaning in an innocent way that could not possibly give offence. She was then in her early twenties, short and invitingly plump, as demanded by standards of feminine beauty at the time. Offenbach's judgement was vindicated by the career on which he launched her. Some years later she was earning over a million francs a year. Though her voice was little to speak of, her manner was inimitable.

Le Roi Carotte attracted audiences not so much to hear Offenbach's music as to gape at the elaborate transformation scenes, one of which depicted magnificently the last days of Pompeii. Then, at the Théâtre des Variétés, he mounted a new operetta, *Les Braconniers*, with Zulma Bouffar and other familiar names.

The exhilaration of once again finding himself in a theatre directing rehearsals after a silence of nearly two years made up for all the unpleasantness of the last few months and gave him fresh vigour. His rheumatism was so bad that he could only manage a hobbling crawl up to the rostrum. Often it was easier for him to be carried, shivering in the depths of a voluminous fur coat, from auditorium to stage. Once the music began it was as if the disabling pains had been charmed away. He danced, mimed, sang in a throaty squawk, his arms flailing the air, his swollen gouty fingers bunched in reproving gestures at the orchestra. The sweat splashed in a stream down his gaunt features and he beat out the rhythm with his stick at such a pace that the wood shattered abruptly and fragments whistled to left and right.

There were tempestuous arguments with the management over *Les Braconniers*. Offenbach chafed at the direction of others Before the war he had been his own master. He would, he resolved, be so again, and on a grander scale than ever. The Théâtre de la Gaîté was leased and redecorated at hair-raising expense. He spruced up the vast interior with entirely new seating, luxurious carpets and oceans of gilt. Having contracted debts that soared beyond the limit of imagination he blithely opened with a play that crashed immediately.

Eventually there came the inevitable moment when revivals could no longer fill the bill. The Théâtre de la Gaîté, awful in its cavernous immensity, had a ruthless appetite for novelties. It sprawled like some greedy monster, daring Offenbach to feed it with new productions that would absorb its seating capacity. He responded by staging a new play, *La Haine*, which his friend

Sardou had written. A fortune was spent on costumes and scenery to mount a spectacular entertainment replete with exciting battle scenes. The snow of a harsh winter kept audiences from attending in any number. Rows of empty seats stared grimly at Offenbach. However much he 'papered' a dwindling house, he could not blot out those ominous gaps. *La Haine* was removed from the stage and yet another revival of *Orphée aux enfers* took its place.

At the same time as he grappled with mounting difficulties in his theatre, Offenbach was still turning out operettas for other houses. He had made another discovery, a nineteen year old café-concert singer called Louise Théo, a childlike blonde whom he launched in *Pomme d'api*. It was a light-hearted diversion that enabled Louise, as a spirited maid-of-all-work, to exploit her attractive husky voice and mischievous look.

Another of his protégées, Anna Judic, was given the title rôle of *Madame l'Archiduc*, a satire on principalities and powers, which lacked the bite of *La Grand Duchesse de Gérolstein*. The most memorable number is a quartet in Franco-English, or Anglo-French, which includes the words: 'Oh! yes splendid *l'Italie*, *London y préfer*, Oh! Yes *moi comme vous y préfer* Birmingham and Manchester, *Oh! Venise elle est jolie*, Very beautiful, *y préfer Dublin*. Oh! Liverpool! Very Nice Liverpool . . . ."

Neither these, nor *La Jolie parfumeuse*, which owed a great deal to Louise Théo, did anything to improve Offenbach's reputation. He seemed to be losing his touch. Before the war he had always been able to keep just that little bit ahead of the public taste. A sure intuition had guided him. He possessed the gift of anticipating fashion, of sensing in advance what people would like and of giving them what they wanted.. Now, in these difficult, puzzling times, he no longer saw as clearly. He, as it were, limped behind the public and was always too late with his ideas.

Certainly he must give up the Théâtre de la Gaîté. His optimistic venture on an impresario's career foundered in ruin. He would never, as he had hoped, rule the Paris theatre as gloriously as he had once ruled it with his operettas. Bankruptcy was the only way out.

What savings he had, a mere drop in the ocean, were realized and handed over. Royalties were mortgaged for years to come. The Villa Orphée was let — though whatever economy this produced was quickly nullified since Offenbach set up himself and his family in a hotel nearby.

The 'Friday evenings' continued. There were still charades and burlesques and all-night parties. Offenbach presided from an armchair, his withered frame wrapped in a dressing-gown. On his doctor's advice he took a cure at Aix-les-Bains, where his idea of rest was to compose three different operettas at the same time. In 1875 alone there were five of his works running in Paris theatres.

His dwindling flair and his gargantuan debts were not alone in darkening the horizon. A new and dangerous rival had gained the favour of the public and was already displacing him as a master of light entertainment. Even before the war Charles Lecocq had established himself with *Fleur-de-Thé*. In 1873 *La Fille de Madame Angot* brought him the greatest success of any musical production since *Orphée aux enfers*. Second Empire audiences had wanted rakishness and parody. They enjoyed satire and burlesque. Republican theatregoers preferred a more genteel brand of comedy with sentimental trimmings and Lecocq was the man to provide it.

Offenbach noted the changing trend and sought to adjust his course. He approached Meilhac and Halévy who had been playing truant and writing libretti for Lecocq. With some reluctance they agreed to work with him on *La Boulangère a des écus*, for they reckoned, harshly but not incorrectly, that their old friend, however much they liked him as a man, had been overtaken by his competitors. Offenbach also managed to persuade Schneider back into the fold. The old team was in business once more.

But not for long. Soon Hortense staged one of her temperamental exits. This time she was taken at her word, and when she deigned to arrive at rehearsals again she discovered, to her speechless fury, that a younger singer with the inviting name of Aimée had been engaged to replace her. At the first night of *La Boulangère*, anxious to see how her rival fared, she was unable to get a seat in the packed house. She then made one of the few witty comments associated with her. She would forgive the theatre manager, she punned, *'parce qu'il a Aimée'*.

La Boulangère, a good-humoured tale of a newly enriched baker's wife, brought a temporary lift to Offenbach's fortunes. There is more than a hint of the Lecocq method in its treatment, and this obeisance to the spirit of the age may have helped to keep it running. But Halévy knew that the old days of triumph were over. 'Offenbach, Meilhac and I can't do it any longer, and that's the truth,' he wrote sadly. 'And besides, we aren't twenty years old any longer, nor even forty . . . We no longer have the daring of inexperience . . . '

Offenbach did not allow himself time for nostalgia. A week after *La Boulangère* he staged a pantomime, based on a Jules Verne novel, which featured a trip to the moon. And the week after that he produced another piece in the vein of Lecocq, a historical comedy entitled *La Créole*, for which Anna Judic browned her quaint little face and sang in patois. Offenbach still had the febrile vigour and the urgent industry that could deliver an operetta ready for production within a matter of days. All he lacked was that indefinable spark which in times gone by could astonish and galvanize an audience from pit to gallery.

viii

The last illusion

Suddenly there exploded into his life a voluble and persuasive South American called Lino Bacquero. He was an impresario, a fixer, a dealer in fantastic schemes. To a bemused Offenbach he explained that 1876 was the hundredth year of American independence. There was to be an exhibition in Philadelphia. The French Government planned to offer a Statue of Liberty. Why, even Richard Wagner was writing music to celebrate the anniversary. Many thousands of dollars would be Offenbach's if he agreed to tour the USA and give concerts.

In April 1876, the composer set sail from Le Havre. When he reached New York harbour clouds of journalists descended on him. A lively throng besieged his hotel and shouted 'Vive Offenbach!'. He stepped onto the balcony and carefully mouthed: 'Thank you, Sir'.

Though at home his star might have dimmed, in America the vogue for Offenbach was at its height. Banquets, receptions, dinner-parties marked his triumphal progress. In New York and Philadelphia he conducted some very profitable concerts. There was even time for a lightning visit to the Niagara Falls and the purchase of 'genuine' souvenirs — probably, mused Offenbach, the result of sales of bankrupt stock.

He was charmed by America. An expert in publicity himself, he marvelled at American advertising methods. The jungle world of the New York theatre, where promoters could survive as many as half a dozen financial crashes, seemed to him a place of epic adventure on a scale much larger than life.

His pockets bulging with American gold, he rushed joyfully back to Paris and his home in the rue Laffitte. On the boat he had written a lot of new music: a full-length operetta based on a fable by La Fontaine, a curtain-raiser for yet another discovery of his, and a fantasy once more taken from Jules Verne. His name appeared everywhere on the theatre posters that season.

He needed all his energy for composing. In between he lay quietly on a sofa, husbanding his strength for rehearsals at which he shaped and fired the current production with relentless vivacity. Never, openly, would he admit that he had lost favour with the public. He lived in hope: hope that his next operetta would repeat the triumph of *La Belle Hélène*, hope that he would regain the crown he used to wear before 1870. He never gave up. 'I shall die with a tune at the end of my pen,' he said.

The Exhibition of 1878 revived memories of his success with *La Grande Duchesse de Gérolstein* on a similar occasion eleven years before. This time, however, Meilhac and Halévy did not respond to his overtures. When writing to Halévy he signed himself 'Charles Lecocq' in a tart reference to their desertion of him. It was not Offenbach who carried off the laurels in that Exhibition year with *Maître Péronilla* to a libretto he cobbled up himself. It was the inevitable Lecocq who dominated the season with *Le Petit Duc* and words by Meilhac and Halévy.

In the summer Offenbach revived *Orphée aux enfers* again. His early benefactor and rival, Hervé, agreed to play the part of Jupiter — provided Offenbach conducted. The composer was well enough only to direct the second act, but even so *Orphée* did well.

The interlude gave him new heart. He composed *Madame Favart*, a graceful work about the eighteenth-century prima donna that blended humour with sentiment quite as deftly as in earlier days. When it was produced in London Bernard Shaw referred justly to the Offenbach style and its 'restless movement, the witty abandonment, the swift, light, wicked touch, the inimitable *élan* stealing into concerted pieces as light as puff paste. The operetta, Shaw decided, had 'grace, gaiety and intelligence'.

A year later the obstinate suitor of a fickle public had the indescribably sweet reward of hearing enthusiastic applause once again, of seeing a crowded house rise to acclaim his music. *La Fille du Tambour-Major* had all the elements calculated to please: romance, a picturesque historical setting and a flavour of patriotism.

Faintly echoing Donizetti's *La Fille du Régiment*, it presented a flamboyant and endearing heroine: *'Je suis mam'zelle Monthabor, Ra ra ra fla, La fille du tambour-major'*. Other good things included a playful 'donkey' song and a lilting waltz in Offenbach's catchiest manner. What, though, brought audiences to their feet was a clever piece of showmanship at the climax. A knowing hand inserted into the finale the stirring tune of the *'Chant du départ'*. This traditional song, rich in Napoleonic association, evoked the same frenzy at the Théâtre des Folies-Dramatiques as 'Rule Britannia' does on the last night of the Proms.

Offenbach had done it again. Strangely, he was not all that moved by a triumph so long and so laboriously sought. The operetta stage seemed to have receded. His eyes, now, were not fixed on the bright and boisterous little world peopled by Orpheus, the Grand Duchess and the Drum Major's daughter. His mind was filled with another vision, one of an eccentric toymaker, an evil doctor, and three beautiful women whose experience of life suggested that everything, even love, is a bitter delusion.

Years ago, as a young man, he had been intrigued by the fantastic stories of E. T. A. Hoffmann, the alcoholic writer and musician who adopted the name of Amadeus in homage to Mozart. Offenbach had always thought that here was an admirable subject for opera. Perhaps, to a certain extent, *Les Contes d'Hoffmann* reflected something of his own life. He could truthfully say that he had gloriously achieved the ambition of his youth. The penniless immigrant had become one of the most famous men in all Europe and beyond. His music was played everywhere, his name stood as a universal symbol of French wit and gaiety. And yet . . . where was the reality and where the illusion?

He, who adored Mozart, secretly longed to be a great composer. A fatal gift condemned him to write operetta. One side of him took pride in the throught that he could set the whole world dancing to a breathless galop. The other regretted that he did not give his talent to better, more serious things. Time was running out. He must show, by one supreme effort, that the composer of *La Belle Hélène* and of *La Grande Duchesse de Gérolstein* was able to write music worthy of a master.

Les Contes d'Hoffmann consists of three episodes. The first, which Delibes also used for *Coppélia*, tells of the mechanical doll with whom Hoffmann falls in love, so beautiful is she. But her creator destroys her, and all that remains is a jumble of springs and wheels. In the second episode Hoffmann is spurned by the courtesan Giulietta. Finally comes Antonia who, eaten up by a fatal disease, moves a step nearer death each time she sings.

Offenbach must have felt a link with Antonia as he worked on his opera, for he knew himself that he was doomed, that the tremendous effort he was making would inevitably shorten his life. Whereas he had been used, once, to write an operetta in a matter of weeks, *Les Contes d'Hoffmann* took him several years. Even then he did not complete it.

In his music he went back to the German masters of his youth. Weber is the model for Olympia's aria *'Les oiseaux dans la charmille'*. The German influence comes through also in the minuet, the drinking choruses and the romantic legend of Kleinzach. Gounod provides the main French element, notably in the brilliant waltz of Act II and in the chorus where Antonia's mother and Dr Miracle encourage her to sing. Most original of all are the duet between Hoffmann and Antonia, and Hoffmann's *'Ah! vivre deux'*, with its exquisite modulation. The famous 'Barcarolle', of course, more than justifies its rescue from the unsuccessful *Rheinnixen*.

As Offenbach scribbled and erased and rewrote, his favourite dog, Kleinzach, dozed at his feet. Sometimes the composer would caress him. 'My poor Kleinzach,' he said. 'I'd give everything I have if only I could be present at the first night.'

In the old days he could only write when in the middle of noise and laughter. Now he wanted silence. Early in 1879 he took rooms in a hotel at Saint-Germain and worked there utterly alone.

Offenbach lived and dreamed *Les Contes d'Hoffmann*. He grudgingly found time for a couple of operettas, later to be finished by Delibes, but chafed to get back to Hoffmann. He ate very little and preferred his strong black cigars to food. In the hottest days of a tropical summer he kept the windows shut and stoked up a huge fire in the room. Though he wore a thick fur dressing-gown he shivered uncontrollably.

His body was like a skeleton. His joints ached perpetually. Bouts of dry coughing echoed through the stillness. From time to time he dragged himself over to the piano and tried out a harmony. Gasping for breath, he scrawled the notes on his manuscript paper.

By September of 1880 he was home again, the Saint-Germain

apartment having proved too expensive. News came from the
Opéra-Comique that plans were being made for *Les Contes
d'Hoffmann*. He feared that death would prevent him from com-
pleting it.

On 25 September he did not have the energy to get out of bed.
He fiddled with the sheets of music strewn over the counterpane.
His whole frame was stiff with gout. *Les Contes d'Hoffmann*, he
whispered to Herminie, would be a success. Their grandchildren
would be rich.

He wasn't well, he declared on 4 October. Could he have
another look at his score? There were changes to be made in the
last act. The end, he feared, would come that night. It arrived, in
fact, at half-past three the following morning. He was sixty-one.

Later in the day one of his actor friends, the comedian who
had been Pluto in *Orphée aux enfers*, called at the door to ask after
him. He was told that Offenbach was dead, but that he had died
very gently, without knowing what happened. 'Well, well,' said the
actor, 'how annoyed he'll be when he finds out.'

Les Contes d'Hoffmann was produced on 10 February 1881.
The orchestration, which Offenbach left unfinished, was
completed by the musician Ernest Guiraud. On that snowy first
night a large audience called for encore after encore. Offenbach
was vindicated. He had, at last, attained respectability and a place
of honour at the Opéra-Comique.

Two years later his beloved son Auguste, for whom he had
dreamed of a wonderful future, died at the age of twenty-one. In
1887 Herminie went too. Like her husband, she was sixty-one at
the time of her death.

Les Contes d'Hoffmann had meant a great deal to the
composer. The pathetic circumstances under which he wrote it
tend to give it an importance among his works that is undeserved.
Admittedly it was, for Offenbach, a major achievement and
contains some charming music. Yet one has only to compare it with
anything by his idol Mozart to see how short he fell of his aim. It is
a swansong, not a masterpiece.

His lasting fame depends on the operettas. It was Offenbach
who shaped the form and became its undisputed master. With
Orphée, *La Belle Hélène*, *La Grande Duchesse*, *La Vie Parisienne*
and *La Périchole*, he showed himself to be an entertainer of genius.

No one can deny that his musical technique was poor. When
he set the French language he often treated it with extreme

brutality. His orchestration is frequently defective when it is not scanty. He relied, at more times than he cared to admit, on the treatise by his old enemy Berlioz as an aid to solving problems which his own training could not help him surmount.

With all these faults against him his music has survived down the ages. While other, more academically correct works have long since disappeared, Offenbach's live triumphantly in all their original freshness. What is their secret? It is to be found in the wit, the bubbling inventiveness and the sheer theatrical skill. Above all, it is due to the vitality which pulses and surges with the rare, the buoyant love of life that sustained their creator throughout an existence of crippling pain that would have silenced a lesser man forever.

ACT II

THE AGE OF RESPECTABILITY

i

The cripple and Dr Miracle

From the top of a hill where the patron saint of Paris has her square, the rue de la Montagne Sainte-Genevive leads down along an ancient Roman way to the noisy boulevard Saint-Germain. It passes through one of the oldest districts in the capital. Round the corner lived Descartes. His house is there still. Not far away Pascal died.

In that narrow street, throughout the eighteen-thirties, an ill-paid copying clerk tried hard to support his large family. He found it difficult to keep a wife and five children on the meagre wage he earned in the law courts. One of those children, born on 3 June 1832, caused extra anguish to his struggling parents, for he was afflicted with a disabling hip disease. Neither money nor art was available to cure it. From the age of six onwards, Charles Lecocq could move about only with the aid of crutches.

At school he kept apart from other boys. Someone had given him a flageolet on his birthday and he took to playing it. His memory was perfect and he reproduced exactly the popular songs he heard. While his schoolmates exercised at leap-frog and chased each other through the playground, he leaned in a corner and produced a thin stream of melody. No one else in the family seems to have had his musical gift. Charles was alone in this as in so many other things.

A few years later the household moved to another dark and winding street, this time in the Île Saint-Louis, to be nearer a school so that Charles might be spared painful journeys. Here a music master discerned the boy's talent and suggested he learn something other than the flageolet. Given the choice of violin or piano, he opted for the second.

He learned quickly and, by the age of sixteen, was competent enough to give lessons himself. Up long, merciless stairs he toiled awkwardly, his crutches banging and sliding, and from omnibus to omnibus he trailed doggedly on his round of pupils. Fortunately he made the acquaintance of a musician who, a failed composer, had reconciled himself to teaching harmony. So well did this obliging friend train Charles that when the young man presented himself at the Conservatoire in 1849, he was immediately accepted.

The formidable Cherubini, who gave Offenbach such a harsh reception, had abdicated some years before. His iron rule was succeeded by the much more easy-going reign of Auber who did not mind, and probably with indolent cynicism approved, when his staff seemed more concerned with the operas they wrote than with their teaching duties. It was not unknown for some of them to be absent for a week or more while they finished a work urgently needed by an importunate theatre manager. Lecocq's harmony teacher was often elsewhere on such errands.

Composition lessons with Fromenthal Halévy were apt to be just as infrequent. Lecocq regarded him with much less affection than had Offenbach. Afterwards he claimed that Halévy taught him nothing whatsoever. 'It's not bad, but I don't like it,' he would remark vaguely whenever Lecocq showed him a composition. Yet he never said why he did not like what he saw. He was too busy with his own operas, too wrapped up in his public work as secretary of the Académie des Beaux Arts, to bother much with a not very prepossessing cripple.

More congenial to him was the sociable Georges Bizet who also figured in the group that year. Lecocq did not get on very close terms with him. His nearest friend was Saint-Saëns, a young student three years his junior. Saint-Saëns, too, had been a sickly child, and perhaps their mutual sympathy sprang from this common experience. For the rest of their long lives they kept up a warm friendship, discussing their work, exchanging ideas and even, once, collaborating on a song that had words by Lecocq and music by Saint-Saëns.

Lecocq graduated from the Conservatoire having collected a second prize in counterpoint and an honourable mention for organ playing. A career as church organist, often in those days a useful start for a musician, was denied him since his twisted legs could not manipulate the pedals. Neither could he attempt the Prix de Rome because, after the non-productive years of training, he was obliged to keep both himself and his parents.

Back he went to the dull routine of giving lessons. He played the piano in dance-halls and wherever else he could earn a small fee. His real ambition was to compose. An excellent chance offered itself in 1856 when Offenbach, newly established as impresario of the Bouffes-Parisiens, announced a competition for new composers. They were invited to set a libretto called *Le Docteur Miracle*. The prize would be a sum of money and a stage performance of the successful work.

Seventy-eight entries were received. A selection committee whittled them down to two: those by Lecocq and by the eighteen year old Bizet. Gounod and Halévy were among the judges. They both knew Bizet. The final decision was that the two scores had equal merit and should be performed alternately for a short run.

Lecocq was disappointed and embittered. He knew Halévy's partiality for Bizet and concluded that his old teacher had swayed the committee's decision. But for that, he learned later, he would have had the prize to himself. He protested when it was decided to stage Bizet's version first. So they assembled in Offenbach's little room at the Bouffes and drew lots. Lecocq won. 'Halévy, my master and Bizet's', he commented bleakly, 'did not do me the honour of coming to hear my operetta, but he came to Bizet's.'

Le Docteur Miracle, Lecocq's first work to appear in public, was given on 8 April 1857. Thereafter it alternated with Bizet's piece. Lecocq was in his twenty-fifth year. He saw the episode as confirmation of his view that success was only to be achieved by a constant battle with hostility and injustice. He never forgave Offenbach, whose behaviour towards him he thought extremely unpleasant, nor did he pardon Halévy. What pleasure he might have gained from the little triumph was spoiled by the manoeuvres and ill-feeling which envenomed the affair.

Several one-act operettas followed, none of them leaving much trace except for the inventive *Ondines au champagne*. This featured water sprites with names like 'Acquamarine' and 'Coral Flower'. 'Acquamarine' herself was given a wistful little romance to sing. The piece ends with a *'Galop final'* which, though a distant cousin of the one in *Orphée aux enfers*, is decidedly more genteel. The style which was to distinguish Lecocq from Offenbach had started to form itself.

In that same year of 1866 he wrote an operetta called *Le Myosotis* with a libretto by the caricaturist Cham and a phenomenon known as William Busnach. An Italian with names both Germanic and English, Busnach had been born in France of an Algerian father. He was one of those incessantly versatile workers often to be found in the theatre. As a play doctor, as a collaborator, as a freshener-up and adaptor, Busnach could always be relied upon to deliver the goods. At any given moment he would have several plays in rehearsal at different theatres and a dozen others on the stocks with various collaborators. Drama? Tragedy? Comedy? Farce? Revue? Busnach was your man, guaranteed to run up just the thing you wanted and with rôles tailored perfectly for everyone in the company. The hundreds of plays in which he had a hand are now buried in history. He is remembered only for his stage adaptations — workmanlike and effective, as was everything from his one-man factory — of Emile Zola's novels.

Apart from his terrifying activity Busnach was an affable man and one ready to do a favour to a young composer, always provided there was a little something in it for himself. A rich banker had just constructed the Théâtre de l'Athénée. With the idealism that sometimes infects even the most successful financiers, he planned to alternate in his beautiful new theatre symphony concerts and lectures on cultural topics. It very soon appeared that audiences did not share his interest in these matters. He gave up and leased the theatre to Busnach and an associate. Busnach knew everyone, had valuable contacts everywhere in Paris, and could be relied on to handle the situation with flair.

For his first production at the Athénée Busnach decided on *L'Amour et son carquois*, a two-act operetta he had written with a partner. He asked Lecocq to provide the music. The plot features Cupid, who, banished from Olympus on account of his escapades, descends to earth and enrols in a girls' boarding-school — that favourite setting of nineteenth-century playwrights in search of comic incident — where he falls in love with the principal's daughter.

L'Amour et son carquois did not have much success, despite the presence of Léonce and Désiré, two comedians who had made themselves famous in Offenbach productions. The music was generally considered to be well written and too good, even, for the mediocre libretto. It lacked, said critics, the necessary verve.

Lecocq had not yet learned to harness his musical gift to the demands of the stage.

Through Busnach, however, Lecocq met Henri Chivot and his collaborator, Duru, a flourishing team who wrote *La Fille du Tambour-Major* for Offenbach and *La Mascotte* for Edmond Audran. They were, like Busnach, inexhaustible. At that moment they were looking for a composer to set their *Fleur-de-Thé*, a full-length three-act piece. They liked what they had heard of Lecocq and asked him to oblige. Within two months he produced a score.

He had not at first been very impressed by the work. Originally entitled *Le Mikado*, a name hastily changed when the Japanese ambassador to Paris made a polite intervention, it concerned a ship's cook ordered by a powerful mandarin to wed his daughter. The obstinate cook is about to be executed when his own wife plies the troops with champagne and fuddles them long enough for a French ship to arrive and rescue him. It was, thought Lecocq, a dated piece of tat, and he only agreed to write the music because Busnach and the authors were so persistent.

Fleur-de-Thé was Lecocq's first triumph. It was helped by the inimitable clowning of Désiré and Léonce, the one bushy-eye-browed, red-faced and corpulent, the other thin, pallid and gaunt, with a genius for adding impromptu gags. Their duet. *'Je vois tout — Il voit tout!'* creamed off the applause every night. This, together with a drinking song and other numbers, helped to make Lecocq's name reasonably well known.

Fleur-de-Thé was the only one of his first nights he ever missed except through illness. Usually, whether the occasion developed into success or failure, he stayed to the end, listening backstage to what was going on out front. He disliked being among the audience. It meant that he often heard and saw unwelcome things. During the run of *Fleur-de-Thé*, for example, a spectator roared with appreciative laughter at the actions of Léonce and Désiré. When the music began again he turned away sulkily, impatient for it to be over so that the buffoons could entertain once more. Moving through the audience afterwards, Lecocq overheard, with annoyance, a woman declare: 'Only a man like Offenbach could write music such as this!' Worse still, on that same evening a friend who wanted to compliment him on the drinking song innocently hummed, by way of illustration, a number from Offenbach's *Les Bavards*. Such incidents deepened his loathing of the composer who had rapidly became his pet aversion.

ii

The father of Madame Angot's daughter

Throughout the Franco-Prussian War and the siege of Paris Lecocq and his widowed mother kept to their flat in the Place Pigalle. This area of Montmartre was not then riddled with the night-clubs and tawdry cabarets of our own age. It still had a faintly rural air. Some years were to elapse before the old windmill of the Place Blanche actually turned into the 'Moulin Rouge' and Auguste Salis founded his 'Chat Noir' in a nearby boulevard.

Madame Lecocq and her son managed to survive the horrors of the conflict. When the revolutionary Commune was established they felt they had had enough of Paris. The middle-aged cripple and his ancient parent left the city to stay in Argenteuil with relatives. Not yet built over with factories and workshops, the vineyards and market gardens had a peaceful aspect welcome to refugees from the bloodied tumults of Paris. If the wind were right they could hear the boom of guns in the capital. They saw, too, the flames of buildings put to the torch by the Communards.

At the height of the terror imposed by the Commune Lecocq realized that, so far as Paris was concerned, the theatre would be inactive for a long time yet. He now thought of Belgium. Before the war he had made the acquaintance of a Brussels impresario called Humbert, proprietor of the Fantaisies-Parisiennes in that city. Humbert, always alert for new talent, always fashioning new projects, spent most of his time on the train between Brussels and Paris arranging deals, contracts, agreements. He was a giant of a man, a non-stop talker who drank generously to lubricate his perpetual discourse. *Fleur-de-Thé* had received its Belgian première in his theatre and he asked Lecocq to write something else for him.

As soon as the Commune was over Lecocq returned to Paris and composed *Les Cent Vierges*. Humbert accepted it and staged the first performance at the Fantaisies-Parisiennes on 16 March 1872. It was well received. Later that year it had an equally good reception in Paris. *Les Cent Vierges* was soon to be heard in Germany and also in England, where it was chastely titled *The Island of Bachelors*.

The idea of *Les Cent Vierges* is that a hundred Englishmen living on a desert island resolve to populate it. They ask the

Admiralty to send them a hundred maidens for the purpose. The boat goes astray. Meanwhile another ship arrives with women aboard, including two married ladies. The latter are followed by their husbands, who, as the plot develops, are obliged to disguise themselves as women and find themselves chosen, respectively, as brides for the governor of the island and his secretary. The original boat containing the hundred virgins turns up just in time.

The music was deft and, as always with Lecocq, thoroughly craftsmanlike. A waltz ('There's no happiness away from you, my fair one') struck the note of inoffensive sentimentality that his admirers soon learned to enjoy. Throughout the chorus of the hundred virgins he showed his usual adroitness at ensemble writing. The operetta, in short, demonstrated that he had by now acquired all he needed to know of stage craftsmanship.

The expansive Humbert, radiant with success, became· a frequent guest of the Lecocq household and a particular favourite of the composer's mother, who looked on him almost as a second son. One day he burst in through the door, his customary exuberance inflated to such a state of delirium that Lecocq feared for his sanity. The excited impresario hurled three manuscript notebooks onto the table. 'My dear Lecocq,' he trumpeted, 'I'm bringing you wealth!'

The manuscript was the libretto of *La Fille de Madame Angot* which Humbert had conjured out of a team of three librettists. It had emerged, as these things will, from a series of exhausting conferences which began with the idea of turning *Romeo and Juliet* into an operetta.

'Madame Angot' was a popular type created during that period of French history known as the Directoire and lasting from 1795 to 1799 when Napoleon wearied of hindrance to his power and took over everything himself. A fishwife, a raucous daughter of the people, she was a comic character who, having become a member of the nouveau riche, found herself quite thrown out of gear by the sudden contrast between her coarse origins and her unexpected wealth. This legendary character provided the excuse for much topical satire in the songs and plays which she inspired. She was often acted by a female impersonator with a great crow's beak of a nose, a voice that quacked like a duck, and a flow of working-class language only checked on occasion by absent-minded attempts to 'talk proper'.

Madame Angot's daughter Clairette is the heroine. An

orphan, she has been bred up by rough but kindly fishwives and market fruitsellers who are unaware of her parentage. She thinks she is in love with Ange Pitou, and, to avoid the marriage that has been arranged for her with an amiable wigmaker, she loudly sings in public some of the chansonnier's most violent couplets against leading Directoire politicians. She is imprisoned. She repents. And she is released in the end to marry the wigmaker whom, she decides, she really loves after all.

The charm of *La Fille de Madame Angot* does not spring from the tenuous plot. It is to be found in the music which Lecocq wrote at the height of his power and in full control of his talent. Somehow he captures the very flavour of the period with refrains that hark back to popular tunes of the seventeen-nineties. At the same time, with a romance like *'Elle est tellement innocente'*, he restores that simplicity and freshness of the eighteenth-century French opéra-comique which it was Offenbach's ambition to achieve. He can be robust, as in Clairette's 'Political song' and in the 'legend of Mother Angot', or lightfooted, as in the duettino *'Voyons, Monsieur'*, and in the trio where Clairette decides at last that her wigmaker is *'charmant'*. The obligatory waltz, *'Tournez, tournez!'* though it lacks the feverish vigour Offenbach would have supplied, starts off with a splendid swoop that pretty well carries it through.

The Belgian audience at the première of *La Fille de Madame Angot* forgot its traditional reserve and demanded encore after encore. It was the same story in Paris the following year. At one o'clock in the morning Lecocq was dragged onstage to acknowledge endless applause. His operetta had been heard with delighted absorption — so deep, indeed, that a fire broke out and went completely ignored. In the ballroom scene whirling dancers created draughts and fluttered candle flames which set fire to background drapes. Under the spell of Lecocq's waltz, the audience remained oblivious to members of the cast who hastily tackled the flames.

Not since the legendary triumphs scored by Offenbach had the musical theatre known such overwhelming success. Lecocq's new style set the fashion. It was very French, as indeed Offenbach's had been, though in a noticeably different way. Sizzling excitement was replaced by a lucid gaiety, charm and sentiment took over from parody and satire. If Lecocq was not as carelessly prodigal of melody, at least his orchestration and harmonies were richer. The approach was quietly humorous and tolerant. The nearest he and

his collaborators came to political satire in Offenbach's manner
was a mild remark *'Voila comment cela se mène / C' n'était pas la
peine; c' n'était pas la peine / Non pas la peine assurément / De
changer de gouvernement!'* ('That's the way things go — no, it
really wasn't worth the trouble to change governments.')

La Fille de Madame Angot ran and ran. At the three-
hundredth performance one of the librettists commented
humorously that the operetta had already worn out 'six Clairettes'
and 'three Pitous' among others, a total of twenty-two actors, thirty
musicians and 'five or six ministers and three governments as well.'

The work was many times revived and attained the ultimate
distinction of performance at the Opéra-Comique. The tunes were
played in drawing-rooms everywhere and inspired countless
waltzes, polkas and quadrilles. Every sort of adaptation and
arrangement made them known up and down Europe. Lecocq's
star had risen. Offenbach's was irretrievably dimmed.

iii

A little Duke

Between 1873 and 1888, except for the year of 1880 which was a
time of illness, Lecocq produced over twenty operettas. He chose to
follow Madame Angot with *Giroflé-Girofla*. (A *giroflée* is a gilly-
flower.) By playing around with the term the librettists created
charmingly memorable names for the twin sisters who are heroines
of the piece.

Lecocq, usually an impartial judge of his own work,
considered *Giroflé-Girofla* to be among the scores he had written
'with the most pleasure and, I must also say, with the greatest
facility'. He did not wish merely to repeat the technique of
Madame Angot and deliberately sought to make his new operetta
as different as possible. 'It is,' he wrote, 'one of the best works
among my output, full of dash and high spirits.'

One cannot entirely agree with his estimate. The dash and
high spirits are certainly there — as in the swaggering quintet
'Matamoros, grand capitaine', for example, or in the 'Moorish'
march — but the score is not so uniformly excellent as that of
Madame Angot. In any case, it would have been extremely
difficult to cap such a triumph. That having been said, *Giroflé-*

Girofla still proves Lecocq superior to his contemporaries in the field of operetta. The pirates' chorus has the same happy inspiration as the conspirators' ensemble in *Madame Angot*. The 'Brindisi' make a scintillating contrast to the innocent appeal of *Giroflé fleur d'innocence'*.

Giroflé-Girofla had its première in Brussels. Thereafter the composer did not need to go outside his native country to launch a new operetta. When it came to Paris the cast included a new face, that of twenty-two year old Jeanne Granier. She had been spotted in Etretat by Offenbach who, with untypical slowness, gave her only walk-on parts. When the star of his *Jolie Parfumeuse* fell ill, Granier took over at very short notice and made a brilliant début. She was quickly snapped up by Lecocq for *Giroflé-Girofla*.

She was built on the stocky, generous lines then much favoured by connoisseurs. Her musical education had been classical and she had never until then had much to do with operetta. For nearly a month she came to Lecocq's flat and sang, at his request, everything she knew. He listened in silence. Eventually, unnerved by the lack of any decision about her engagement, she blurted out: 'I can see, *cher Maître*, that I don't suit you for *Giroflé!*'

'What do you mean?' asked Lecocq. 'If I make you sing every day it's because I get rare pleasure, a musician's pleasure from hearing you. And I assure you I shall never be able to find anyone better than you to create my *Giroflé*.'

The contract was signed next day. Just as Hortense Schneider became identified with Offenbach's music, so Jeanne Granier, destined for a splendid career, was to be associated with Lecocq's as his favourite interpreter.

Despite the success of *La Fille de Madame Angot*, the Paris manager who put it on still did not have much faith in Lecocq and he turned down *Giroflé-Girofla*. The operetta was accepted for the Théâtre de la Renaissance. This new theatre, built in 1872 and as typical of the Republic as Garnier's Opéra was of the Second Empire, is still to be found in the boulevard Saint-Martin. *Giroflé* began something of a tradition there, and Lecocq was to produce half a dozen new works in succession at the Renaissance.

His relations with publishers were what might be expected of a successful composer. In those days, before television, recording and film interests usurped their domination, music publishers were all-powerful. Upon them depended almost exclusively the circulation of new music. Amateurs who lived in Paris and the big provincial cities with opera-houses or theatres at least had the chance of hearing it for themselves. Elsewhere, they had to rely on sheet-music to keep up with the latest successes at the parlour pianos. As Gounod did with *Faust*, Lecocq sold the score of *Madame Angot* much too cheaply. He did not forget this and sold the score of his subsequent operetta, *Pompon,* at a vastly higher price. Here the fortunes of the theatre gave him an ironic revenge for *Pompon* did not last for more than fourteen performances.

He coasted along over the next few years, his name appearing on theatre bills as the composer of a new work at least once and often twice a year. *Kosiki* was an attempt to profit from the current fashion for things Japanese and featured rival mikados. That it lasted for some three months was due rather more to Zulma Bouffar, once the star in Offenbach's theatre, than to Lecocq's music. *La Marjolaine* did little better: it depended on the attractions of Jeanne Granier.

Both were produced at the Renaissance, which Lecocq had come to look on as 'his' theatre, much as the Bouffes-Parisiens had been Offenbach's. A sympathetic management listened to his views and carried out his wishes. 'Ah!' he wrote later, 'how easy and pleasant was the composer's profession under the conditions in which I followed it at the happy time of the Renaissance! What rehearsals and what first nights! Everything went smoothly as if on wheels. With what vigour did leaders and soldiers march into battle! Those sweet memories are so far away already and seem like a dream!'

In 1878 he rewarded his friends at the Renaissance with a piece that was to rival *La Fille de Madame Angot* herself. It was called *Le Petit Duc* and had an excellent libretto by Henri Meilhac and Ludovic Halévy. 'Meil' and 'Hal' no longer worked with the composer of *La Belle Hélène*; they had seen that the future belonged to Lecocq and their belief was vindicated by *Le Petit Duc*.

This was a story set, like *Madame Angot*, in the historical past. The period is that of Louis XIV and the glorious days of Versailles. The hero is a young duke who weds, for dynastic and financial reasons, an even younger heiress. Once the marriage is over the politicians and courtiers are satisfied. The boy and girl, they decide, are too young to live together so the child-wife is packed off to a convent for several years and the boy posted to a

ADOLPHE ADAM,
a pioneer of operetta who
cheerfully bankrupted himself
in the cause of music.

HERVE, the "loony composer",
who was conductor, producer,
scene-shifter, actor and singer,
as well as composer of more than
a hundred stage-works.

OFFENBACH—"I shall die," he said, "with a tune at the end of my pen."

Caricature of Offenbach astride the four Paris theatres where, at the height of his career, he had different operettas running simultaneously.

HORTENSE SCHNEIDER, an Offenbach star . . .

. . . as were ZULMA BOUFFAR . . .

A scene from Offenbach's
Le Voyage à la lune
featuring Zulma Bouffar.

LEONCE, the comedian of the troupe,
in Offenbach's *Le Docteur Ox*.

DESIRE, another popular comic actor,
in Offenbach's *Les Géorgiennes*.

JEANNE GRANIER as Eurydice in the 1887
production of *Orphée aux enfers*.

ROBERT PLANQUETTE,
Composer of *Les Cloches de Corneville*.

CHARLES LECOCQ, parrot-lover
and Offenbach's successful rival.

EDMOND AUDRAN,
creator of the "schocking" *Miss Helyett*.

ANDRE MESSAGER,
consummate musician and man of the theatre.

The versatile JEAN PERIER again,
this time at Coppélius in the 1911 Opéra-Com
production of *Les Contes d'Hoffmann.*

JEAN PERIER and MARIETTE SULLY
in the "donkey duet" from the
first production of *Véronique.*

DEARLY
aude Terrasse' *Chonchette*.

RI CHRISTINE, whose *Phi-Phi*
ed a new vogue for one-steps and fox-trots.

REYNALDO HAHN,
elegant musician of the Belle Epoque.

SACHA GUITRY, prince of the boulevard theatre,
who wrote witty words that Messager,
Hahn and Oscar Straus set to music.

ALBERT WILLEMETZ,
collaborator in over two hundred
and fifty revues and operettas.
(Caricature by Sacha Guitry.)

YVONNE PRINTEMPS,
the second Madame Sacha Guitry.

A scene from *Mozart* with Sacha Guitry, left, as Baron
and Yvonne Printemps, centre, as the boy Mozart.

dragoon regiment where he can play at soldiers. But the little duke longs for his duchess. He lays siege with his troops to the convent and rescues her by a clever stratagem. Suddenly war is declared. While the duchess stays in camp, he fights bravely on the battlefield. His valorous deeds win him the king's forgiveness and the youthful couple are allowed to set up house.

Lecocq's music had the benefit of a libretto written by two old masters. Their last joint work of a military flavour, *La Grande Duchesse de Gérolstein*, had been quite different. In *Le Petit Duc* there was no hint of satire. They recounted the little anecdote with grace and a touching humour. If the third act, as Lecocq sensed, did not entirely work, the total impression was good.

As the little duke *en travesti*, Jeanne Granier, wrote Lecocq, was 'dazzling with charm and verve'. There were few problems involved in the production and *Le Petit Duc* soared easily to the height of popularity. The composer himself revelled in public favour as never before. For the time being he was master of the unpredictable world of operetta.

Le Petit Duc has the same musical quality as *Madame Angot*. Justly famous was the singing lesson in the middle act. It is prefaced with a delicate madrigal-like introduction, sweetly sincere yet comic in effect, which reminds us what an adroit musician Lecocq was and how thoroughly he had absorbed the lessons gained from close study of the old French composers. Another example is the gavotte in Act I, a melody that contains the sort of exquisite nostalgia distilled by a Rameau or a Lully. Soon afterwards the pages' chorus, *'Il a l'oreille basse'*, shows that Lecocq's gift for memorable tunes was as strong as his talent for pastiche.

Alternately reflective, as in the *Lamento* of Act III, or boisterous, as in the little hunchback's song and the peasant rondeau, Lecocq handles each passing mood with a sure and accurate touch. The chorus he wrote for the dragoons is as stirring as the 'idyll' duet is tender. Hardly anywhere does his flair betray him, and the result is a score that embodies his own sort of perfection.

The hundredth performance of *Le Petit Duc* was celebrated with a banquet in a chic hotel at Saint-Germain. The colonel of a dragoon regiment stationed nearby gallantly sent a mass of flowers inscribed to *'le colonel duc de Parthenay'*, which was the rôle played by Jeanne Granier. She, enchanted by the gesture, fell upon the young dragoon who delivered the bouquet and kissed him on both cheeks. Of all the events in his military career, this was the one for which his training had least prepared him, as, blushing and stammering, he underwent an experience many theatregoers would have envied.

iv

Old friends and a parrot

Lecocq was forty-seven at the time of *Le Petit Duc*. The years of struggle and poverty were over. He could now afford to take a flat in the rue de Surène, a fashionable street near the Madeleine, and to live, if not in grandeur, at least in solid comfort. Towards the end of his long life he was to have as neighbour, in the rue d'Anjou just round the corner, the young Jean Cocteau, who shared his mother's home there. Next door to Cocteau was an equally youthful Sacha Guitry, still a penurious actor and not yet the prince of the boulevard theatre. By the time Lecocq died in 1918 they had both been well launched on their careers.

Unlike his waning rival Offenbach, Lecocq avoided publicity. He left such things to impresarios. Whereas Offenbach had a genius for publicising himself and his colourful personality as a means of advertising his theatre and his latest operetta, Lecocq preferred to live his private life in private. Nor did he emulate Offenbach by choosing his mistresses from among his leading ladies. His crippled legs, twisted and painful, in any case restricted his ventures into society. He married and settled down, so far as is known, to a quiet domestic existance with an attentive wife. When he was not working on an operetta he was just as happy to stay at home writing songs or studying Rameau.

He was blessed with the gift of friendship. Saint-Saëns, whom he had met in his student days, remained an intimate. Over the years they exchanged hundreds of letters. Lecocq watched the development of Saint-Saëns's career with affectionate envy. He would himself have so much liked to achieve renown as the composer of symphonies and operas. His talent for light music decreed otherwise. Ironically enough, Saint-Saëns, whose work was played in concert halls throughout the world, in turn envied Lecocq his success with operetta.

Another friend was the irrepressible Emmanuel Chabrier,

composer of *Espana* and much else of originality. He had met Lecocq in the eighteen-eighties. A civil servant at the Ministry of the Interior, a largely self-taught musician, Chabrier was often dismissed by conventional opinion as an amateur of little worth. Lecocq, together with other discerning musicians, was among the few who appreciated his novel inspirations. 'Chirpy as a finch and melodious as a nightingale' was how his friend Verlaine described Chabrier. He had a wide acquaintance. His taste in painting was as adventurous as his music, and his private collection included dozens of pictures by Manet, Monet, Cézanne, Renoir and Sisley.

Lecocq read Chabrier's manuscripts and gave helpful advice. 'Thank you, my dear Lecocq, thank you, dear friend,' replied Chabrier, 'You're kindness and understanding itself, and what's more you're always right! I've corrected everything, even the question marks . . . "

In Lecocq's home and Chabrier's they played Grieg piano duets ('Marvellous stuff!' exulted Chabrier) and, as a special treat, four-handed music by Schubert. Lecocq, ever modest, recognized Chabrier's superior quality as a composer and prided himself on their friendship. His reward came in the letters he received from Chabrier, letters which he treasured, for Chabrier wrote prose with as much verve as he did music. *'*Mes chers coqs*,' Chabrier would begin, preluding in his letter to Lecocq and his wife yet another burst of wit and fantasy.

The comradeship of musicians like Chabrier and Saint-Saëns, and the peaceful household in the rue de Surène, were enough for Lecocq's happiness. To these must be added the company of a parrot. The bird had been given him by Zulma Bouffar, the star of some of his major operettas. It was old even then, and no one had ever been able to estimate the precise age of the venerable creature. Whenever a singer came to rehearse or audition, the parrot cocked a watchful ear. If what it heard was satisfactory, it did not open its beak. If, however, it detected a mistake — for it seemed somehow to have acquired a perfect knowledge of its master's compositions — it would dash itself angrily at the singer's feet squawking 'That's wrong, that's wrong! Oh Charles, come, come!' Often Lecocq

---

*Some of Chabrier's letters have been admirably translated by the late Edward Lockspeiser in *The Literary Clef* (John Calder, 1958) — itself a valuable anthology in English of selected correspondence by French musicians.

would have to exercise considerable diplomacy to make up for the offence caused by his outspoken pet.

The parrot had a grudging and jealous nature. More than one singer who greeted Lecocq with an affectionate kiss was to find herself attacked by an angry bundle of feathers whizzing through the air and pecking at her feet. When it was obvious that Lecocq was about to leave the flat on some errand, the bird would fly down from its perch and dance about in front of him like a gaoler keeping a convict under watch. There was no better proof of Lecocq's good nature than the patience with which he bore the parrot's tantrums.

v

To end with Ali Baba

To follow up *Le Petit Duc*, which had scored over three hundred performances at the Théâtre de la Renaissance, Lecocq brought out *La Camargo*, an operetta featuring the eighteenth-century French dancer. Not only was she famous for her delicate style of dancing, for the ravishing portrait by Lancret and for the dish, '*Bombe Camargo*', named after her. She also introduced an important change in ballet dress by shortening her skirt and preparing the way for the tutu. As well, and this may have endeared her to Lecocq, she also had a much beloved pet parrot.

La Camargo made unusual demands on Zulma Bouffar who took the lead, for she had to dance and perform convincing entrechats in addition to singing. As always at the Renaissance, Lecocq had complete control of a theatre possessing 'a good troupe, a good orchestra, a well disciplined chorus . . . ' Since then, he remarked grimly, 'a host of composers without authority have allowed managers to elevate tampering to the level of an institution; but I don't think they've ever been successful. If, in a work under rehearsal, modifications become necessary, the writers should be the first to realize it.' All his working life he had fought for the supremacy of the creator. He never willingly surrendered authority to interfering producers or dominating singers.

In 1879, as a result of a contract signed years before and forgotten by the composer until then, he briefly interrupted his tenure of the Renaissance to write an operetta for the Théâtre des Variétés. *Le Grand Casimir* featured the comic actor Baron, a great favourite with audiences. He was subject, however, to disabling attacks of stagefright, especially where music was concerned. In Offenbach's *Les Brigands,* playing the chief of police, he missed his cue on the first night and had to gabble, in his rusty, thunderous voice, the words of the famous chorus *'Nous sommes les carabiniers'*. Eventually he caught up with the orchestra and both finished at the same time. The effect was even funnier than Offenbach had intended.

For *Le Grand Casimir* Baron had a song which, stricken with fear, he was totally unable to sing at rehearsals. On the first night and thereafter, nonetheless, his uproarious bungling of Lecocq's music stopped the show.

With a sigh of relief Lecocq went back to the Renaissance. Even here all was not well. A tempting offer by the manager persuaded him to agree, against his usual practice, to set libretti as yet unwritten by Meilhac and Helévy. Normally he would not write the music until all the words had been completed. The first act of *La Petite Mademoiselle* proved excellent and well up to standard. The two remaining acts, when delivered, turned out to be a sharp disappointment. Crude, exaggerated, they were completely different from the first act.

Bitterly regretting the terms of his contract, Lecocq set about his task. In the end he believed the score of *La Petite Mademoiselle* to have been 'one of the best, in my opinion, that I have written'. This was not quite true, and the talent of Jeanne Granier in the leading rôle was necessary to give the piece a measure of success.

La Jolie Persane, a comedy about Persian marriage customs, had the same sort of mixed fortune. It was designed for Jane Hading, a young performer with a pretty voice and a keen musical instinct who later became a very well-known actress. She soon afterwards married Lecocq's impresario at the Renaissance. Despite her undoubted charm, audiences were disappointed at the absence of their idol, Jeanne Granier, and although *La Jolie Persane* brought the owner of the Renaissance a wife, it did not bring him much in the way of box-office receipts.

For a year and more Lecocq remained silent. Domestic problems and a long illness kept him away from the theatre. By 1881 he was just well enough to struggle to rehearsals of *Janot*, his last collaboration with Meilhac and Halévy, and also his final production at the Renaissance. The theatre with which his name was so closely identified, 'his' theatre where he had felt so much at home, was abruptly denied him. A happy association dissolved under threats of legal action and angry disputes. Ill and reluctant, Lecocq painfully scrawled the music of *Janot* because it was a part of his contract to do so and for no other reason.

Under these circumstances *Janot* was one of the poorest operettas Lecocq ever wrote. He fully realized this and himself scribbled his own harsh judgements throughout the score. 'An idiotic song,' he wrote against one of the numbers. 'Stupid' he declared about another. His comments sprawl across the pages: 'not up to much . . . wretched . . . horrible! . . . silly as a goose'.

Exhausted by the preparations for *Janot*, he fell ill again and his next operetta, *Roussotte*, had to be completed by Hervé. The happy days at the Renaissance were over. Luckily he found a new home at the Théâtre des Nouveautés and, within two months, had written *Le Jour et la nuit*. This fanciful romance, set in an imaginary Spain at the beginning of the eighteenth century, recalled the qualities of *Giroflé-Girofla* and gave Lecocq some compensation for the collapse of *Janot*. 'Total takings at the first hundred performances', he noted gleefully, 'were 432,119 francs, 50 centimes.'

Le Jour et la nuit was the début of Marguerite Ugalde, daughter of a famous opera singer and on the threshold of a very successful career in operetta. Lecocq was unable, through illness once more, to see the first night and only managed to attend the fifteenth performance. It was an unfortunate choice, as the audience that evening was cold in the extreme. He had, moreover, the unpleasant experience of sitting near a couple of spectators who did not cease to criticise, in vigorous terms, both words and music. By the third act, to his relief, they had fallen silent. Perhaps someone had told them the composer was nearby?

With *Le Coeur et la main* he attempted to repeat his success. Again the setting was ancient Spain and the theme one of princely romance. The score was distinguished by an 'orange blossom' song in Lecocq's best manner and a neatly written love duet. But the public, suspicious of the similarity with *Le Jour et la nuit*, did not show much enthusiasm.

After *La Princesse des Canaries*, a joke about a princess who disguises herself as a village girl in order to regain her lost throne. Lecocq could do little right. From the mid-eighteen-eighties

onward he gradually drifted out of touch. It was inevitable. Public
taste had changed and no longer favoured the cosy, sentimental
comedy in which he specialized. Just as he had superseded
Offenbach at a given moment, so he was in turn overtaken by
younger rivals. Among them was André Messager. The extent to
which Lecocq failed to appreciate the new style is shown by his
reaction to Messager's *Les Dragons de l'Imperatrice*. 'It's original,
it's interesting, but it belongs,' he remarked surprisingly, 'to a
genre that bores me because there's too much talent in it and not
enough imagination.'

He went on to write an operetta taken from an Aristophanes
play, and then another with Ali-Baba as its hero. In 1894 he
composed a music-hall number for the Casino de Paris. The final
years of his career saw an operetta which anticipated Rostand by
casting Cyrano de Bergerac as the leading figure, a ballet that told
the story of Bluebeard, and, here and there, various one-act trifles.
He was written out. The grace and fine workmanship of his best
years were still there, but inspiration had flown.

By the turn of the century Lecocq had reached his sixty-
eighth birthday. Although he was naturally disappointed that his
reign must now be thought of as over, he continued to write music.
Four volumes of piano pieces and a violin sonata testify to a love of
his art that had lost none of its keenness. His output of more than a
hundred and fifty songs included some delicate settings of La
Fontaine and of Verlaine's *Green* which was to attract Debussy and
Fauré too. All his life he worshipped Gluck. One of his greatest
pleasures he derived from adapting Rameau's opera *Castor et
Pollux* as a vocal score.

Shyness made him appear reserved and a little cold. He was
not a volatile boulevardier as Offenbach had been, an eager
frequenter of clubs and restaurants. His physical handicap and a
sensitivity bruised by early struggle created a barrier against the
world outside. Yet a sympathetic remark would quickly thaw his
iciness. A discreet reference to one of his operettas that had failed
to conquer the public won his friendship. The big hits — *La Fille
de Madame Angot, Le Petit Duc, Giroflé-Girofla* — were of
interest to him only for the royalties they earned. It was of his
frailer brain-children, *Fleur-de-Thé* or *La Petite Mademoiselle*,
for example, that he spoke most readily. Then he showed that,
despite a lifetime spent in the rough surroundings of the theatre, he
had preserved the simplicity of boyhood.

It is true that he made no great innovations. He inherited a tradition and turned it to his own elegant use. Neither did he leave a model to be imitated or a school to continue his influence. He had charm. He had an unaffected gaiety. His craftsmanship, much greater than Offenbach's, carried him through many a scene whence originality had fled. Only the absence of supreme melodic vitality kept him in a rank inferior to the composer of *La Vie Parisienne*.

The years of retirement melted quietly away among the books and music which, ever the soul of order, Lecocq methodically catalogued and arranged. Most people thought he was dead. He did not receive the Légion d'Honneur, which he could justifiably have expected, until more than a quarter of a century after *La Fille de Madame Angot*. The minister responsible believed that he had died long before. In 1910 a group of friends, as is the custom, solicited his promotion to the rank of *Officier*. Only the intervention of the President brought this about. The Second Empire had lavished distinctions in plenty on Offenbach. The Republic was not so generous towards its composers of operetta.

One afternoon Lecocq went to a dress-rehearsal and heard, on coming out of the theatre, that an evening newspaper had just reported his death. He bought the paper and, having chosen a prominent seat on the terrace of a much-frequented café, read his obituary over a glass of beer, his eyes flashing mischief behind the pince-nez. This sort of thing happened several times. Journalists seemed not to credit that a man could outlast his fame. On each occasion Lecocq declared that they were signing a new lease of life for him.

At last the end came on 24 October 1918. He was eighty-six years old when he died in his rue de Surène flat. So much else was going on at the time that the long-awaited fact of his death caused little stir. Behind him he left fifty-three stage-works and a parrot in mourning.

ENTR'ACTE

Higher fliers

If the clown traditionally wants to play Hamlet, why should not Hamlet feel like playing the clown? In other words, if Offenbach wanted recognition as a composer of grand opera and wrote *Les Contes d'Hoffmann*, what is there to prevent 'serious' composers from cherishing a whim to dabble in operetta?

This frequently happened with nineteenth- and twentieth-century French musicians. Saint-Saëns, as we have already seen, was one example. His career presented an almost unbroken series of triumphs. Starting as a child prodigy, he wrote his first work at the age of little more than three. When he was eleven he made his début as a pianist and offered to play, as an encore, any one of Beethoven's piano sonatas from memory.

His friendship with Lecocq, together with his own ambition, encouraged him to try his hand at operetta. He wrote two, one quite early on in his career and the other much later. The first, *La Princesse Jaune*, belongs to 1872. It had a derisory run of five performances at the Opéra-Comique. This is sad because it shows a light-handed talent which, had it not been squandered on attempts at Meyerbeerian epic, might well be attracting audiences today. Over a decade before *The Mikado* this agreeable work has a Japanese setting and an imaginary 'yellow princess' as its heroine. Indeed, Saint-Saëns, like Debussy, admired Sullivan and, when in London, made a point of visiting the current Savoy opera. One of the numbers in *La Princesse Jaune* has a strange resemblance to Josephine's 'Sorry her lot who loves too well' in *HMS Pinafore*.

The overture, which at the time was thought 'advanced' by some, is an appealing hors d'œuvre crafted with Saint-Saëns's usual dexterity. The final duet echoes Offenbach, though with greater musical refinement. Fauré described the work as 'witty tender and splendidly coloured . . . an exquisite *divertissement*' — which it is. Later in the century Messager was to venture into *japonaiserie* with his exotic *Madame Chrysanthème*.

The other operetta Saint-Saëns wrote was *Phryné*, a two-act piece given at the Opéra-Comique in 1893. The setting is ancient Greece and the heroine a beautiful courtesan with whom a young man falls in love. His uncle, an elderly magistrate, is outraged at such folly — and promptly becomes infatuated by the lady himself. The music is as witty as the libretto. It includes an effective number satirizing the magistrate's pomposity, and, in the reprise, an Offenbachian refrain *'On raconte qu'un archonte'*. Saint-Saëns, being much occupied with other commissions at the time, gave his young friend André Messager the task of orchestrating the first act while he completed the second. *Phryné* was, over the years, to have a hundred and twenty performances at the Opéra-Comique and four revivals, the last in 1935. *La Princesse Jaune*, by contrast, certainly as accomplished, though perhaps not so worldly, has been five times revived there since its initial brief run and was most recently heard in 1946.

These two operettas reveal the composer's sense of fun. So do his unpublished *Gabriella di Vergi*, a *'drame lirico, pochade carnavalesque en parodie d'un opéra italien'*, and a spoof entitled *Les Odeurs de Paris*. The latter is scored for piano, harp, trumpet, bagpipe, tin whistle, cricket, cuckoo, quail, big drum, pistol and humming top. Better known as an example of Saint-Saëns's Parisian humour is the *Carnival des animaux*. He only allowed *'Le Cygne'* to be printed in his lifetime, fearing, rightly, that the other numbers might harm his reputation as composer of the ambitious Organ Symphony and of the grand operas.

In private, before he grew old and disillusioned and notoriously bad-tempered, Saint-Saëns was a genial party entertainer. His most popular turn was an imitation of Madame Carvalho, the famous singer of Marguerite in Gounod's *Faust*. Decked out in a bonnet and with plaits of false hair which assorted oddly with his black beard and huge nose, he sang in a falsetto voice, and with precision, all the trills and cadenzas which adorn the passage where Marguerite sits at her spinning-wheel. Such was his uncanny musical sense that he perfectly captured the slightly off-pitch tone that Madame Carvalho, now past her best, was apt to produce.

Saint-Saëns as Marguerite was a regular attraction at the parties given in Emmanuel Chabrier's home. The accompaniment was provided by a most unusual organ, an instrument which could also imitate the noises of canon and drums. In springtime, when the windows were open, crowds gathered outside in the street to hear the extraordinary melodies that floated on the air. The Impressionist painter Manet, a close friend of Chabrier, painted several pictures of that street. He also did two portraits of the composer and, into the bargain, featured him amid his group in *Un Bal masqué a l'Opéra*. His famous *Bar aux Folies-Bergère* hung for many years above Chabrier's piano.

As a schoolboy in his native Ambert — appropriately, for a gourmet like Chabrier, the home of a flavoursome cheese — he took music lessons. He composed even then. A piece entitled *Le Scalp!!!*, (the trio of exclamation marks are Chabrier's own), was possibly suggested by a youthful reading of Fenimore Cooper. When he graduated from his law studies and took a post at the Ministry of the Interior, his bourgeois family predicted for him a safe and comfortable career, ending with a pension. Eventually he was to throw it up for music.

He brought a turbulent enthusiasm to everything he did. His piano playing was titanic. A picture by Detaille shows him, top-hatted and swathed in a voluminous overcoat, attacking the keyboard with powerful stubby fingers. As a destroyer of pianos he can have been equalled only by Liszt. He battered the instrument with hands, elbows, stomach, feet. He made it yield up a torrent of sound and left it, keys broken and strings snapped, a pathetic ruin. His improvisations were famous. A friend would show him a newspaper item about some crime or accident and he would dramatize it instantly with, say, a terrifying galop, a funeral march, a vindictive jig. The only example that has come down to us of his talent for improvisation is the entertaining quadrille for piano duet on 'favourite themes from Tristan and Isolde'. Even his infatuation with Wagner could not damp his bubbling humour, and he transformed the sacred themes into jaunty quadrille movements with a brio at once tremendously comic and ingenious.

Chabrier travelled much, notably in Spain, his favourite country after France. He loved the colour and the sound of the tangos, the malaguenas, the zapateados he heard at night in crowded cafés. 'The women are pretty,' he wrote home, 'the men are well-built, and on the beach the senoras, who have fine bosoms, often neglect to fasten up their costumes; from now on I'll be carrying buttons and thread with me. I'm always keen to be of service.' *España*, bold and boisterous, was his Gallic tribute to the country.

He had a sharp wit. 'There are,' he once said, 'three sorts of music: good music, bad music, and the music of Ambroise Thomas.' Benjamin Godard, a facile and now almost entirely forgotten composer, observed to him: 'What a pity, my dear Emmanuel, that you took up music so late.' Chabrier replied: 'It's an even greater pity, my dear Benjamin, that you took it up so early.'

With Verlaine as librettist he wrote two operettas, *Fisch-ton-Kan* and *Vaucochard et fils l^{er}*. Neither was published, though they may have been privately given. (In 1941, at the Conservatoire, Francis Poulenc took part in a performance of extracts, one of which he described as 'genuine Chabrier'.) Remembering the collaboration, Verlaine was to write:

> *Chabrier, nous faisions, un ami cher et moi,*
> *Des paroles pour vous qui leur donniez des ailes*

He gave Chabrier the scenario for another operetta. Later, in 1877, Chabrier met the librettists who had worked with Lecocq on *Giroflé-Girofla*. Verlaine's scenario, including the verses of a song he had already written, was taken over and built up into *L'Etoile*. This, performed at the Bouffes-Parisiens, Offenbach's old theatre, won Chabrier a deserved reputation.

The plot is vague and sprawling. The music, on the other hand, has spontaneity. The 'inspired amateur' for whom composing was a tedious struggle hit on ideas that give *L'Etoile* a clear advantage over the usual type of operetta. The satire of Donizetti (Italian opera had been a favourite with Offenbach) in particular amused Debussy, who had a special affection for *L'Etoile*. If the *'Chanson du pal'*, believed to have been written by Verlaine, has the gaiety of an Offenbach, in general the music shows a greater depth of feeling. Chabrier may have been a jester, but he was a jester with a heart.

Two years later, with the same librettists, he wrote *Une Education manquée*. A young man, who has been educated by an immensely learned tutor, marries the lady of his choice. On his wedding-night he finds that, for all his erudition, he is ignorant of what he is required to do. The obscure science and arcane knowledge he has imbibed have never enlightened him on his duty in such circumstances. His tutor is called and instructed to look up the answer. Almost immediately a thunderstorm breaks and the frightened bride flies into her husband's arms. A sudden intuition reveals to the hero his course of action.

The little anecdote was illustrated with music that is delicate and economically written. The rôle of the bridegroom was played *en travesti* by Jane Hading, whom we have already met as the wife of Lecocq's impresario. *Une Education manquée* was to be revived by Diaghilev close on half a century afterwards. At Erik Satie's suggestion he asked Milhaud to turn the spoken dialogue into *recitative*. With scenery by Juan Gris and production by Diaghilev, it must have been a spectacle to treasure.

After *Une Education manquée*, apart from a couple of fragments called *Cocodette et Cocorico* and *Monsieur et Madame Orchestre*, Chabrier wrote no more operettas. He was too involved with his Wagnerian experiments. He had, however, shown that he could, if he chose, have been a master of this *genre*.

Another composer of the time who produced many operettas but who, like Chabrier, is remembered for other types of work, was Léo Delibes. Before he wrote those classic ballets, *Coppélia* and *Sylvia*, and the operas, *Le Roi l'a dit and Lakmé*, he served a rigorous apprenticeship in the light theatre. He wrote, while he was learning his trade in this hard way, sixteen operettas. Delibes was a country-boy afflicted with a dual passion for music and the stage. At the age of eleven he had arrived in Paris to study at the Conservatoire. City life did not agree with him. The lack of freedom, compared with the liberty of the meadows at home, irked him and turned him into an unruly prankster. His uncle, who was responsible for the child at the time, had him placed in a class run by a teacher noted for his severity.

Léo did reasonably well, though he could never find much enthusiasm for harmony, fugue and counterpoint. He also needed to earn extra money, as his mother had made many sacrifices to keep him at the Conservatoire. Until his voice broke he sang in the choir at the Madeleine. On weekday evenings, at Opéra performances of Meyerbeer's *Prophète*, he again appeared as a choirboy, this time in the cathedral scene. Often he played the piano for dances which began at nine o'clock and did not end until six in the morning. "Don't forget I'm entrusting you with my little nephew," his uncle used piously to admonish the organisers. "Be careful with him and don't wear him out."

One of his teachers at the Conservatoire was our old friend Adolphe Adam. When Delibes' voice broke a useful source of income vanished, so Adam came to the rescue by having him

appointed organist in a church and also accompanist at the
Théâtre Lyrique. The second of these posts was the more fruitful.
At Adam's theatre Delibes came to know many popular stage
composers of the time, among them Victor Massé, who, very
behindhand with his latest opera, *La Reine Topaze*, only yielded
up instalments of the score day by day. A musician of keen
intelligence was needed to interpret his sketches and direct
rehearsals. The experience was useful training for Delibes.

He was now, and remained for the rest of his life, hopelessly
stagestruck. His admiration for Meyerbeer, then the superman of
grand opera, was intense. Often, when he glimpsed his hero
strolling on the boulevards, he would follow him at a distance,
respectful and worshipping. Meyerbeer himself became a little
nervous. Who was this tall burly young fellow who shadowed him
so mysteriously?

Delibes was shy and modest. Reluctant to make up his mind,
he needed some outside influence to force decisions on him. He
might never have decided to compose for the stage had not chance
impelled him. Opposite the Théâtre Lyrique where Delibes was
employed as accompanist stood Hervé's headquarters, the Folies-
Nouvelles. In that year of 1855 the prolific Hervé had written
twenty one-act operettas alone. Perhaps he was tired and could
not, for the moment, face up to writing another. For one day his
librettist, Jules Moinaux, (who was Courteline's father) crossed the
road, called in at the Théâtre Lyrique, and enquired if there was
anyone at home able to compose music for a new operetta. The
diffident accompanist did not know what to reply. He said he must
consult his master, Adolphe Adam. Delibes was then nineteen
years old. Adam laughed at his irresolution and urged him: 'When
you get an offer like that at your age, you thank your lucky stars
and accept.'

Within a few days the music of *Deux sous de charbon*, sub-
titled '*Asphyxie lyrique*', was ready. Hervé took the rôle of the poet
who strikes a suicide pact with his girlfriend. Having arranged to
gas themselves with the fumes of 'two pennyworth of coal', they are
interrupted by news that the death of a rich uncle has removed the
need for the poet to leave this world. Such threadbare nonsense at
least gave Delibes a start in the theatre.

His next operetta, by a pleasing symmetry, was a commission
from Offenbach. Hervé's rival also found that sometimes his own
industry was not enough to keep the Bouffes-Parisiens ticking over

week after week. *Les Deux vieilles gardes* started an association
with Offenbach that was to last for a decade or so. Throughout
that time many of Delibes's operettas were played at the Bouffes.
The cast of three included Léonce, a stalwart of the troupe
Offenbach had assembled around him, and they made *Les Deux
veilles gardes* the success of the season. A polka danced by the two
old guards was invariably encored and became very popular. It
cropped up everywhere: at concerts, at dances, in cafés and
parlours. The twenty year old composer had written his first hit.
Years later, in 1911, the piece was revived. The polka still had
plenty of kick in it.

Delibes, a few months later, kept the pot boiling with *Six
demoiselles à marier*. As the title suggests, a widower encumbered
with six marriageable daughters is anxious to find husbands for
them. An attractive young man, an amateur violinist, appears as a
likely candidate for at least one of them. But he turns out to be the
widower's long-lost son and ends up by proposing to marry the
cook. The most engaging feature of the score is a dashing bolero
with violin obbligato. A 'knife sharpening' duet recalls a trio on a
similar theme in *La Grande Duchesse de Gérolstein*.

Through Offenbach's influence Delibes was able to have two
operettas staged at Ems. One of them, *Les Eaux d'Ems*, included
an Englishman called 'Lord Grosborn' and his wife's harebrained
lover 'Arthur de Fauxbrillant'. Fiddle-faddle of this nature was not
to occupy Delibes much longer. In 1866 he was asked to add scenes
to a ballet, *La Source*, partly written by the German Minkus.
The passages from Delibes's pen became most popular with
audiences. He had found his true destiny as a superlative composer
of ballet.

Some of the operettas he wrote during those early years merit
revival. *L'Omelette à la Follembouche*, perhaps, and *La Cour du
Roi Pétaud*, which contains a pretty serenade, would stand hearing
again. The craftsmanship in general rises higher than Offenbach's.
Harmony and melody often have pleasant surprises to offer. Yet, as
with Lecocq, if the purely musical content outshines Offenbach,
the vital pulse and frenetic humour are sometimes lacking.

Delibes never ceased to be surprised at the public favour which
greeted his ballets and later operas. Though shy and diffident, in
appearance he was big and powerful. A massive brown beard
cloaked his chin and confirmed the impression of solidity. His eye,
light and clear, betrayed, though, uncertainty and a sensitive

spirit. Envy was unknown to him. He had plenty of mischief, but no malice.

Some composers can write anywhere and at any time. Milhaud, for example, has been known to compose a violin sonata on a train journey. Others need a piano. Delibes belonged to the second category. 'Reading scores and the pleasure it brings aren't enough for me,' he used to say. 'The piano, the voice, the orchestra, are absolutely essential in my experience to bring them to life. Often, when composing, I'm obliged, inevitably, to run to my keyboard, to sing, to make music by myself. My imagination lights up, my ideas take shape. That's when, in truth, I really feel myself to be a composer.'

His technical ability was formidable. After the Théâtre Lyrique he was appointed to the Opéra as chorus-master. One day the director of the Opéra came back from a mysterious journey, summoned Delibes, carefully shut the door, and pointed to a large parcel on the table.

'My dear Delibes,' said he gravely, 'prepare yourself for one of the greatest emotions in your artistic life. Please sight-read this manuscript for me.'

It was the orchestral score of Meyerbeer's latest work, *L'Africaine*, and the Opéra, for an immense sum, had just purchased the rights. Delibes sat himself down at the piano and began the marathon of playing it through, not only transposing and arranging the orchestral layout at sight as he went along, but also grappling with the countless well-nigh indecipherable scribblings and hieroglyphics in Meyerbeer's own hand. He played continuously for over four and a half hours.

When he had finished, the director cried: 'What a masterpiece, isn't it?'

'*Monsieur le directeur*,' replied Delibes, exhausted and trembling, but determined to be honest, '*Monsieur le directeur*, it's . . . it's awful!'

He had come a long way since, with youthful adoration, he followed the great Meyerbeer on his rambles around the boulevards.

ACT III

A LATE FLOWERING

i

Miss Eliot's bottom

By the eighteen-eighties a growing population sought amusement in the theatre. Fifty years before, the stage had been the preserve of the aristocracy and the upper classes. Its appeal was now much broadened. More and more theatres were built throughout France. Every provincial city was soon to have its 'Grand Théâtre'. While the State-run Comédie-Française maintained a traditional repertory of the classics, it also presented the farces of Labiche, the problem plays of Dumas *fils*, and the comedies of Pailleron. In the musical theatre, operas by the all-conquering Massenet won a large following. The less dignified operetta enjoyed even greater audiences.

Operetta had become an industry on its own. Its popularity inspired the building of new theatres, kept them profitably in business and created employment. There was plenty of work for singers, actors, dancers and orchestral players. Scene painters and stage managers were needed, as were dressmakers, shoemakers and designers. Backstage operations called for scene shifters and stage hands, property masters and wardrobe mistresses. Front of house cashiers, usherettes and cloakroom attendants were required. In this way operetta sustained a whole world of workers who depended on it for a living. During the winter, most provincial centres had their own operetta troupe which provided entertainment throughout the season. When summer arrived, the company moved off to play in the casinos of watering-places or seaside resorts.

Local theatres acquired a stock of scenery which could be

adapted for every sort of production. A ready supply of drawing-rooms, open-air settings (garden, inn yard, highway), barracks, convents, throne rooms and offices ensured that the scenic demands of any operetta could speedily be met, thanks to the deft plying of saw and paintbrush. Orchestras learned versatility and could switch from Gounod's *Faust* one week to Offenbach's *Grande Duchesse* the next. The musicians were recruited locally. Much depended on the conductor, who often made them play with smooth professionalism, although sometimes they were lamentable.

At this period Lecocq's name still figured often on provincial bills. *La Fille de Madame Angot* and *Le Petit Duc* went on touring year after year. The provinces remained faithful to him for many seasons. In Paris things were different. The capital had tired of Lecocq. The man of the moment now was Edmond Audran.

The son of a well-known tenor, he came into the world at Lyon where his father happened to be on tour in 1842. Music and the stage surrounded him from his earliest years. His younger brother, also a tenor, made his début in a revival of *Girofle-Girofla*. Edmond was sent for his musical education to the Ecole Niedermeyer. This establishment deserves a word in passing, since it made an unusual contribution to nineteenth century French music.

It had been founded by a Swiss Louis Niedermeyer with the aim of improving the low standard of church music in France. By training young musicians in the glories of such then-neglected composers as Palestrina, Vittoria and Jannequin, he hoped to provide organ lofts throughout the country with a team of keen reformers who would restore plainchant undefiled and purify services in cleansing draughts of Bach and Lassus. This he succeeded in doing. But an unwelcome irony dictated that his school should also become something of a nursery for composers of secular operetta, among them Audran and later André Messager, not to mention Léon Vasseur and Claude Terrasse.

After working through the Ecole Niedermeyer Audran took a post of which the founder would have approved. He became organist at a church in Marseille where his father had settled. Like the young Hervé, though, he found that his mind kept straying towards the theatre. Between mass and vespers, as it were, he started composing operettas. These little works gave him a local reputation when they were mounted at the Gymnase theatre in Marseille.

The Franco-Prussian War for a moment damped his interest in light music and his thoughts turned to more serious things. He wrote a mass and an oratorio which he conducted himself at the first performance.

After the war operetta revived and once again Audran was tempted by the *genre*. A playwright friend of the family offered him a libretto. *Le Grand Mogol* was produced in 1877 at Marseille with an eighteen year old leading lady by the name of Jeanne-Alfrédine Tréfouret, better known as Jane Hading, who immediately caught the eye of Paris theatre managers and of Lecocq in particular. We know the rest.

Le Grand Mogol, which was to repeat its success in Paris, is the story of an Indian prince who will succeed to the title of Grand Mogol provided he remains chaste. He has, meanwhile, fallen in love with a Parisian girl, Irma (not 'la Douce'). The villain of the piece, an English agent by name 'Captain Crakson', attempts a little pimpery with the aim of making him lose his inheritance. Of course the wicked Britisher fails. Audran illustrated the plot with music very much in the style of Lecocq and tinted with a shade of exoticism.

He made his assault on Paris with *Les Noces d'Olivette*. The public took to this unpretentious offering. Even more successful was *La Mascotte* in 1880. It played over four hundred times at its first appearance and established Audran in his own right. No operetta since *La Fille de Madame Angot* had so caught public fancy.

The heroine of *La Mascotte* is a shepherdess who brings luck to all around her on condition that she keeps her purity. It was the theme of *Le Grand Mogol* again. She sings with her peasant swain of how she loves the turkeys and sheep in her charge — 'When gently they go gobble, gobble, gobble', 'And each one goes baa!' adds the boy — to one of those yodelling refrains, absurd yet persistent, that stick like burrs in the memory. (Gounod exploits in a similar way the comic potentialities of the expression "glou glou glou" in *Le Médecin malgré lui*, though fortunately he does not give them yodelling form.) It is a snatch of period whimsy that can still charm if you are in the right mood.

Among the stronger features of the score are an 'Orang-outang' song and a number given to the Prince of Piombino, who defines in a zingy waltz the power of superstition. It has been said that Audran is a 'sub-Lecocq'. There is something in this.

Although both were well-trained musicians, the work of Audran carries a hint of writing down to the public. Whereas Lecocq thought in terms of full orchestra, Audran gives the impression that he is catering for smaller groups, that he always has at the back of his mind the 'fit-up' ensembles that the now much wider appeal of operetta necessarily entailed. Ideas are given more obvious treatment, effects which in Lecocq would have been subtle are imperceptibly broadened. The new and larger audience for operetta contained many people whose education and background were not of the most refined. They had to be remembered.

Audran continued working until 1899, two years before his death, when his latest work fizzled out after only twenty-eight performances. *La Mascotte* is one of some twenty-five operettas. Among them was the lavishly produced *Reine des Reines* (1896) in which Paulette Darty sang for the first time. She was later billed as 'Queen of the Slow Waltz', for after delivering the words of her song she would gracefully waltz around the stage in hypnotic circles. Her statuesque figure and dominant bosom quelled the unruliest of audiences. In her repertory were Erik Satie's music-hall song *'La Diva de l'Empire'* and the slow waltz *'Je te veux'*. That eccentric composer dedicated to her one of his outlandish piano pieces. What Paulette made of it one cannot imagine. She died, after appearing among other things in the French version of Leslie Stuart's *Floradora*, in 1940.

Monsieur Lohengrin, a parody of Wagner, did not fare very well. Audran was happier with the more simple amusements of, for example, *La Cigale et la fourmi*, inspired by La Fontaine's tale of the grasshopper and the ant. It has a grasshopper's song, light and skipping, and a really well-written gavotte that manages to be plaintive and jolly at the same time. Sung by Jeanne Granier, once the star of Lecocq's operettas, it was invariably encored. The harmonic development is very prettily done.

The same trick is deftly managed in *Miss Helyett* which is the Gallic form of 'Miss Eliot'. Here the pastiche takes the shape of a *'Cantique'* sung by the heroine. She is the daughter of an austere American clergyman, whence the unexpected presence of a canticle in an otherwise frivolous work. Niedermeyer, one feels, would have approved the idea, though he may have felt dis-ease at the unclerical spruceness of the tune. Another echo of Audran's early training is heard in the opening theme of the overture, which borders on a fugal subject. Once more there is a gavotte, linked with the *'Cantique'*, and a rattling quadrille. The 'Spanish' duet is a neat bit of local colour, and a terzetto is distinguished by some bewitching modulations.

And the plot of *Miss Helyett*? It is quite, as the French say, *'schocking'*. The respectable young heroine, on vacation in the Pyrenees, falls from a rock and is caught, fainting and upside-down, in a tree. An artist rescues her — but not before he has quickly sketched a view of that which respectable young ladies keep hidden at all costs. (*'Ah, ah! Le superbe point de vue! Ah, ah! perspective imprévue!'*) When she emerges from her faint she swears to marry her rescuer, for he has beheld what only a husband should be allowed to see. Neither of them knows what the other looks like. All the artist has to guide him is his sketch. The mis-understandings, and the climax, are easily imagined.

Such naughtiness proved most acceptable to London theatre-goers as well as Parisians. Audran soon gained an English following. As early as 1880, a version of *Les Noces d'Olivette* began a run at the Strand Theatre of more than four hundred and fifty nights; *La Mascotte* for a long time filled the Comedy Theatre; at the Lyric, *La Cigale et la fourmi* kept going for over a year. F. C. Burnand, a famous editor of *Punch*, adapted *Miss Helyett* for the Criterion and veiled in suitable coy terms all reference to the heroine's behind.

Most of all to the taste of Victorians was one of Audran's last operettas, *La Poupée*, which at the Prince of Wales Theatre in 1896 held the stage for close on six hundred evenings. It was set in a monastery, than which nothing could be more blameless, and there was no mention of ladies' bottoms. Nothing here suggested those Offenbachiades liable to raise a blush on a maiden's cheek. The atmosphere was very genteel, very well behaved. If Audran showed in the score a rather higher standard of musicianship than elsewhere, the tone was irreproachably moral. Operetta domesticated for Victorian consumption lost something of its vitality. Audran took to their natural conclusion the petit-bourgeois tendencies of Lecocq.

ii

Gallimaufry

They pullulated, those composers of nineteenth-century French operetta. By the eighteen-eighties there were dozens of them. Like Hollywood script-writers, like the purveyors of television serials in our own time, they scribbled busily to keep pace with the demands of a greedy machine that was rarely satisfied. New theatres which had sprung up in Paris and the provinces needed fresh material. At any time an urgent request was likely for a successor to a current production that had ceased to draw. A closed theatre brought no-one profit. And the general public, which had now acquired a taste for operetta, wanted constant novelty. At the start of the decade, in 1880, no less than twenty-three new productions were mounted in the capital alone. Throughout the nineties a yearly average of forty was not unusual.

There was a musician called Robert Planquette who wrote songs and sketches for café-concerts. He had been in so much of a hurry to set up as a composer that he left the Conservatoire before his training was properly at an end. Still, he was, in spite of his abbreviated studies, a good pianist and a singer with a fine tenor voice.

He discovered that he had a talent for writing military marches as well as the popular songs he confected with such easy skill. In 1867 he wrote the march 'Sambre et Meuse' which, with patriotic verse tacked on, became a very famous number. It is still famous today and one would find it difficult to avoid 'Sambre et Meuse' at military occasions and parades. First sung on the stage of the music-hall known as Ba-ta-clan after the Offenbach operetta, this jaunty item quickly found its way into the repertoires of brass bands throughout France. Planquette composed many others.

While still in his twenties he had written several one-act operettas. By chance he was given the opportunity of setting a full-length piece called *Les Cloches de Corneville*. The librettists had at first offered it to Hervé. He, as usual anxious to stamp his personality on it and give himself openings for his own brand of crazy humour, declared that there were not enough puns in the text. As for a number which celebrated the virtues of apples and the good Norman cider they produced, he suggested turning it into a big scene featuring every historical character to be associated with the fruit: Adam and Eve, Paris, William Tell . . . the authors hastened elsewhere.

Planquette was himself a Norman and had always wanted to pay musical tribute to his birthplace. Within a few months he had written *Les Cloches de Corneville*. It was put on in 1877 at the Théâtre des Folies-Dramatiques to replace Offenbach's latest, *La Foire Saint-Laurent*, which was limping badly. Where Offenbach had failed to delight an audience, Planquette succeeded. His operetta was an instant hit.

The well-constructed libretto invokes an ancient legend which tells that one day the haunted castle in the Norman village of Corneville will be claimed by its heir and rightful owner. The hero is a handsome young scion, the heroine a nobleman's long-lost daughter, while the plot is nicely complicated by a miserly old retainer who stores his vanished master's treasure in the castle and keeps nosy villagers at bay with talk of ghosts and spectres.

The most famous number is *'Digue, digue, digue'*, a tinkling melody that recounts the legend of the bells. It is based, rather charmingly, on the sounds produced by what bellringers, with affectionate contempt, call a 'ting-tang'. The Marquis de Corneville has an even more attractive song to put over, a nostalgic waltz, *'Dans mes voyages, combien d'orages'*, where he recalls the storms and shipwrecks he has had to go through before gaining his native Normandy and entering on his inheritance.

Though listed in publishers' catalogues as an opéra-comique, *Les Cloches de Corneville* is actually a mixture of opera, melodrama, comedy and farce which may, for convenience's sake, be qualified as operetta. Perhaps it was this disconcerting blend which moved the critics to be so harsh in their judgements. Planquette's reputation as a composer of popular songs gave one of them the excuse to write that the new piece was little more than 'a bundle of polkas, waltzes and refrains that are so many reminiscences'. His colleagues mostly agreed with him.

Yet the public ignored critical opinion. Thousands of them took *Les Cloches de Corneville*, cider-apples and all, to their hearts. A year later it crossed the Channel and, as *The Chimes of Normandy*, won as great a success with London audiences. Under the management of H.B. Farnie it ran for over seven hundred performances. Farnie was an enterprising man who had helped to make Offenbach popular in England. He now took an interest in Planquette and encouraged him to write *Rip van Winkle* in 1882.

Based on Washington Irving's famous tale, *Rip*, as it was known in France, started its career in England. A certain immortality was given to the catch-phrase *'C'est un rien, un soufflé, un rien'*, (*'It's a trifle, light as air, the merest trifle'*), when Erik Satie incorporated it, as he often did with popular music of the day, into a piano piece, the second of his *Chapitres tournés en tous sens*, which is a long way removed from the innocent fun of Planquette. *Rip* also has a 'toothache' duet which, one cannot help thinking, would have appealed even more to Satie's macabre sense of humour.

Planquette was never again to repeat the triumph of *Les Cloches de Corneville*. Such was the effect it had made that it received the compliment of being parodied under the punning title of *Les Cornes de Clochenville*. None of his other works achieved this distinction. In 1903, after emerging one chill January day from a rehearsal of his most famous operetta, he took cold and died.

At the time of his death he had just completed a new piece eventually called *La Paradis de Mahomet*. The production was notable for the appearance of a young actor called Max Dearly whose performance marked the beginning of a career that flourished both on the stage and in films for over half a century. The elongated features looked as if a flat-iron had been passed over them. The voice crackled like a rusty hinge. He had the stature and air of a jockey (a particularly sharp one, you'd have thought), and indeed as a youth had been undecided as to which of the two passions in his life, racing or the theatre, he should adopt as a living. While his parents believed he was following art classes, the devious boy was in fact playing walk-on parts at the Théâtre du Vaudeville. In later life, when established as an actor and in a position to indulge his racing tastes, he liked to pose for offstage photographs wearing a Norfolk jacket and a trainer's flat cap, and holding the bridle of his favourite horse.

After a catastrophic début in a Parisian café-concert he went to Marseille and fell in with an English mime troupe known as 'Les Willi-Willi'. One of their members suddenly left and Max took his place. To avoid changing the printed programmes he also took his name, which was 'Dealy', and afterwards changed it to 'Dearly'. Experience in the provinces was followed by a return to Paris and better luck this time on the music-hall stage. He sang ditties like *'Tra-la-la-la-voilà les English'* and played small parts in revues.

Around 1900 his most famous number was *'Le Jockey Américain'*. He also gained renown by dancing the *'valse chaloupée'* with Mistinguett, then a wide-mouthed dark-haired beauty who, like him, was a favourite with Moulin-Rouge audiences. Both on stage and off, Max was adored by women. 'The most virtuous woman', he used to say, 'can't resist a sympathetic little chap who knows how to make her laugh.'

There was something tragic about his impassive face. Like the writer Alphonse Allais, he adopted an 'English' manner of coldness and straight-faced humour. In his music-hall years he had perfected an acrobatic talent which enabled him to build up the whirling climax of a riotous dance number with the zest of a dervish and the gravity of a high court judge.

He was a little too early for the cinema, having reached his late fifties when sound-film emerged. Even so, he created a memorable series of character parts — as, for instance, in Sacha Guitry's films, where he personated, at one time or another, a threadbare nobleman down on his luck, or a steel-eyed tycoon. When you saw his name on the cast list you felt a pleasurable stir of anticipation. You were never disappointed. His admirers thought that, had the chronology been different, he might have become the French Charlie Chaplin.

As well as helping to launch Max Dearly as a husky-voiced Grand Mufti, *Le Paradis de Mahomet* represented an extra chore for that hard-working musician Louis Ganne. Planquette had not been able to orchestrate his operetta before he died and Ganne was called in by a desperate theatre manager. He was an oddly appropriate choice. Even more than Planquette he had specialized in military marches. Among the most famous are *'Le Père la Victoire'* and the *'Marche Lorraine'*, which, written for a gymnastic display in 1892, was to acquire a special resonance during the 1914-18 war.

After a spell directing the orchestra at the casino in Royan he settled down at Monte Carlo. His 'Concerts Louis Ganne' had a large following. Naturally the gregarious conductor made many friends among the patrons of Monte Carlo and its gaming tables. It was equally inevitable that he should write a great quantity of dance music for events that studded the social calendar. His mazurkas and waltzes gave as much pleasure as the ballets he composed for the Casino de Paris and the Folies-Bergère.

Les Saltimbanques was his first big operetta. It is a story of travelling circus people, of a clown and a strong man in love with a girl in the troupe who turns out to be the long-lost daughter of a count. The setting has always given producers an excuse for incorporating extra numbers: clowns, jugglers, acrobats. It has not been unknown for a menagerie to fill the stage, odorous and alarming.

The music, as one would expect from a dealer in martial rhythms, is bold and thickly textured. The march heard in the overture sets the tone. It is redolent of sawdust and spangles. The brass belches with innocent vulgarity and the drum knocks out a swaggering tempo. This is the circus atmosphere portrayed, with more sophistication, by Erik Satie in *Parade* and by Henri Sauguet in *Les Forains*. Then the march dissolves into a sentimental waltz of the type heard in casinos and spa concert halls at the turn of the century — the sort of thing, in fact, that Ganne conducted every season at Monte Carlo.

The waltz and the march are principal themes in *Les Saltimbanques*. They are typical of the broad effects that characterize Ganne's style. A rare moment of subtlety is achieved in a second-act chorus based on the old song *'Auprès de ma blonde'*. Elsewhere the music relies largely on the vigour of military rhythms and galops. The public liked it very much indeed.

Les Saltimbanques was a close rival of *Les Mousquetaires au Couvent*, an older work by Louis Varney, a much more prolific musician than Ganne and the composer of some forty operettas. He was the son of Alphonse Varney, Offenbach's assistant in the heroic days of the Bouffes-Parisiens. Alphonse conducted, arranged, adapted and often wrote operettas to fill vacant spaces on the programme. When Offenbach, drowned in debt, withdrew from the Bouffes-Parisiens, Alphonse took over. He was, as events later showed, rash to do so.

Basically Alphonse was a conductor. He had links with Bordeaux where an opéra-comique of his, to a libretto by another of his sons, Edouard, had been performed. His best-known composition remains the *'Chant des Girondins'* (*'Mourir pour la patrie'*) which became nothing less than a musical symbol of the 1848 revolution. The words had been written for a drama by Alexandre Dumas. Even this, however, Alphonse's one great triumph, has been queried. The observant have pointed that it bears a strong resemblance to a patriotic number by Rouget de Lisle, composer of 'La Marseillaise'.

Some confusion exists as to the birthplace of his son Louis. One authority gives New Orleans. Another says Paris. We know that his father travelled widely. Whatever his origin, Louis emerged as a conductor in musical theatres after the 1870 war. Managers gave him various chance commissions and in 1880 he wrote *Les Mousquetaires au Couvent*.

The time is the reign of Louis XIII. A dashing young musketeer officer loves a young person who has been shut up with her sister in a convent by her stern father. The musketeer and his friend dress up as monks and wheedle themselves into the convent. Unwisely they drink too much at dinner and are locked away in a tower by the outraged nuns. They are saved from disgrace when it is revealed that the two monks whose robes they stole are conspirators plotting the assassination of Cardinal Richelieu. The hero wins the heroine and his friend marries her sister.

Convents and girls' boarding schools had an irresistible attraction for nineteenth-century plot-makers. Mr Pickwick's embarrassing adventure in the establishment for young ladies is part of a long tradition. The possibility of confusion and innuendo offered by settings like these were gratefully taken up by librettists. A typical example, as here, is the presence of musketeers, and handsome ones at that, in a nunnery.

The music is lighter of touch than Ganne's. It has a particular delicacy in the scene where the girls, ordered to confessional by their Mother Superior, compile a list of sins which they may decently avow. The blend of gaiety and seriousness is attractive. Individual numbers often recall Offenbach with their nonchalance, and the finale of Act I comes very close to the nervous exuberance of the old master himself. The third act falls off badly. Unable to complete the score in time, Varney was obliged to call on his friend Achille Mansour to help out with half a dozen of the items required. Even so, the earlier part of *Les Mousquetaires au Couvent* is good-quality neo-Offenbach.

Varney is something of an enigma. Mr Gervase Hughes, a shrewd commentator, has pointed out that he produced little before *Les Mousquetaires au Couvent* (1880), by which time he was already thirty-six years old.* From that point onwards he wrote operettas at a remarkable rate, often two a year. Could it be, Mr Hughes goes on, that his father, Alphonse, had left a supply of unpublished manuscripts which the son Louis dipped into for odd

*In *Composers of Operetta* (Macmillan, 1962).

numbers here and there? This would explain the persistent flavour of rather dated conventions, not to mention Offenbach whose assistant Alphonse had been, which occurs so frequently in Louis's curiously prolific work.

There is, on the other hand, no mystery about Gaston Serpette whose name is the French word for 'pruning knife'. He came from Nantes, qualified as a lawyer, then switched to music and, at the Conservatoire, studied composition under Ambroise Thomas. Serpette graduated as a brilliant winner of the Prix de Rome with a cantata on Joan of Arc, a lady who has suffered much from the attentions of prize-winning composers.

Soon afterwards an operetta of his was accepted for the Bouffes-Parisiens and he devoted himself to the *genre* for the rest of his life. Scholars lamented his desertion of serious music for the lighter stage. The qualities he showed in *Jeanne d'Arc*, they argued, deserved better. Nonetheless he stuck to his choice of career. It was obvious that he was beyond salvation when he wrote a piece called *Shakespeare*, in which the hero was not the dramatic poet but a dog of the same name. Strange, how performing dogs haunted the men of operetta, from Offenbach to Varney and Serpette.

Few of Serpette's many works enjoyed long runs. *Madame le Diable*, richly costumed and luxuriously produced at Lecocq's old theatre, the Renaissance, might have lasted for some time had not contractual engagements forced the manager to take it off after a hundred and twenty nights. Serpette came back undaunted with *Fanfreluche* and Jeanne Granier, only for the theatre to go bankrupt shortly afterwards. *Le Château de Tire-Larigot*, featuring Berthelier, a member of Offenbach's legendary troupe, had better luck and stayed in fashion for several years.

Adam et Eve continued the trend, though audiences were more impressed by the sight of plump little Louise Théo as Eve, in flesh-coloured tights garnished with strategic tufts of ivy, than by the qualities of the music. There were less revealing opportunities in *La Demoiselle to Téléphone* of 1891 and its exploitation of the novel speaking instrument which had begun to be installed throughout Paris.

In later years Serpette was more and more tempted by fantasy — Japanese exotica, Gilbertian imbroglios, flirtations with the Devil, Greek legend — of the sort in which the Folies-Bergère specialized. So much emphasis was put on revolving stages, elaborate machinery and under-dressed girls that the music was quite submerged. This was not difficult, for his talent, at the best, remained slim, and little is heard nowadays of this ingenious Prix de Rome winner.

He worked, once, with Victor Roger on *La Dot de Brigitte*. Perhaps collaboration stimulated his gift, for *La Dot de Brigitte* gained both artistic and financial success. Roger was a graduate of the Ecole Niedermeyer, and, remembering the exalted principles animating that school, it was suitable that his first major work should have a Biblical link, however remote. *Joséphine vendue par ses soeurs* translated the episode of Joseph to modern Paris and changed the sex of the characters. 'Mother Jacob' is a concierge blessed with twelve daughters, of whom her favourites are Joséphine and Benjamine. Joséphine, a singing pupil at the Conservatoire, is persuaded by her jealous sisters to accept an offer from an Egyptian impresario. His 'theatre' in Cairo, she finds on arrival, is a harem . . . Despite which she is eventually united with her true love. Unpretentious, never aiming high, Roger's music illustrated the tale with competence.

The operetta world being a close-knit one, even perhaps a shade incestuous, composers often worked together, sometimes to meet an unforgiving deadline, sometimes because an importunate theatre manager believed that two heads were better than one. Roger was no exception and collaborated with Paul Lacôme d'Estaleux on *Mademoiselle Asmodée* in 1891. Lacôme was by then quite as well known a figure as his colleague, though by no means a Parisian. He preferred his native Gascony and was only to be seen in the capital when one of his operettas was being staged. Like his ancestors, he was a man of the fields whose true delight came from farming and vine-growing. As a child he adored music and each day walked several miles to a neighbouring village where he had organ lessons. When a music magazine organized a competition and invited readers to set a one-act opera for performance at the Bouffes-Parisiens, the youthful Lacôme took first prize.

In the meantime, since he loathed teaching, he earned his living by writing music criticism for a wide range of papers. He also composed at length. A taste for unusual combinations showed itself in a quartet for cornets. He wrote, too, a polonaise for the same instrument and a pastorale for tenor saxophone. His inclinations were a little more erudite than those of his contemporaries. An admiration for Destouches led him to revise and produce one of the old French master's operas. A collection of seventeenth- and eighteenth-century songs appeared under his name as editor.

But his heart really lay in the theatre. A good chance came his way in 1876, when Offenbach relinquished the libretto of *Jeanne, Jeannette et Jeanneton* because he was unable to recruit Judic, Granier and Théo for the three main women's rôles. The trio of 'Jeannes' includes she who became the royal mistress, Madame du Barry, a second who found fame as the dancer, Guimard, and a third who ended up running a famous inn. It was a neat little plot and graced by Lacôme with unpretentious music. The ancestry of Lecocq is evident. With *Ma Mie Rosette*, Lacôme continued to exploit a small but agreeable talent. At one time he was rumoured to have, in his bottom drawer, three operas. Did these more ambitious works ever see performance? He is now remembered, if a little dimly, for the dozen or so operettas that found their modest way into the Paris theatres. After each first night he would return gratefully to his Gascon smallholding, there to watch the crops and dart an anxious eye at the weather.

Lacômes' prize-winning operetta had not been given a chance to save the Bouffes-Parisiens from decline. This was something that had once been done during an early vicissitude after the Franco-Prussian War of 1870 by Léon Vasseur's *La Timbale d'Argent*. Vasseur was the son of an organist and had dutifully studied at the Ecole Niedermeyer. He then played the organ at a Versailles church, but acquired, in between, the regrettable habit of frequenting café-concerts. Here he produced his first, unsuccessful, operetta.

Although he was later appointed organist at Versailles cathedral and wrote much religious music — offertories, masses, oratorios — he at the same time composed nearly thirty operettas. In 1879 Vasseur even ran his own theatre, combining within his person the qualities of composer, impresario and cathedral official. *La Timbale d'Argent* had a subject unusually licentious for the time. The inhabitants of a Tyrolese canton have, through debauchery, lost their voices and are unable to compete for the silver cup offered by a local dignitary. In the neighbouring canton another worthy citizen has imposed bachelorhood on the lads and continence on the husbands in order to preserve their vocal powers. Upon this situation is built a romance between two young members of the rival choirs.

Vasseur's music was helped by the presence of Anna Judic. She was delightfully plump, not yet mountainous, as she became with age, and had Marie Lloyd's gift of singing innocent words and giving to them apparently unspeakable meanings, as Offenbach had discovered. 'Mademoiselle Judic', wrote a critic who appreciated her gift of naughtiness, 'plays with the fig-leaf as if it had been a fan.'

Edmond Missa, though he lacked a cathedral in his background, possessed academic credentials no less impeccable than Vasseur's. He had been a pupil of Massenet and, like Serpette, won the Prix de Rome in his time. All his life he tended to waver between operetta and opéra-comique. Perhaps for this reason he was to find fame with neither. His choice of subject was certainly original. *Dinah* was based on Shakespeare's *Cymbeline*. And *Muguette*, which had twenty performances at the Paris Opéra-Comique early this century, took as its starting-point Ouida's *Two Little Wooden Shoes*.

With the possible exception of Farmer Lacôme, all the composers mentioned up to now have been full-time theatre musicians. There were, however, others who, while turning out occasional operetta from time to time, prudently relied for their living on steadier employment. This meant, in most cases, teaching.

Emile Jonas was an early example. He seems to have enjoyed collaboration on the grand scale, for he once worked with no less than six other musicians, including our old friend Clapisson, when writing *La Poularde de Caux*. Since it consisted of one act alone, the mass-production technique must have dispatched it very quickly.

One of his colleagues at the Conservatoire was the harmony teacher, Ernest Guiraud. Like his father before him, Ernest won the Prix de Rome and so established a family record not equalled before or since. He improved on this by composing, at the age of fifteen, an opera which was given in New Orleans where his father had settled for a while. His ballet, *Gretna Green*, and the operetta, *Madame Turlupin*, which verges on opéra-comique, have charm and facility. Eventually he was to be better known as the musician who added the recitatives to Bizet's *Carmen* and who finished Offenbach's *Contes d'Hoffmann*. In the later years of his academic career he proved a sympathetic teacher to the young Debussy and, on several legendary occasions, was baffled by the presence in his class, like a cuckoo in the nest, of Erik Satie.

Yet another Prix de Rome victor was Emile Pessard who also taught harmony at the Conservatoire. He was born in Montmartre at a time when that district was an independent commune and had

not yet been swallowed up by Paris. (Even today one hears of
elderly Montmartrois talking of 'going down to Paris'.) His father
was a flautist and the child showed early musical talent. Unable for
a long time to establish a footing in the theatre, he consoled himself
by writing religious music. At last he gained a hearing with *Le
Capitaine Fracasse*, a version of Théophile Gautier's novel and
probably one of Pessard's best works. He then perpetrated an
Armée des Vierges. This army of virgins contrived to march for
only ten performances. His *L'Epave* ('The Wreck') only kept afloat
because it was included on the same bill as Leslie Stuart's *Floradora*. It was as well that, in addition to his Conservatoire post, he
could depend on his salary as inspector of singing in the Paris
schools.

A pedagogue, too, was Antoine Mariotte. He started, as had
Rimsky-Korsakov, as an officer in the navy. A change of mind led
him to study under the formidable Vincent d'Indy at the Schola
Cantorum. After working as an organist and conductor, he taught
at the Conservatoires of Lyon and Orléans. It was his bitter
misfortune to write an opera called *Salomé* at the same time as
Richard Strauss. Even his operettas, people agreed, were too
solemn, too laborious. A work of Rabelaisian inspiration called
Gargantua seems to have brought him a trifle of success. Mrs Viva
King, that irrepressible hostess and veteran opera-goer, records
once having seen, at the Opéra-Comique, a spectacle where
'Gargantua is born on the stage behind the curtain of a large
four-poster bed, from which the moans and groans of his mother
are sung by a full-throated tenor'. Could this have been Mariotte's
work? I confess that I have not had the courage to enquire further.

The famous pianist Raoul Pugno had a love of operetta which
came a close second to his passion for food. In time his stomach
grew so enormous that he could only reach the keyboard by sitting
with his legs sideways. In spite of this his playing, especially of
Mozart, was better than that of most who sat at the piano in the
usual way. In youth he had somewhat imprudently identified
himself with the wrong side during the Commune, but his career
soon recovered from this unwise association.

As a composer he was dogged and ever hopeful. An oratorio
on the resurrection of Lazarus was followed by operas, ballets,
pantomimes and much else. In particular he clung to operetta and
made half a dozen ventures in the form. Few of them achieved
more than a handful of performances, and those that did owed

their success to the presence of stars such as Louise Théo. His name
remains in the memory for the delicacy of his Mozart playing and
for that enchantingly small and overcrowded music shop on the
quai des Grands Augustines, beside the Seine. It was opened by a
nephew of Pugno, and a photograph of the pianist's florid visage,
heavily bearded and pince nez'd, looks benignly down on the
milling customers squeezed between counter and bookshelf.

The last name to be mentioned here is that of a man who was
neither teacher nor virtuoso. He deserves a place, however, because
he was responsible for giving an early chance to a composer who,
eventually, was to be classed with Offenbach as a master of French
operetta. Firmin Bernicat arrived in Paris from his native Lyon
and wrote a number of one-act pieces that were performed in café-
concerts and at the Folies-Bergère. He was a good musician and
several times helped Planquette with his orchestration. In 1883,
though suffering from a chest illness, he began work on a new
operetta called *François les Bas Bleus*. He had written only ten of
the numbers when he died suddenly at the age of forty. It was then
summer, and the first night had been arranged for early autumn.
Bernicat's publisher, anxious to find someone who would finish the
score, remembered a promising young man whose work he had just
started to bring out. The young man, who was called André
Messager, agreed to take on the commission.

iii

Success in blue stockings

In the tenth century the town of Montluçon, which stands at the
heart of France, grew up around a castle built by its first lord and later
restored by Henri IV. By the time André Messager was born there
in 1853, coalmines and a nearby canal had totally industrialised
the place. Today the ancient castle on the mound and its little town
of narrow winding streets are overwhelmed by factories making
aluminium, plate-glass and car tyres.

There were soldiers in his ancestry. Messager inherited his
difficult character, it was thought, from a maternal grandfather
who had been in the King's personal service and whose temperament,
like April weather, could very quickly move from sudden anger to

unexpected charm. His great-grandfather was landlord to the eighteenth-century hostess Julie de Lespinasse.

There was, until the arrival of André, no musical talent in the family. His father, a tax collector, arranged for him to have a few lessons when he started school, for as soon as the boy was tall enough he had begun to tinkle on the keyboard of piano. He needed discipline, his elders found. At the age of seven he could be charm itself and could wheedle endless favours out of indulgent grown-ups. When frustrated he would, though dressed in his best suit, roll frenzied with anger in the mud and dust of the street.

He was sixteen years old at the time when financial problems overtook the family. There was now no question of his embarking on the long and expensive studies that would have qualified him for some official post. Music up to then had been a hobby. In the new situation that arose it must become, as soon as possible, a means of earning a living. On the strength of a bursary André was sent to that famous school which has appeared before in these pages, the Ecole Niedermeyer.

A few years previously Gabriel Fauré had studied there with a teacher, Saint-Saëns, who was not much older than his pupil. From this early acquaintance developed a life-long friendship between the two men. Shortly afterwards Fauré went back to the Ecole Niedermeyer, this time as a teacher himself. Saint-Saëns was still there, and they both welcomed the obviously talented Messager as a student.

The school was then situated in a noisy spot near the place Clichy. Despite the strict régime — pupils were up at half-past five in the morning and immediately set to work, with a single break on Thursday afternoons when they were let out for a walk — Messager enjoyed his stay there. This was chiefly due to his lessons with Fauré and Saint-Saëns. The latter was an exciting teacher. Beak-nosed like a parrot, short and squat, his voice lisping in a foghorn boom, he opened up, in Messager's words, 'horizons until then closed to everyone', and stimulated his hearers with revelations of new music by Wagner, Schumann and Liszt.

His teaching was not always serious. On occasion a member of the class would be asked to provide incidental music for a farce written by Saint-Saëns. It was both fun and a useful exercise. Saint-Saëns, who was a gifted parlour entertainer, once appeared as Rosina in *The Barber of Seville*. Messager accompanied him at the piano, delighted as was everyone else by the perfection and malice of the satire on prima donnas.

The friendship and guidance of Saint-Saëns and Fauré were invaluable to Messager. He never lost touch with them, and their affection became allied to a mutual respect. When Fauré completed a new work he would submit it for judgement to what he called his 'tribunal', a group consisting of Messager, Saint-Saëns and the song writer Henri Duparc. 'Tell Messager,' wrote the young Fauré once, 'that I tremble at showing him my latest compositions. He frightens me almost more than Saint-Saëns even.'

On leaving the Ecole Niedermeyer, Messager took over Fauré's post as organist at Saint-Sulpice, that old, very large church, one of the biggest in Paris and further distinguished by some unique Delacroix murals. In this game of musical chairs Fauré moved on to become Saint-Saëns's deputy at the Madeleine.

Organ playing, then, as now, was not overpaid. After Saint-Sulpice Messager conducted for a time an orchestra in a Brussels theatre. He came back to Paris as organist at yet another church, and for a few years worked as musical director at Sainte Marie des Batignolles. He was not a religious man — rather, a young musician who needed to earn a living. In after years, when it was noted that he hardly ever attended church, he would reply that in his struggling youth he had heard enough masses to last him a lifetime, and inhaled the odour of sanctity so deeply that he had no wish to breathe it again.

At the time there was only one possible way of earning large sums through music, and that was to be found in the theatre. A composer who succeeded on the stage could, like a writer of film music today, look to quite a substantial income. Without necessarily feeling any great love for it, Messager went into the theatre. He became conductor at the Folies-Bergère and wrote occasional ballets there.

The Folies-Bergere of the eighteen-eighties was by no means the house of lewdness and vulgarity Puritans have supposed it to be. The ballets Messager wrote for his employers were innocent little things. Huntsmen pursued shepherdesses across the stage with admirable decorum. Clorinda, veiled in a skirt that descended to her calves, blushingly surrendered to Damon an orange-flower from her corsage.

There is no doubt that Messager had 'serious' ambitions. He belonged to the Société Nationale de Musique which Saint-Saëns and others had founded, and which played an important part in the renewal of French music. Chance directed him elsewhere. Asked to complete Bernicat's *François les Bas Bleus*, he wrote thirteen of the twenty-five numbers and orchestrated the whole of it. Bernicat's name was featured in large type and Messager's only briefly mentioned. Rehearsals were gloomy and everyone predicted failure. As often happens in such cases, the first night was a complete success.

Around this time Messager was in Le Havre deputising for Saint-Saëns in a number of concerts. There he met a girl, Edith Clouet, and married her soon afterwards. Following the honeymoon he wrote a group of songs which he dedicated to Fauré who had played the organ at his wedding. As bride and bridegroom processed solemnly down the aisle, the mischievous Fauré included in his improvisation a theme from one of Messager's Folies-Bergère ballets.

Now, with a household to sustain, Messager was glad of any theatrical opportunities that offered themselves. *François les Bas Bleus* made him attractive to theatre managers. During the last months of 1885 he had three works running in Paris. One of them, *La Fauvette du Temple*, was a fashionable 'military' piece. Another, *La Béarnaise*, starred Jeanne Granier in the title rôle and slipped in one or two sly touches of the Gregorian mode. Both showed signs of an original gift for harmony. A year later Marie Tempest played the Granier part in an English version of *La Béarnaise* by Sir Augustus Harris at what is now the Palace Theatre.

Saint-Saëns now did him another good turn. Temporarily in high favour at the Opéra, he persuaded the powerful director to commission a ballet from Messager. *Les Deux Pigeons* emerged from this happy intervention. Based on the La Fontaine fable, it is set in Roumania and peopled by gypsies who provide a reason for exotic dances. *Les Deux Pigeons*, still in the repertory today with its vivid colouring unfaded, is the first of Messager's important works. There is, in the second act, a Hungarian dance with a vigorous trumpet theme which was particularly admired by the composer Albert Roussel who always awaited, greedily impatient, the return of this virile melody. One knows what he felt. It is a magnificent inspiration and a good example of Messager's brilliance with the orchestra.

Messager's next production, which was based on the historical episode of the burghers of Calais, taught him the sharp lesson that, in the theatre which he had embraced as a career, failure was as much to be expected as triumph. For nearly two years afterwards he sought in vain for a librettist to work for him. No one liked to be associated with a flop. His joy when Catulle Mendès agreed to write the libretto of *Isoline* was a measure of the desperation he had reached. For Mendès, though classified as a poet, was a versifier of the lowest rank.

In youth a bright-haired giant with the aquiline features of a Nordic god, by middle age Catulle had degenerated into a flabby, mountainous heap of a man, piggy-eyed and epicene. His first wife Judith, daughter of the poet Théophile Gautier, deserted him to become the mistress of Wagner. By the composer Augusta Holmès he had three daughters, one of whom married the novelist Henri Barbusse. Among his descendants is a former prime minister of France. When not at home, where he lounged, puffy-faced and ashy-bearded, in a tent-like kimono shaded mauve and green, Catulle haunted editorial offices, restaurants and theatres. His poetry, his plays and his novels did not make enough to keep him in the champagne and mistresses he needed, so he turned out journalism at great speed, editing, publicising, and writing dramatic criticism. It is all forgotten now. Even the abysmal poetry he wrote did not merit the unpleasant death that finished him. By misstake one night in a railway tunnel he opened the carriage door and was smashed to pieces by an oncoming train.

Sumptuous tableaux and a ballet in the magic forest of Brocéliande failed to save *Isoline*. Almost immediately after the first night in 1888, the manager of the theatre, the Renaissance, which had achieved prosperity with Lecocq, saw bankruptcy overwhelm him. After that the score lay in obscurity for many years until 1930 when Reynaldo Hahn put on the ballet at Cannes. The complete work was revived in 1958 at the Opéra-Comique and again failed to hold an audience, although the ballet, unencumbered by Mendèsian affectations, became a part of the repertory. As Reynaldo Hahn perceived, while the absurdity of the libretto harms the rest of the work, the dance interlude is finely planned and written.

Messager was a working musician who depended for his living wholly on the success of his music. He did not waste time complaining over the fate of *Isoline* but set about writing the music for an operetta which, it was hoped, would profit from the visitors and tourists crowding into Paris for the Exhibition of 1899. It did not.

A more reliable occupation was conducting. The fees, though modest, were guaranteed, and Messager had perfected a technique which made him one of the best French conductors of his day. During the Exhibition he directed concerts of new Russian music. He was also to gain a reputation as a Wagnerian. Early in the eighteen-nineties, at Marseille, he conducted *Die Walküre*. Himself well acquainted with the methods of Bayreuth, he succeeded in transmitting them to a provincial orchestra which had never before been confronted with such complicated music.

Everything can go wrong in the theatre. Curtains may rise or fall unexpectedly. Singers can miss their cues, make false entries and, suddenly, in a panic, forget whole phrases. Scenery collapses. There is the classic story of the conductor at the Opéra who, when the diva petrified him by skipping no less than twenty pages of the score, lost his head, stopped the orchestra and rushed out. He never returned and ended his career in the provinces. Messager did not panic like that.

His manner was precise and undemonstrative. The baton flicked neatly here and there in a way that meant little to the audience behind him but conveyed volumes to the orchestra. Before stepping onto the rostrum he would have familiarised himself with every aspect of the music. Composers do not always make good conductors, as Debussy and Ravel were to prove. Messager was the exception. He had the ability not only to grasp the spirit of a score, but also, equally important, to communicate that spirit to the orchestra and, through the strange mystery that lies at the basis of the conductor's art, cause it to be reproduced by the players.

No crisis, no emergency was allowed to ruffle his serenity. With Messager in charge both singers and orchestra knew that he would carry them through difficult passages, that he would rescue them when disaster struck and would smooth over mistakes and faults of memory so that no one in the audience would suspect the awful things that might have happened. He did not lose control for a moment of the elements it was his job to fuse together: orchestra, soloists and chorus. When he conducted the first performance of Poulenc's ballet *Les Biches* in 1923, the light on his desk abruptly went out. Quite undeterred by the sudden darkness, he relied on his memory to guide him through the intricacies of the score and nursed the work to a successful end with few people realizing what had happened.

He did not conduct the first performance of his own *La Basoche* in 1890, though ten years later he directed the revival at the Opéra-Comique. It was to have, all told, more than two hundred performances there, and at each new production it became something of a tradition for Messager to take the rostrum. 'Basoche' is an old word for the Paris students who, throughout many years since the fourteenth century, were authorised to form themselves into a guild and to elect their own 'king'. The operetta goes back to the year 1541 and imagines that the poet Clément Marot has been chosen for the honour.

The portrait of this young man in *La Basoche* is elegantly done. Credit is due to Albert Carré, later to be a director of the Opéra-Comique, who wrote the libretto and gave it a delightfully archaic tang as well as cleverly interweaving quotations from Marot's own poetry. According to the plot, the nineteen year old Marot has been elected king of the Basoche for the statutory year and will preside over all deliberations and festivals. Now King Louis XII, an ageing widower, has chosen as his bride Princess Mary, sister to Henry VIII of England. She arrives incognito in Paris. Never having met Louis, the naïve princess takes 'king' Marot for her royal bridegroom. From this situation flows a narrative of great good humour and wit.

The music is the best Messager had written to date, and there can be no doubt that *La Basoche* is one of his finest works. Colette, Marot's secret wife, has a *pastourelle* of ravishing wistfulness. She also sings a most lovely *andantino*, '*En l'honneur de votre hyménée*', which is shot through with a pure silver thread of beauty. This is not pastiche but the intelligent use of old forms to express true emotion. *Villanelle* and *passe-pied* are touched in with a deft and sympathetic technique. The orchestral writing throughout is, within the terms of reference Messager set himself, distinguished and subtle. One of his mannerisms, a liking for chromaticism, is to be found in the number '*Ah que ne parliez-vous?*' sung by the Duc de Longueville who is Princess Mary's escort. It must have impressed the magpie Francis Poulenc, since many years later he stole half-a-dozen bars and incorporated them wholesale in his own operetta *Les Mamelles de Tirésias*.

Messager described *La Basoche* as an opéra-comique, a term he gave to several of his other works. This is justified, since the craftsmanship is far superior to what may be found in the operettas of composers such as Planquette and Ganne. The vocal writing is skilled and inventive. The handling of solo and concerted numbers, as well as of the linking passages, has a fully rounded operatic quality. *La Basoche* gave him his rightful place as a leader in the theatre.

iv

A second marriage

In 1891 the award of the Légion d'Honneur to Messager confirmed the popularity he had begun to enjoy. A letter from Chabrier congratulating him, in a mixture of Spanish and French, on having obtained *'el hocheto della vanitade'*, added to his delight.

His circle of acquaintance widened. Saint-Saëns remained a true friend, as did Fauré. Messager played the piano in an early performance of César Franck's Quintet, and though he had little in common with the dreamy composer of *Les Béatitudes*, he respected his talent. Once, Messager and other mischievous colleagues took the unworldly Franck to the Folies-Bergère. He looked around him in bewilderment at seeing no one he knew, and, noting the ladies who stalked the promenade, observed with ingenuous surprise: 'Who are these people?'

Gounod was sometimes the occasion of a respectful visit, though Messager found more congenial company in Chabrier. Massenet he did not much care for. In Bayreuth he saw Wagner, and at Brussels he had observed the ageing Liszt. On a visit to Paris, Rimsky-Korsakov revealed to him that he had discovered the themes of his 'oriental' music in a French collection of Algerian popular songs.

Orchestrating was a welcome relaxation for Messager. He composed with ease, regularly and methodically. For composition, though he wrote fluently, he demanded complete silence, but when orchestrating he was untroubled by noise or distraction. It was a pleasure, after the rigours of original work, to turn to orchestration. The handling of instruments, the balancing of different sonorities, the grouping of colours, and the structuring of effects were a source of enjoyment. Musical ideas, he said, came to him already clothed in the appropriate instrumental shades.

One reason for his embarking on no major works at this time was a highly eventful private life which resulted in the break-up of his marriage. The guileless provincial of ten years ago was now a seasoned inhabitant of the easy-going backstage atmosphere where liaisons were formed as casually as they were dissolved. His adventures did not make for a steady marriage. He was a man of the theatre with success to his credit, which meant that there were many young singers anxious to gain his favour. Moreover, he was by no means an easy companion to live with. The tantrums of his childhood were still likely to explode at any moment. Though he possessed immense charm, he could without warning fly into terrible rages.

The gentle Edith divorced him. Soon afterwards, she contracted a lingering but fatal illness. Messager, contrite, visited her every day. Long before the end came they had forgiven each other the wrongs done on both sides.

After surviving this emotional crisis Messager appears to have recovered his appetite for writing large-scale works. At the beginning of 1893 his new 'comédie lyrique', Madame Chrysanthème, was produced at what had formerly been known as the Théâtre de la Renaissance. It was based on a novel by Pierre Loti, the naval officer who, during his career and between turns of duty, wrote many books which became bestsellers of his time. His travels around the world gave him material for stories which he set in Turkey, Senegal, Tahiti and other favourite far-off places. He also wrote well about the hard life of Breton fishermen and Basque peasants. The style, impressionistic and, to modern readers, a little flaccid, has a disillusioned vein of resignation. You may be sure that whenever a native girl falls in love with a foreign visitor to her country, she is bound to be tragically disappointed.

Loti himself liked to create an exotic impression and to encourage belief that he had experienced the strange adventures through which the heroes of his novels passed. As he grew older he attempted to preserve his youthful romanticism by the discreet application of make-up. It is not by chance that one of the persistent themes of his books is the relentless passage of time. By his late sixties he had become desperate. Towards the end of the 1914-18 war he was glimpsed, an old doll in resplendent naval uniform, his withered features running with grease.

Madame Chrysanthème was one of his most successful novels. The Japanese heroine, a 'mousmée' or waitress, gives her heart to a French naval officer — who enjoys the amorous episode and then sails away, leaving her desolate on the quay. The story is slim enough, and in the book it is eked out by those evocative passages he did so well. But the stage demands action. For lack of dramatic incident Messager had to fall back on creating the atmosphere which Loti established in his prose. It was not his fault, nor that of his librettists, that very little happened in the course of this 'comédie lyrique'.

The new work followed the line inaugurated by Saint-Saëns in *La Princesse Jaune* and by Lecocq in *Fleur-de-Thé*. The grand finale was to be provided by *Madame Butterfly* a few years later. It is possible to feel that Messager showed more subtlety than Puccini. Exoticism is hinted at and the 'Japanese' effect obtained by understatement. Maybe his very discretion has prevented *Madame Chrysanthème* from surviving, for Messager was handicapped by a libretto that kept all too closely to the original source. Puccini's collaborators had no such scruples and filled their opera with action guaranteed to hold an audience's interest.

At the end of the year Messager brought out *Miss Dollar*, an operetta of no great distinction. By way of relaxation, on Boxing Day, he presented a little burlesque called *Amants éternels*. Romeo and Juliet, it seems, never really died and have returned to life from the tomb. Now they are married and destined to an eternity of happiness which they find hard to bear. Mercutio helpfully becomes the third member of the party. When they hear a street organ grinding out Gounod's famous duet, the eternal lovers start fighting. This diverting piece of cynicism has, unfortunately, never been published.

For some time now Messager's fame had been growing in England after *La Béarnaise*, with Marie Tempest, had planted the seeds of his reputation. *La Basoche*, as *King of the Students*, followed it at Richard D'Oyly Carte's English Opera House. At the Savoy, in 1894, D'Oyly Carte presented Messager's new operetta, *Mirette*. It had a short run, was taken off, revised and put on again, but did not succeed in rivalling *La Basoche*.

The libretto had been written by a lady who chose to be known professionally as Hope Temple — a wise move since her real name was Dotie Davies. Her pseudonym, though Queen Victoria still ruled England, had a curiously Edwardian ring. As Miss Temple she sang in polite London drawing-rooms. Many of her songs she had composed herself, and she touched in her own sketchy accompaniment at the piano. They were pleasing little ditties, light, sentimental, easy to hear at tea-time and calculated not to upset the digestion after dinner.

In the summer of 1896 she came to France with Messager. He introduced her to startled friends as 'Miss Hope Temple, the new Madame Messager'. For he had been charmed by her beauty and her lively Irish temper to the extent of marrying her. She also had wit and the gift of quick repartee, as he soon found in the skirmishes that began to arise between them. She was undaunted by his bursts of irritation. His cutting remarks were lobbed back at him in the shape of tart ripostes which did not lack irony or effectiveness. For days they would exchange, tirelessly, insults which were devised with an elaborateness that suggested a certain relish for battle. A thoughtless comment would grow into a quarrel that was nurtured with loving care. They were experts in the art of domestic warfare.

Her English accent and her occasional misuse of the French tongue which, during their courtship, had so delighted him, ended by turning into a source of annoyance. Like the hero in the Maupassant short story who married an Englishwoman, he reproached her for those very qualities which, at the beginning, he had adored and even encouraged. She, too, had many faults to find. Her husband, she claimed, was stifling his musical talent. Deceived by his facility at composing quickly, she accused him of being an idler.

Madame Messager became resigned to his long absences and his entanglements with other women. She gathered round herself a circle of friends who helped console her in the realisation that her own musical gifts were far outshone by his. Often she would do what she could to further his career and, through her English connections, was able to assist him in his London projects. Before, at long last, they separated, weary of perpetual bickering, she gave birth to a daughter. Dotie kept on her cottage beside the Thames at Maidenhead, where, after their wedding, they had come for a time to enjoy the peace of the English countryside.

Messager's career seemed to have reached a full stop. His new work, *Le Chevalier d'Harmental*, had been a dispiriting failure. It was based on a novel by Alexandre Dumas, and in it Messager had tried to develop the type of Wagnerian continuity he essayed in *Madame Chrysanthème*. Everything was against it: a poor libretto, an uninteresting plot, and an impresario who kept meddling at rehearsals and even, to Messager's blazing fury, attempted to alter the orchestration which the composer had worked at for three years. Its failure, he said, 'was all the more painful to me in that I set great store by the work and believed that I had given in it the full measure of what I could do. I was so discouraged by this lack of success that I wanted to write no more and tried to retire to England.'

v

Véronique and the battle of Pelléas

It rained in Maidenhead. Passing showers dimpled the surface of the Thames. Messager brooded in his study. He wrote a few songs to English words that a London publisher had commissioned. Most of the time he read. The hours melted into a long grey boredom. He had decided to quit the theatre which, in any case, he had not been so keen on entering in the first place. But, despite himself, he kept thinking of the footlights, of the first-night atmosphere, of the disturbing though not unpleasant thrill he always felt when the curtain rose on a new production.

One day the manuscript of a new libretto came through the post. It had already been refused by three other composers. Messager looked at it idly. Interest stirred. Soon, absorbed by its wit and ingenuity, he felt growing enthusiasm. Within a few weeks, all melancholy forgotten, he had set *Les p'tites Michu*.

The plot is Gilbertian and concerns two girls who have been brought up together in the same family and believe themselves to be twin sisters. Blanche-Marie is, in fact, the daughter of a marquis who has gone to the wars. He gave her, as a baby, into the care of the pastry-cook, Michu, and his wife. The pastry-cook, bathing the child with his own newly born daughter Marie-Blanche, confuses the two infants, and from then on neither he nor his wife is able to distinguish between them. The complications, mostly romantic, that arise in time from this error are skilfully plotted.

The music attempted none of the elaboration Messager had spent three years lavishing on *Le Chevalier d'Harmental*. It was as if he had resolved to avoid all experiment and to compose simply, from the heart, in whatever mood the words of the libretto suggested to him. *Les p'tites Michu* was, accordingly, the best of his operettas yet written, full of gaiety and verve. The sentiment is discreet, and an occasional echo of churchly diction recalls the composer's Niedermeyer training. Rigadoons and other contemporary dances evoke, with much grace, the atmosphere of

Paris early in the nineteenth century. There is also a minuet which, appearing at a crucial moment in the action, is both exquisite and of genuine dramatic value. The craftsmanship is civilized and does not call attention to itself. Melody flows easily. If the harmonies are tactful they are no less original and well found. *Les p'tites Michu*, first heard at the Bouffes-Parisiens in 1897, was a total success and quickly travelled to the provincial theatres. It took eight years to reach London as *The Little Michus* at Daly's Theatre in 1905.

The orchestration is exquisitely turned. This was something on which Messager, with justice, prided himself. As he said, the orchestration of light music demands a tact and dexterity which composers in the medium do not always possess. He pointed out that those who had their music orchestrated by others were little concerned if the journeyman who did the task for them lacked that indefinable sixth sense which would indicate the right combination of sonorities to carry out the original intentions of the composer. Often a passage depended for its significance or flavour on the orchestral writing alone.

Messager's orchestral gift was shown perfectly in *Véronique*, his best-known operetta, which succeeded *Les p'tites Michu* in the following year. Even before the opening act had ended it was clear that *Véronique* was his greatest success. A fusion, strictly speaking, of opérette and opéra-comique, it had a good and witty libretto that enabled Messager to deploy his talent fully. The scene is Paris in the eighteen-forties under the rule of the worthy Louis-Philippe. The action begins in the picturesque setting of a flower shop. The hero is the Vicomte Florestan de Valincourt, lover of the florist's wife. The portrait of the deceived husband, incidentally, is an amusing study in pomposity: having introduced himself as the 'god' of the surroundings, he then, with the aid of a quotation from Virgil, presents his wife as the 'goddess'.

Florestan, riddled with debt, is engaged to a rich beauty from the provinces. She overhears him when he incautiously tells his flower shop mistress that he will have to marry 'some provincial little silly-billy', so she resolves to teach him a lesson. The annoyed fiancée and her Aunt Ermerance disguise themselves, are given employment at the flower shop, and, as 'Véronique' and 'Estelle', lead on both Florestan and the amorous tradesman. Of course, when Véronique decides that Florestan has been teased enough, she reveals her identity and they are married after all.

The score is of the highest quality throughout. The overture gives a foretaste of good things in store with the march, a tune of glorious virility which recurs during the first act. The curtain rises on a women's chorus that has a quite Gounodian purity. Florestan's 'Allons, allons' contains all the dash associated with Offenbach, though the contour of the melody and the cunning insertion of a grace note preserve it from exploding into the breathless delirium that the prince of the can-can would have achieved. With Messager, balance and restraint are all.

This is beautifully demonstrated in the small but important matter of ornamentation. Messager uses the device not just for the sake of prettiness but as a genuine part of musical characterization. The 'Chut! Chut!' chorus ('Hush! Hush!') introduces a serio-comic number sung by Véronique's aunt, a middle-aged spinster of whom Gilbert would have made heartless fun. She laments being left on the shelf in a gentle parody of the type of sentimental ballad popular in Louis-Philippe's time. While it is funny that she should express herself with grotesque exaggeration, it is sad, too. The turns and grace notes which, in the original, would have been nothing more than embellishment, are here used to shape and colour the character. Besides which, Messager gives her a concluding heartfelt tune that no ballad-monger could have equalled.

When *Véronique* arrived in England with a first performance as the quaint little Notting Hill Coronet Theatre in 1903, the two most popular numbers were undoubtedly 'Trot here, trot there' and the 'Swing Song'. When Florestan treats Véronique to a donkey ride, their duetto *'De çi, de là'* had an attractive busy-ness that Edwardians adored. They also delighted in the *'Chanson de l'escarpolette'*, where Florestan pushes her back and forth on a swing to the rhythm of the neatest waltz Messager ever wrote, together with an accompaniment suggesting the rustle and movement of the swing. Altogether the stage picture recalls, and was probably meant to, that famous painting by Fragonard, with the girl soaring demurely through the air to reveal a tantalizing flash of white stocking.

With *Véronique* the composer showed himself to be a master of French operetta. The libretto may have aged a little and taken on period charm as an Edwardian view of the eighteen-forties, but the years have done nothing to harm the music. It was built to last with a solid craftsmanship and a deep practical knowledge of stage and orchestra. The richness of accompaniment, the wealth of

luscious harmony (among dozens of examples may be quoted the
ronde 'Lisette avait peur du loup' and the swinging 'Allure
martiale'), and the immaculate blend of humour with tenderness,
give Véronique its place as one of the finest productions of its kind.

Soon after Véronique had made her bow, Messager's friend
Albert Carré invited him to become musical director at the Opéra-
Comique. Over the next six years Messager was able to develop the
curiosity for new music which, together with composition,
remained his chief professional interest. There were murmurs at
the appointment of an operetta composer to such a lofty post, but
he soon displayed remarkable ability in the new sphere. During his
time there the Opéra-Comique was distinguished for the originality
of its programmes and the quality of performance.

When Messager began at the Opéra-Comique it had just
taken up residence in its third home, a solid, much ornamented
building in the appropriately named place Boieldieu. The façade
coyly turns its back on the boulevard and looks out elsewhere. In
the main entrance hall there are statues of Manon and Mireille,
two heroines respectively Massenetic and Gounodian who helped to
establish the Opéra-Comique in its heyday. Upstairs, in the Grand
Foyer, a dazzle of mirrors, polished floors and brightly coloured
paintings on ceiling and walls breathe of past glories.

The new musical director of the Opéra-Comique had known
Debussy for several years. They first met in the offices of Debussy's
publisher, the sympathetic Georges Hartmann. Messager was
instantly attracted to the younger man, whose Prélude à l'après-
midi d'un faune he had already conducted. When he heard of the
new opera Debussy had on the stocks he immediately wanted to
know all about it. He took Carré with him to Debussy's flat, and
there the opening scenes of Pelléas et Mélisande were played over
from the manuscript. Persuaded by Messager's excitement, Carré
agreed to accept the work.

On the day of the first performance Messager had had to
attend the funeral of his beloved elder brother. He arrived at the
theatre distraught and weary. Every single omen was unpropitious.
Debussy had quarrelled with his librettist, Maurice Maeterlinck,
who now openly declared his hope that Pelléas et Mélisande would
fail. Maeterlinck's wife, the singer Georgette Leblanc, was furious
that she had not been asked to take the part of the heroine. The
evening was tumultuous. Hostile pamphlets were distributed at the
doors of the theatre. As the music continued people laughed and

joked aloud. Cries of disapproval were met by cheers from Debussy's supporters. In the orchestra pit Messager urged on players and singers with an implacable eye, his look and his gestures sustaining those who faltered. Some people behind him in the audience made derogatory remarks. He turned and quelled them in a sharp dry voice.

Messager could not allow himself too many luxuries in the form of *Pelléas*. He had only a limited subsidy to finance new productions, and his box-office cashier provided a more ruthless and objective guide to the state of public favour than did high artistic ideals. With admirable conscientiousness he put on the old tried and trusted crowd-pullers in the repertory and did not allow himself to be bored by their familiarity into routine performances. If he derived more pleasure from conducting *Don Giovanni* than the hundredth representation of a current Massenet success, he did not let it show.

While he was still in charge at the Opéra-Comique Messager had also taken on a similar post at Covent Garden in London. As the historian of that theatre has remarked, 'this was an odd appointment, which has never been satisfactorily explained'.* Perhaps the acquaintances he had been making there since 1894, the year of *Mirette*, were responsible. Lady de Grey, whose brother-in-law was chairman of the Grand Opera Syndicate which then ran Covent Garden, is known to have patronized French musicians, among them Reynaldo Hahn, and she may have been involved in the matter. Messager also, through his English wife, knew various people in England and had stayed in London for long periods.

As the seasons progressed he began to appear quite often at Covent Garden. Gluck's *Armide* and Massenet's *Le Jongleur de Notre Dame* were heard under his baton. His own ballet, *Les Deux Pigeons*, was billed and he conducted *Don Giovanni* as well as standard favourites like *Carmen* and *Faust*. At the end of 1906 he decided to resign and was succeeded by the well-known English musician, Percy Pitt. For he had now been offered the musical direction of the Paris Opera House, that brooding monument described by Debussy as having the exterior of a railway station and, inside, the appearance of a Turkish bath.

*Harold Rosenthal, *Two Centuries of Opera at Covent Garden* (Putnam, 1958).

Even more than at the Opéra-Comique Messager was here caught up in government politics. The Opéra was the subject of parliamentary manoeuvre. It was not simply a place where music could be heard. The fact that it received a large state subsidy — though never large enough for the artists concerned — turned it into a target for every deputy and every senator who wanted an excuse for making himself known to the electorate. The replacement of Messager's predecessor touched off dispute at the highest Cabinet level and opposed Aristide Briand to Clemenceau. The names of their protégés were closely argued at meetings and dinners and in private houses. Briand won. Messager was appointed, and, to supply the administrative experience he was deemed to lack, was partnered by Louis Broussan, who had formerly managed several provincial theatres.

Messager entered a domain far vaster than that of the Opéra-Comique. An army of fifteen hundred people worked there, all jealous of their rights and prestige, all ardent to protect the little empires which over the years had been built up through custom and tradition. The grandiose façade of Charles Garnier's elaborate edifice sheltered a host of warring groups, alive with rumour and suspicion. The stagehand who fought to preserve his territory was inspired by the same motive as the prima donna who waged vendettas to ensure bigger billing for her name. Trade union squabbles over demarcation lines at the Opéra are nothing new. The staff employed there in the nineteen-hundreds would not have been at all surprised to hear of a recent director who complained, with bitter frustration, that to buy a comb for use as a stage property it was necessary to obtain the written authorization of at least a dozen people.

Symbolic of the weird mixture of politics, art and personality that create the distinctive atmosphere of the Opéra is the design which André Malraux commissioned in 1962 from Marc Chagall. This, like the cleaning of Paris monuments, was in itself a political act. The original panel which decorated the lofty ceiling of the auditorium was a typical Victorian perspective of nymphs and vaguely Olympian figures careering about in a riot of mists and draperies. It had a quaint attractiveness similar to that of the discreetly unveiled dancers which Carpeaux sculpted for the exterior. Chagall replaced it with a shower of vivid blues, greens, reds and yellows symbolizing the great musicians. (Adam is the only representative of operetta, and he is included on the strength of *Giselle*.) One of the sections is devoted to *Pelléas et Mélisande*. Behind a window Pelléas looks out. He has the unmistakable features of André Malraux.

So far as possible Messager left administration to Broussan. In order to keep his partner happy he agreed to mount trusty box-office successes, as he had at the Opéra-Comique, so that he might also be able to experiment safely with more daring works. Yet he could not escape entirely from the chores administration implied. When he complained to his wife about the interminable procession of time-wasters who pestered him in his office, the unsympathetic Dotie replied, with brutality, and some truth: 'You say they bore you? But that's what you're there for, my friend.'

A signal feature of his period at the Opéra was the frequency of memorable Wagner performances. For *Rhinegold* he engaged Weingartner. One of the massive drop curtains failed to operate at the precise moment, and Weingartner, annoyed at the delay, stumped backstage. The offended German claimed that if he did not receive a personal apology from the staff concerned he would leave the theatre at the interval. Messager tried to calm him. Weingartner became more and more aggressive. Finally Messager interrupted him in barrack-room tones: 'If you don't get back there and conduct, I'll take over myself.'

'What? You?'

'Yes. I've already conducted the work twenty-five times. This will make it the twenty-sixth.'

'But . . . I didn't mean . . . .'

'Right. Will you conduct the orchestra, yes or no?'

'I will.' And he did.

The level of box-office takings, though important, was not the only factor that dictated what Messager produced at the Opéra. There were all sorts of pressures from outside as well as internal regulations which limited his choice. No other explanation than the crudest of string-pulling can account for the appearance of that grotesque opera, *Le Vieil Aigle*, by Raoul Gunsbourg. He was director of the Monte Carlo opera house and had put together the absurd spectacle with the aid of the conductor there. It was typical of the peculiar works that, along with the more hackneyed items in the repertory, Messager was forced by circumstance to accept.

He was able, nonetheless, to bring in various reforms. One with which he is credited involves the placing of the conductor. Until quite late in the nineteen-hundreds the conductor, leaning on the prompter's box in the middle of and immediately at the front of the stage, would stand with his back to the orchestra the better to direct singers and chorus. Only during overtures and when the applause began did he turn and face the audience. The new system removed him to the front of the orchestra where he has remained every since.

During Messager's régime the 'claque' also disappeared, at least officially, though it continued a surreptitious life until 1939. At the beginning of this century, in return for a fee of a hundred and fifty francs a night, the leader of the claque would spread his team throughout the auditorium and, at the right moment, give the signal for enthusiastic applaus of the singer who had paid. If a member of the cast happened not to have contributed the fee and responded to the genuine cheers of the audience, it was agreed that he should compensate the claque with the sum of fifty francs. This would explain why prima donnas often seemed untypically reluctant to give encores.

By 1913 Messager had had enough. Many times he had threatened resignation and been persuaded to change his mind. Weary of trade union disputes, shocked by a corps de ballet that went on srike in the middle of a performance, constantly harassed by plots, intrigues and money worries, he at last departed in 1914. For his swansong he conducted Parsifal with all the skill and love the work evoked in him. As a result he left the Opéra feeling not quite so bitter as he might have been.

He was still able to work regularly elsewhere as conductor. For some time he had been director of the Conservatoire orchestra, a position to which, following custom, he was elected by the individual players. It may be that some of them regretted their choice, for they soon nicknamed him 'the pike' because of his swift and merciless descents upon those who were lazy or who made too many mistakes. Gradually, however, they came to respect his high standards.

Often demanding and severe, Messager trained his orchestsra and raised it to a level that surprised foreign audiences when they heard it on tour. After the outbreak of war in 1914, he took his band of players to give concerts throughout Europe. Although his latest enthusiasm was for new Russian music, he still included Wagner on his programmes, much to the annoyance of super-patriots at home who called for a ban on German music so long as the war lasted. From Europe he went to the Argentine and concluded the tour in America. By the time Messager ended his travels in New York he had convinced Americans that music was not entirely the domain of the Germans.

vi

Some very Parisian talents

Messager's duties as an opera administrator left him few opportunities to write music. *Une aventure de la Guimard*, produced in 1900, was a ballet featuring as heroine the eighteenth-century dancer who, notorious for her skinny body and ugly pock-marked face, yet had many lovers. It was said that even in her mid-forties she could look, on stage, no more than fifteen years old. The score, including rigaudon, sicilienne and tambourin, is an amiable tribute to Rameau.

Five years later he wrote *Les Dragons de l'Impératrice*, a romantic anecdote which took place, as did *Véronique*, at the time of the Second Empire. It was composed in the country home his wife had created in Normandy. Originally a house of little comfort or amenity, it became, under Dotie's influence, a retreat as welcoming as the cottage at Maidenhead had been. Here, beside the lively crackle of an autumnal wood fire, he drew on memories of his own youth for the quadrilles and waltzes he needed to give his new operetta period colour.

Flavoured with an amused but delicate nostalgia, scored with purity and economy, *Les Dragons de l'Impératrice* deserved to succeed. That it achieved only forty performances must be due to sheer bad luck.

Messager was happier with *Fortunio* in 1907. This 'comédie lyrique' was based on Musset's little play, *Le Chandelier*, which had also served Offenbach for *La Chanson de Fortunio*. It was obvious that comparisons would be drawn between the two versions of Fortunio's song which is an important feature of the action. Some critics preferred Offenbach, others Messager. Both are acceptable, in fact, and it is impossible to say that one is better than the other: they are simply different.

Monsieur Beaucaire signals a clear return to operetta and is actually termed an '*opérette romantique*'. It was taken from a successful novel by the American, Booth Tarkington, who painted a romantic picture of Bath in the eighteenth century. The hero, a Duc d'Orléans who has been exiled to the Georgian city, hides there disguised as a wigmaker called Beaucaire. His love for the grand Lady Mary inspires rivalry, intrigue, duels, and eventually, a royal pardon at Versailles.

The operetta, which dates from 1918, was originally given in English at the Prince's Theatre, London, with the incomparable Maggie Teyte, fresh from singing in *Pelléas et Mélisande*, as Lady Mary. The 'book' is an uncharacteristic piece of work by Frederick Lonsdale, better known as the author of epigrammatic drawing-room comedies like *On Approval*. Since the lyrics were written by Adrian Ross, the worldly-wise Lonsdale is presumably not to be held responsible for such rhymes as 'Beware, Beaucaire!' and '*Beaucaire, mon cher*'.

French critics have been rather hard on *Monsieur Beaucaire*. They tend to dismiss it as Messager's 'English' operetta and conclude that he over-sugared the mixture to cater for Anglo-Saxon tastes. When it came to Paris in 1925 one commentator remarked that the production had been deliberately got up in the broad colours of an English Christmas card. It is true that the music deliberately aims at an English flavour. Beau Nash, who is one of the characters represented, has a hearty song, 'When I was king of Bath', which is pure Edward German, foursquare and unashamed. The 'Red Rose' number is openly sentimental. On the other hand, the duet, 'A little more', has typical Messager charm.

The score is filled with pastiche, of which the 'Rose Minuet' is a well-turned sample. The 'Philomel' pastoral, though sung to waltz tempo, succeeds in its rather obvious 'nightingale' effect. *Monsieur Beaucaire* was very popular both in England and America. Even in Paris, despite critical objections that Messager had betrayed himself to the English, it played over two hundred times and enjoyed a long life in provincial theatres.

The same versatility enabled Messager, in 1920, to write a music-hall sketch for a well-known comic actor. *Cyprien, ôte ta main d'là* ('Cyprien, take your hand away from there!') tells all in the title. Then, for just over a year, he became musical director at the Opéra-Comique again. During that time he conducted Mozart's *Cosi fan tutte* with a brilliance that evoked unanimous admiration. 'To have been the accomplished interpreter of Debussy, Wagner and Mozart is surely enough to set the seal on a conductor's reputation,' exclaimed one normally severe critic.

In the post-war years of the , nineteen-twenties Messager became something of an elder statesman. His experience covered every domain, from operetta to Wagner, from music hall to concert hall. His appetite for music was insatiable. Often, at night, he would sit up late in bed devouring a new score that had come his way. Bach was one of the unexpected composers whose work he loved to study, and among the scores that figured most often on his piano at home were those of Mozart, Beethoven, Chopin, Rameau, Debussy and Chabrier.

Gradually he ascended the ranks of the Légion d'Honneur and in 1927 was promoted to Commandeur. He had already achieved the ultimate in prestige and respectability by his election to the Institut des Beaux-Arts. Honours were now descending upon him in a cloud. One that especially pleased him was chairmanship of the Société des auteurs-compositeurs et éditeurs de musique, an organization founded in the eighteenth century by the dramatist Beaumarchais, gun-runner, harpist, financier, secret agent and author of *Le Mariage de Figaro*. Having suffered himself from the double-dealing of theatre managers, Beaumarchais saw that authors and composers who worked in the theatre needed protection for their interests. To this day the SACEM, as it is known for short, controls and licenses the production of musical works throughout France and sixty or so other countries. The arrival of outlets such as radio and television has made its work even more necessary. Messager found that his post was by no means a sinecure. He had little chance of composing at this busy period. Only in 1921 did he return to the operetta stage with *La Petite Fonctionnaire*, based on a comedy by that veteran boulevard writer Alfred Capus. At the first night Messager appeared, beaming, pleased at renewing contact with the public again. Afterwards, backstage, friends crowded round to offer congratulations. They were deceived. Takings began to fall and *La Petite Fonctionnaire* closed down after struggling on for little more than two months.

He tried again with *Passionnément*. This was largely the work of Albert Willemetz, a man whose name and work figured largely in the theatre from the nineteen-twenties until the sixties. As a youth he graduated in law, but, he later said, 'I was predestined to be a man of letters because my first name begins with an A and my surname ends with a Z.' When a theatre was inaugurated bearing the name of the august Eiffel Tower, he celebrated the occasion with a poem and was invited to meet the great engineer Gustave Eiffel. Willemetz asked him a question that had long been argued: why had Eiffel limited the height of his tower to precisely three hundred metres, no more and no less? It was true, replied Eiffel, that he could have made it three hundred and fifty metres or even four hundred. But, he explained, he was a staunch Republican and determined that the tower would have 1,789 steps exactly, to mark the date of the Revolution.

After a short time in the Ministry of the Interior as secretary to Clemenceau, Willemetz left it for the stage. In association with the composer Maurice Yvain and others he wrote a hundred and fifty revues and over a hundred operettas. He was an all-round man of the theatre and in his career played many parts: librettist, producer, playwright and manager. His song hits were numerous and long-lived. 'A popular song,' he wrote, 'is the art of composing with the aid of the public. It's the public that chooses what it likes and retains what it sings.' For Mistinguett he wrote 'Mon homme', one of her most popular numbers. He was the author of 'Valentine' with which Maurice Chevalier will always be identified. Chevalier once remarked: 'Among the writers whose songs I've sung, the most accomplished, the one whose style, grace and lightness were best able to refine my working-class cockiness, was Albert Willemetz.'

Passionnément featured an American millionaire who, like the character in that Chaplin comedy, became an entirely different personality under the influence of drink. Quite unbearable when sober, he turned into the most sympathetic comrade after drinking a bottle of wine (*'Comme on devient bon quand on a bu!'*). The score shows that Messager at the age of seventy-three still possessed wit and ease aplenty. For the central character he wrote a big number of irresistible verve and catchiness, one that goes out on its dancing way with an uncanny prediction of 'I'm gonna wash that man right out of my hair'. A waltz opulently harmonized and couplets fashioned with a precise irony were among the other delights of an operetta which, this time, won the approval and audiences — and of serious critics. Arthur Honegger, a member of 'Les Six' and, like Messager, an occasional journalist, wrote: 'I shall content myself with very simply expressing my admiration for the freshness and melodic invention . . . and above all for that vitality which make of M. Messager a composer as modern as Poulenc and Auric.'

Relieved by the success of *Passionnément*, Messager spent a month in the summer on holiday at Offenbach's old haunt of Etretat where he arranged the score for small orchestra, as the operetta was destined, after its Paris triumph, to tour the provinces. The apparent ease and smoothness of his work were deceptive. Into it had gone many hours of hard and often exhausting labour which, concealed by immaculate techniques, had the effect of making everything look simple. Sometimes he would say, speaking true words in jest: 'I'm no good much longer for writing anything but opera. It's far less tiring. You're carried forward by the words, by the orchestral development, by the conventions; with operetta you need to have new ideas all the time!'

Yet he could not resist another collaboration with Albert Willemetz and, in fact, proposed the original idea which he found in a novel he had been reading. *Coups de roulis*, a title which implies the lurch and roll of a ship at sea, takes place on a cruiser. An important parliamentary figure arrives to carry out an inspection ordered by the government because of excessive spending in naval administration. With him, as secretary, he brings his pretty daughter. She, of course, is an object of rivalry between the captain of the vessel and a humble midshipman. (The latter is the excuse for an excellent number in march rhythm, 'There's no such thing as rank in love, the important thing is to be twenty years old'.) As extra spice to the plot, the MP becomes entangled with an exotic Egyptian actress eager for his influence to get her into the Comédie-Française.

The MP was played by none other than Raimu. More accustomed to his performances as a great character actor, one is a little surprised to meet with him in operetta. Yet he started his career in music-hall as part of a singing act and, before he established himself, had worked in revues and among variety turns. He had, it appears, much success in *Coups de roulis*, especially when he sang '*Quand on est député*', a satirical item including a little chromatic mannerism which had been a Messager 'fingerprint' as far back as *La Basoche*. At one point he tripped and fell into the ship's coal-bunker, much to the enjoyment of an audience that loved to see politicians ridiculed.

In the final decade of Messager's career he was also associated with a friend of Albert Willemetz, one whose name is even more characteristic of the inter-war years of the French theatre. Sacha Guitry then, and for some time still to come, was at the height of his glory. He was the son of France's greatest actor, Lucien, but after a quarrel with his father — which, like every other incident in his private life, was conducted in such a way that all Paris knew about it — struck out on his own as a dramatist. Having experienced some early flops he quickly gained a reputation as the author of light, fast-moving comedies distinguished for their benevolent cynicism, mercurial dialogue and an undercurrent of disillusionment. His first wife, an actress, taught him stage craft and it was not long before he was acting in his own plays. He was known everywhere as 'Sacha'. 'My surname was already made,' he once said in reference to his celebrated father. 'I made myself a first name.'

A Sacha first night was unique. For preference in some small theatre, like the Edouard VII, where his intimate effects and subtle playing could best be appreciated, the atmosphere was gay and indulgent. Even before Sacha made his entrance, the spectators had willingly entered into a conspiracy with him. They played their rôle as brilliantly as he played his, and the collaboration sparkled with humour. His theme, invariably, was women, their lies, their deceptions, their trickery, their falseness — and their utter irresistibility. He was to be married five times, and the adventures he had offstage were reproduced in the theatre, where he adorned the set with Utrillo and Renoir pictures and antique furniture from his own beautiful town house. 'All the others,' remarked Sacha to his fifth wife and indicating, with the gesture of a grand seigneur, his lovely possessions, 'were my wives. You, my darling, will be my widow.'

The theatre remained his first love. Even when, ill and frail at the end of his life, he was confined to a wheelchair, he refused to sacrifice the joy of acting on stage — so he wrote a play with a part for himself as an old man confined to a wheelchair. There was, for him, no difference between life and the theatre. His various homes in Paris and the country, furnished with exquisite things, including a legendary art collection, were the backdrop to a comedy which he acted continually with style and wit. Poet as well as playwright, sculptor, cartoonist and inimitable raconteur, he was the idol of *le tout-Paris*. Women loved it when he murmured, in those deep caressing tones: 'As for the man who runs away with your wife, there's no worse punishment than to let him keep her.' Or when, flipping a white cuff and lighting one of his interminable cigarettes, he mused: 'To be married, to have a mistress, and to deceive her with somebody else makes it look as if one is becoming faithful to one's wife again — more or less.' And, with a sidelong glance at his present wife: 'If one day we want to be bachelors again, we should take care only to marry the most beautiful women.'

Sacha had already written revues in collaboration with Albert Willemetz and was to create an operetta with Oscar Straus. One day in the 'twenties he was approached by a composer called Ivan Caryll, who, though a Belgian with the real name of Félix Tilkin, was responsible for a number of musical comedies very popular in England. His headquarters were in London, where his *The Shop Girl* led the way in 1894 as an early example of musical comedy and gave Seymour Hicks the opportunity of stopping the show with 'Her golden hair was hanging down her back'. *Our Miss Gibbs*, written, as were several others, with Lionel Monckton, also ran well in London. Apart from *Hello Charley!*, a piece which introduced an intriguing new rhythm called the 'wai-ki-ki', he had not made much impression on Paris audiences. He proposed that Sacha write the libretto of a musical comedy for him. This was agreed. Whereupon Ivan Caryll, né Tilkin, promptly died.

For some time the libretto of *L'Amour masqué* sat in a drawer. Then Sacha offered it to Messager, who, always keen for novelty, accepted the commission. The plot features a beautiful young woman who lives a very comfortable life sustained by two elderly lovers. To her horror one of them suddenly announces that he is about to divorce his wife because she is having an affair with someone else. He will, he says happily, at last be able to marry the young woman. She is appalled at a development which threatens her agreeable existence, and hastily warns the guilty couple that the husband is on his way to confront them. And then, at a masked ball, she elopes with a third man who can give her not only money, but love as well.

The musical side presented problems, not the least of which concerned the size of the orchestra. In the little Théâtre Edouard VII there was room for only a small number of players. The chorus was limited to no more than eight singers. The spacious pre-war days of orchestras forty-strong, of many changes of elaborate scenery, of large choruses and numerous extras, had gone. Messager rose to the challenge with ingenuity. His score, using only the simplest of means, gave an adroit impression of fullness and body.

Sacha played the young lover. His second wife, Yvonne

Printemps, took the part of the *cocotte*. He had early recognized her potential, her wide-eyed charm and attractive voice, and had groomed her into an actress of poise and accomplishment. In the twenty-odd plays he wrote for her as leading lady she displayed a grace, a loveliness, which made her unique. The number *'J'ai deux amants'*, which Messager cast slyly in the mould of 'Coquette' from Schumann's *Carnaval*, was sung by her with such vivacity and mischief that every night an enchanted audience insisted on an encore. The clarity of her diction and the warmth of her seductive tone gave an extra quality to the music that made her perhaps the best female interpreter of his work Messager had known. Her voice, he declared, had 'extraordinary lustre and power'.

The tango being then all the rage, Messager paid tribute to fashion in a beautifully written example with luscious harmonies that, by contrast, show up the threadbare nature of most other efforts at the time. He also contributed a waltz, poignant and affectionate. In solo and concerted numbers alike, he wrote with a youthfulness that belied his years and set the airy trifle of a plot in a musical framework that matched its wit. He also allowed himself his own little jokes. One of these he played in the finale, where the chorus, chanting *'L'amour est enfant de Bohème'*, breaks into a quotation from Carmen's *Habañera*.

L'Amour masqué, a skilful blend of two very Parisian talents, stayed a long time at the Edouard VII. It was, as Fauré remarked, 'a great big success'. Now aged and failing, so deaf that he could hear hardly at all, Messager's old friend was unable to get to the theatre. 'However,' he wrote, 'I've been lent your score. Your wit is the same as always — it never grows old — and so are your charm and very personal brand of music that always remains exquisite, even amid the broadest clowning.'

Three years later Messager again worked with Sacha. The occasion was a revival of Sacha's play *Deburau* which had originally been given in 1918. This brought to life again on the stage the great mime Deburau. At his tiny theatre in the boulevard du Crime, he evoked the legendary white-faced Pierrot, a sad, mute commentator on the poverty and suffering of life. His popular art translated into gesture and movement the hard existence of the pedlars and labourers who worked in the streets of Paris. He had come from Bohemia and earned a living on the way across Europe by tumbling and tight-rope walking, often seriously hurting himself when, amid the cruel laughter of watching crowds,

he fell by accident. Since then he had evolved from his harsh
experience an exquisite form of mime that joined comedy to
tragedy in wordless perfection. His admirers included Balzac and
George Sand who came to see him act among the penny-gaffs and
shadow shows and puppet theatres that lined the boulevard du
Crime. In modern times he has been marvellously reincarnated by
Jean-Louis Barrault as a character in the film *Les Enfants du
Paradis*.

Sacha wove all these elements into a fantasy both moving and
poetic. He also gave to Deburau an unrequited love affair with
Marie Duplessis who had lived at the time and was the original of
the heroine of the famous old play *La Dame aux camélias*. Yvonne
Printemps acted both Marie Duplessis and the part of Charles,
Deburau's son. The tragic mime's world of the Pierrot with the
flour-whitened face was re-created in a sensitive and picturesque
vision of the Romantic eighteen-forties. The music was scored for a
cornet, tuba, big drum, two violins, double bass and piano.

Although these are fairground instruments Messager used
them with subtlety. In the first act, where Deburau mimes his
famous number as the old-clothes dealer, the music tactfully
reflects his adventures. Playful at the entry of Columbine, it takes a
dignified turn when the duchess comes on to the accompaniment of
a minuet that begins in stately fashion and then broadens out into a
touching wistfulness. It works in the dealer's traditional street cry,
'Any old clothes to sell?' and concludes with an exuberant waltz,
brassy yet tender.

Even in the wisps of melody that accompany spoken dialogue
Messager shows a delectable inspiration. When Deburau tells the
story of his life, its hardships and its struggles, the music is subtly
married to word and gesture. The double bass plays a tune that
rises from the depths with a sad nobility and then melts into a
Brahmsian dying fall. The song given to Yvonne Printemps as
Marie Duplessis has a fluent melancholy. Between the acts, interval
music sustains the mood of poignance and regret. Messager's
contribution to *Deburau* may not have been the lengthiest of his
works. It is certainly among his most beautiful and concentrated.

He was already, in 1926, afflicted by the kidney disease that
proved mortal. The first agonies were felt when he was writing
Deburau. They redoubled as he worked on *Coups de roulis*, though
it would be impossible to guess from such youthful and light-
hearted music that the composer was undergoing at that moment

the tortures of a stone in his kidney. He refused to let illness defeat him so long as he could hold a pen in his hand. His curiosity about new music remained as keen as ever. The only music he could not get excited about was what he had himself written in the past, and he often forgot it. One evening Yvonne Printemps and some friends asked him to play *Véronique*. 'With pleasure,' he replied. 'But have you got the score? I can't remember a single note of it any more.'

Yvonne Printemps hummed one of the most famous songs in it. Gradually his fumbling fingers picked out the melody at the piano and gathered speed as the tune emerged haltingly from his memory. Even so he did not play very well. The piano was not his instrument and he rarely used it, preferring to compose for the orchestra direct onto his manuscript paper.

There was little music ever written that he did not know. His range of knowledge and appreciation was vast. Politics, however, were outside his scope and, although he enjoyed painting and literature, it was his own art that absorbed him completely. His output was prolific. Yet, as he said, 'if a dozen or so of the acts that I've written for the stage have succeeded, it's only because I've composed over a hundred'. It was his special glory to have made 'light' music respectable and to have shown that it could be written with·taste, skill and art. Both the general public and the professional musician agreed to praise his work. It is ironic that a composer of Messager's quality should be pigeon-holed under 'operetta' with men so inferior to him as Varney, Planquette and the rest. Of the composers discussed in this book so far, he was without a doubt the most consummate musician.

All his life he was dedicated to his art. Gravely ill while engaged on *Deburau*, he remarked: 'Well, I think I'm about to see how music is written from the other side.' Having recovered from the attack, he said: 'Good, now we can get on and make some music.'

But he was also subject to the frailties of human nature, a man of uncertain temper who smoked cigarette after cigarette to calm a state of nerves ever on the boil. He was, too, a man who made his living entirely from music and who, even at the height of his fame, had no protection against the type of shabby misfortune which could happen to the veriest beginner. One day in Nice, with Albert Willemetz, he was going to his table for dinner when the hotel orchestra started playing one of the most popular numbers from

Fortunio. His brow clouded, his moustache bristled, he puffed angrily at his cigarette.

'What?' said Willemetz, a little surprised, 'Aren't you glad to hear that lovely tune being played and sung by the whole world?'

'No,' he muttered thickly behind his moustache.

'Why?'

'For two reasons. First, because they're playing it at the wrong tempo. Second, because it reminds me that I made over all the rights in it to my publisher for the sum of fifty francs.'

ACT IV

DECLINE AND FALL

I

Reynaldo from Venezuela

Somewhere in Caracas during the eighteen-seventies there was a road that led into a square containing a statue of the Venezuelan patriot Simon Bolivar. That, and a memory of sitting on some stone steps in a large garden while a Negress watched over him, was all Reynaldo Hahn could remember of his birthplace.

The garden was his father's, a lavish prospect of native flowers varied with European strains like begonias, jasmine and orchids. For Venezuela, rich in trees and exotic birds, fruits and gold, oil and diamonds, abounded also in flowers of many varieties. Botany was only one of Carlos Hahn's interests. A close friend and economic adviser of the president, he built railways across the land, constructed telegraph systems and established a gas company. In Caracas he put up a huge theatre which opened with Verdi's *Ernani*. He was a clever businessman and also, as his love of flowers and music showed, an amateur of beauty.

No one knows why Carlos had settled in Venezuela. His family had left Holland many years before and taken root in Hamburg. There were brokers and rabbis and merchants among his ancestors. He married a girl from an old Venezuelan family, beautiful, cultured and as fond of flowers as he was. They had twelve children, of whom ten survived — five boys and five girls. Reynaldo was the youngest. His birth certificate recorded the date of 1874. But through coquetry or pure misapprehension, for the rest of his life he gave himself an extra allowance of youth by quoting the date as 1875. Offenbach, it may be recalled, had the same misleading little habit.

Reynaldo's mother tongue was Spanish. He chattered in it fluently from the age of twenty months. Whenever the piano teacher came to give his sisters a lesson he would silently haunt the room. Once his mother found him in tears. Had he hurt himself? she asked. No, he replied, but the music was so sad. 'There's somebody dying in that music.' Two of his sisters had been working through the final act of *La Traviata*.

In 1877 Carlos Hahn's powerful friend, the president of Venezuela, resigned and was succeeded by a weaker man. The latter died, of poisoning, it was thought. Carlos Hahn judged it wise to leave the country, and next year the family set off for Paris. The financier quickly made friends and new business connections. His wife became a graceful hostess. Their luxurious flat, just off the Champs-Elysées, was the scene of many grand receptions.

At the age of three Reynaldo could already find his way around the keyboard. When he was five he played charmingly, and at eight he was composing. His father had used to dandle him on his knee humming Offenbach tunes the way he'd heard the great Schneider sing them. This early experience gave the boy a lifelong conviction of the importance of rhythm. No musical pleasure could exist, he decided, without 'that mysterious and infallible dynamic which rules all the movements of nature, from the motion of the planets to the circulation of the blood.'

The boy Reynaldo made his début in the salon of the formidable Princesse Mathilde, that cousin of Napoleon III who patronized writers and artists with an awesome majesty. Music was not often heard in the gloomy mansion. The piano had to be cleared of numerous ornaments, pictures and draperies before it could be played. Reynaldo, wearing a new black velvet costume, sat there and piped in his boyish treble songs from Offenbach operetta. His career had begun.

He was ten years old when he entered the Conservatoire. There he was nicknamed 'the little Venezuelan', although he very soon learned to speak and write French with complete fluency. Sometimes his teacher would run out of examples for the pupils to sight-read. 'Reynaldo,' he'd say, 'write something for us!' Ten minutes later, having dashed off a few pages, Reynaldo would produce the manuscript and practice could go on.

Perhaps his favourite teacher was Massenet. Certainly he was one of Massenet's favourite pupils. The composer of *Manon* lost no opportunity to help Reynaldo. He introduced him to important people, spoke of him to his friends, confided in him about his latest opera. When the precocious Reynaldo had begun to write songs, it was Massenet's beautiful protégée, Sybil Sanderson, who performed them.

You do not need to have been born in Paris to be a Parisien. Many, in fact, whose birth certificates mention the capital never achieve that airy scepticism, that lightness and nonchalance which are the signs of the true Parisian. Reynaldo, though he first saw the light of day in Venezuela, acquired the title at birth. It is impossible to imagine him in any other setting. As a character of the Belle Epoque he fitted the rôle to perfection.

Reynaldo knew everyone. He moved easily in the world that Colette evoked with *Gigi*. 'Little Hahn' as people called him, was a favourite of the celebrated dancer Cléo de Mérode. She appreciated his fine brown hair, the brilliant velvety eyes, the perceptive knowledge he had of art and literature. She enjoyed, even more, his wit. At the Opéra one evening he was asked what he thought about the singing of the famous tenor Van Dyck. 'I prefer his painting,' murmured Reynaldo.

With Cléo de Mérode he sustained until his death an intense friendship. He gave her copies of his songs bearing extravagant dedications. He wrote her many long letters in which he continually expressed his adoration. 'I love you,' he wrote 'as an admirable, perfect work of art.' His passion remained chaste.

So did his *'amitié amoureuse'* with the notorious *cocotte* Liane de Pougy, one of the most successful among the high-class courtesans of the Belle Epoque. After numerous adventures and after using up several husbands both rich and aristocratic, she took to religion and charitable works. Observed a wit: 'She gave herself to God since men no longer wanted her.'

She, like Cléo de Mérode, was fascinated by Reynaldo's attractive personality. He received her most intimate confidences. Her letters told him of the developments in her love life, of how everything was over with 'Frank' and how she had just begun with 'Max', of how she lamented the death of her first husband and the two hundred thousand francs a year he had taken with him. And then she would exclaim to Reynaldo: 'You are the only man I'd *want* to give myself to and who won't take me.'

It was Liane de Pougy who formed the subject of one of those anecdotes that delighted Paris at the time. Her husband surprised her in bed one day with a lover. He fired his gun and wounded her in each buttock. Fearfully she demanded of her doctor who extracted the lead: 'Will it show?'

'Madame,' he replied with a grave bow, 'that depends entirely on you.'

Such gossip was eagerly collected by Reynaldo, for, as Sacha Guitry has remarked, the Parisian has a duty to use his wit 'fiercely and without pity. An epigram is sacred. You can make an epigram against your sister or your wife, if necessary, provided it's amusing. No one has the right to keep an epigram to himself.'

Reynaldo dined out frequently and was often a guest not only in the salon of Princesse Mathilde, but also in the drawing-rooms of other leading hostesses. It was the daunting custom of Madame Aubernon to assemble a dozen or so guests around her table and to give them a subject on which they were expected to talk. One lady, asked to offer an opinion on adultery, faltered: 'A thousand apologies! I'd only prepared myself to talk about incest.' The dramatist Labiche, wanting to make an observation, was called to order by a tinkle from the bell which the imperious Madame Aubernon kept at her side. Invited to explain himself a moment later, he mumbled: 'I only wanted to ask for some more *petits-pois*.'

When the time for music came Reynaldo would take his seat at the piano. There, a cigarette drooping lazily from the corner of his mouth, he would sing in a light tenor voice. As he sang, his dark, half-closed eyes carefully surveyed the audience to judge the effect he was making. Not the least intriguing feature of his performance was the way in which the cigarette remained immovable while he played and vocalized. Jean Cocteau caught the stance perfectly in one of his sketches. Hostesses loved Reynaldo. He wore a smart grey hat and a pearl-studded tie. As he came in, he handed to the butler his gold-handled walking stick. His manners were admirable.

He had launched his conquest of the salons in the house of Alphonse Daudet, a very popular novelist at the time, who gathered round him a circle of friends that included most of the important names in literature. Though racked by the tortures of syphilis contracted when a young man, Daudet was an engaging talker and, like Reynaldo, charm itself. He wanted someone to write incidental music for his new play, *L'Obstacle*, and asked Massenet to suggest one of his pupils for the task. Massenet indicated Reynaldo.

From then on Reynaldo was the firm friend of Daudet as well

as of his sons, the excitable Léon and the dandified Lucien. He was
then no more than fifteen years old and still at the Conservatoire,
yet he had already composed the *Chansons grises* which are among
his best-known works. These settings of Verlaine poems illuminate
the aching emotion of *'Chanson d'automne'* or of *'L'heure exquise'*
with a discreet and sensitive glow. They pleased Daudet and helped
him forget a little the pains of his illness. Even that crabbed old
diarist Edmond de Goncourt, who was not really fond of music,
had to record: 'Little Reynaldo Hahn sat down at the piano and
played music he'd written to three or four poems by Verlaine.
They're real gems.'

The Verlaine pieces like the Mendelssohnian *Si mes vers
avaient des ailes*, which Reynaldo composed when he was little
more than fourteen, have a crystalline simplicity. They continue
the heritage of Gounod, whom Ravel called the 'true founder' of
the *mélodie*, that type of song as characteristically French as the
lied is German. A cigarette fuming incessantly between his lips, the
ash drooping in a fine arc, Reynaldo sang them with intelligence
and wit. He did not regard himself as a professional singer and took
none of the usual precautions to safeguard his voice. On the
contrary, he revelled in late nights, extended talking and eternal
chain-smoking. Was it, perhaps, his charm rather than his vocal
skill that captivated audiences who heard him singing? Not
necessarily. The great Pauline Viardot, friend of Chopin and sister
of Malibran, had in her time been a very famous prima donna. 'I
like the way you sing,' she told him once after hearing him. 'Yes,
yes, it's simple, it's good.'

He often sang in the drawing-room of Madeleine Lemaire, the
painter who specialized in roses. So many of them did she paint,
day after day, that one of her lovers remarked: 'Only God has
created more roses than she has.' Her salon was very musical and
included the composers Saint-Saëns and Massenet and the singers
Emma Calvé and Jean de Reszke. One evening there Reynaldo was
introduced to Marcel Proust. Reynaldo was twenty years old and
Marcel twenty-three. It did not take them long to discover that they
were both members of what Proust quaintly described in his great
novel as the race of *'hommes-femmes'*.

Unable to respond to the beauty of a Cléo or of a Liane,
Reynaldo was instantly moved by the pale features of Marcel. The
new friends adored each other. Their passion was deep and ardent.
Proust's letters to Reynaldo were written in a private language and

saluted him as *'cher Binchnibuls'*, *'mon cher Petit Puncht'*, or *'cher Gruncht'*. In Salzburg to conduct *Don Giovanni*, Reynaldo found himself addressed as *'mon petit Buninuls chersi'*. Marcel reported with delight that Prince Antoine Bibesco had compared one of Reynaldo's songs with a Mozart trio. Once, already a clever *pasticheur*, he cast his letter in the style of Madame de Sévigné.

Together they wrote *Portraits de peintres*, being music by Reynaldo to accompany the declamation of poems by Marcel in honour of the artists they admired. In the early novel *Jean Santeuil*, the character Henri de Réveillon is Reynaldo. 'I want you to be ever-present in my novel,' Marcel told him, 'but like a god disguised whom no mortal shall recognize.'

Musically Proust was now a Wagnerian and even sympathized with Debussy, allegiances which Reynaldo could not approve. His own models were Saint-Saëns, from whom he'd had private lessons, Massenet, Gounod and, among the classics, Mozart. Proust could never summon up much enthusiasm for Reynaldo's idols, though he did, to please his friend, write a laudatory article about Saint-Saëns. Yet Reynaldo was to have a major influence in the matter of the famous *'petite phrase'* which recurs symbolically throughout *A la recherche du temps perdu*. There is a passage in Saint-Saëns's D minor violin sonata that caught Marcel's fancy when Reynaldo played it over to him. It is one of those simple but haunting themes which Saint-Saëns had a knack of producing.

'Play me that little piece I like so much, please, Reynaldo,' Marcel would often ask. 'You know: the little phrase.' It became 'their' tune, the melody that symbolized his feeling for Reynaldo just as, in his novel, it represented the love of Swann for Odette.

For some time, perhaps as long as ten years or so, the liaison endured. 'Since Mamma will be leaving soon,' Marcel would write, 'you can come and console me after she's gone . . .' Gradually love cooled into a friendship that was warm and profound. When Proust died in 1922, a grieving and exhausted Reynaldo kept watch over his bed.

Proust was not the only literary man Reynaldo frequented. The composer was the subject of one of those joking little quatrains by the Symbolist poet Stéphane Mallarmé — a great honour indeed — in which the whole point was to obtain a rhyme, however far-fetched, for the name of the person addressed. For 'Reynaldo' Mallarmé dug up *'jet d'eau'*. He also wrote a typically mannered prologue to a concert of Reynaldo's music. The child prodigy was fourteen at the time.

Reynaldo travelled much and, among other countries, knew England well. One of his favourite English novelists was R. H. Benson. This now largely forgotten writer, one of three talented brothers, was rather surprisingly described as 'a most original and powerful talent' by Reynaldo, who even translated a novel of his into French.

Among his closest English friends were the Duchess of Manchester, Lady de Grey and Lady Juliet Duff. One evening at the Duchess of Manchester's home Edward VII and Queen Alexandra were expected. Everyone wore court dress, and Reynaldo spent a fraught half-hour trying on his ceremonial breeches. The King arrived and engaged the composer in polite conversation, his eyes flickering constantly to the door where he expected at any moment the arrival of his current favourite, Mrs Keppel. After the performance he asked Reynaldo to sing Offenbach to him as a reminder of his visits to Paris when he was Prince of Wales. Then he went off to play bridge. The Queen, seizing her chance, begged Reynaldo and the orchestra to play over again an earlier item she'd enjoyed very much. This was *Le Bal de Béatrice d'Este*, a suite for wind instruments, two harps and piano. Typical of Reynaldo's liking for unusual combinations it includes a 'Lesquercade' and a 'Romanesque', sweetly archaic and instinct with the atmosphere of a Milanese royal court that vanished three centuries before. The work is dedicated to Saint-Saëns.

In the dedication of *L'Ile du Rêve* he also paid tribute to another of his idols. 'To Massenet, my master,' it reads, 'as a token of affectionate gratitude.' Produced at the Opéra-Comique when Hahn was twenty-three, this 'Polynesian idyll in three acts' had been taken from yet another South Seas bestseller by Pierre Loti. It is very Massenetic.

La Fête chez Thérèse was a ballet which took the famous dancer Carlotta Grisi as a leading character. It had a run at the Opéra of more than forty performances and stayed in the programme long enough for Reynaldo to conduct a revival in 1921. The scenario was by Catulle Mendès, who also wrote the libretto of Reynaldo's opera *La Carmélite*. Much praised on its appearance, when the cast included Emma Calvé and the conductor was Messager, the opera has since failed to keep its place.

Having gained an entrée to the Opéra-Comique and the Opéra as well, something which older composers often spend a lifetime in achieving, Reynaldo awaited the final consecration.

This materialized in 1911: a commission from Diaghilev to write a work for the Ballets Russes. Based on a scenario by Jean Cocteau, who had firmly hitched his wagon to Diaghilev's star, and by Reynaldo's nephew Coco de Madrazo, *Le Dieu Bleu* was intended as a showpiece for Nijinsky to display his virtuosity in steps inspired by Siamese dancing. Reynaldo travelled to St Petersburg, Diaghilev's home that winter, and played his score to the assembled company. His singing and his playing were as well received there as they had been in Paris. And yet, the Russians felt, was not his music for *Le Dieu Bleu* a trifle too mannered, too well bred?

Before the première in Paris, elated by the excitement and the heady atmosphere that always surrounded Diaghilev, Reynaldo snatched time off and fled on an escapade to Folkestone where his name appeared on the register of the West Cliff Hotel as 'William Shakespeare'.

Le Dieu Bleu made no great sensation. It did not measure up to its predecessor, *Schéhérazade*, which had been Diaghilev's reason for seeking another oriental ballet. The choice of Reynaldo as composer was tactical rather than artistic. Diaghilev needed him at the time because he wanted to gain the favour of the Paris drawing-rooms, and Reynaldo, the idol of the salons, was an obvious, though doubtless unknowing ally. His music was too reminiscent of Delibes in *Lakmé* mood and did not possess the barbaric vitality associated with the Diaghilev manner. It was soon eclipsed by the scandal of Nijinksy's over-explicit costume in the *Prélude à l'après-midi d'un faune*.

In 1909 Reynaldo surrendered his Venezuelan passport and took French nationality. When the war came in 1914 he joined up. Since he had fluent English, German, Spanish and a little Italian besides his French, he applied for an interpreter's post. Asked by the British authorities to give references, he quoted the names of those who knew him and had often heard him play: King George V, Queen Mary, the Duke of Connaught . . . .

He was, of course, too innocent for the Kafkaesque ways of the army. Having all the qualifications of an interpreter, he ended up as an infantryman at the front line. In the depths of a winter offensive he sketched plans for an opera called *Nausicaa* and another based on Shakespeare's *Merchant of Venice*. In between reading Carlyle's *History of the French Revolution* he set to music some English poems by Robert Louis Stevenson. He emerged from the war as a fully-fledged corporal with a Croix de Guerre.

Early in the nineteen-twenties he was invited by a friend of his youth, the Marquis Robert de Flers, to write an operetta in the style of *La Fille de Madame Angot*. Flers was a director of the important newspaper *Le Figaro* and author, in collaboration with Gaston de Caillavet, of boulevard comedies whose satirical point has not been wholly blunted by the years. At his *Figaro* office he sat in front of a desk piled high with letters. He believed that one should not answer letters too quickly — one should wait at least a fortnight, after which one realized that in most cases any reply would be pointless. Once, on actually starting to dictate a letter, he began: 'Dear friend . . . ' Then he changed his mind. To his secretary he exclaimed: 'No, I can't call that scoundrel, that rascal "dear friend". Write: dear colleague.'

An operetta? Up to now Reynaldo had composed operas, ballets, and a great deal of incidental stage music. He was not at all sure he had the 'light' touch required. What was the title to be? *Ciboulette*, Flers replied. Now *ciboulette* is the French word for a chive. This, Reynaldo objected, was not the most romantic of names. Flers could think of no better, so Reynaldo in the end agreed. The action of the operetta took place under the Second Empire, and, like Lecocq's masterpiece, was located in the Halles, for a long time the wholesale fruit, flower and vegetable market of Paris.

The shadow of Lecocq hung over Reynaldo's début in operetta. Lecocq had been one of the ten composers — Reynaldo and Messager were among the others — who contributed in 1914 to a joint work called '*Miousic* (a playful French phonetic spelling of the way English people pronounce the word 'music'). After the war Reynaldo conducted a noted revival of *La Fille de Madame Angot*. And had not Claire Angot, like Ciboulette, been the darling of Les Halles?

One of the old market-women tells Ciboulette's fortune. The pretty young girl will, apparently, find her fiancé under a cabbage; will see a dark-haired woman turn white in a moment; and will receive a marriage proposal in a tambourine. The rest of the operetta shows how these incongruous prophecies are fulfilled. Ciboulette's future lover goes to sleep in her cart and is discovered there beneath a pile of cabbages. His former mistress, a dark beauty, is drenched by a bag of flour and goes as white as a sheet. And, at the end, when Ciboulette becomes Conchito Ciboulero,

the Spanish prima donna, she hears from her suitor in the way
foretold.

This may not sound the most exciting of plots. Yet the charm
of the lyrics and the winning grace of the music help to·make
Ciboulette a rightful part of the Lecocq tradition. The tale of how
a simple country girl captures the heart of a dashing nobleman is
told in a libretto shrewdly contrived by Flers and his collaborator,
Francis de Croisset, a pair of experienced old boulevard hands.
The music, while based on Lecocq's formula, rejuvenates the old
technique with a singular brightness of melody and adroit
combinations of voice and instrument. It is matched by dialogue of
a high standard, as, for example, when the heroine recounts her
view of Paris glimpsed as she drives her cart down the hill of
Montmartre. She has a vision of Paris the elusive, Paris the
unseizable: *'Ma pauvre fille, Paris ce n'est pas encore pour
aujourd'hui!'*

For the third act, which takes place at the home of Olivier
Métra, the writer of popular dance tunes, Hahn conceived a waltz
of bold and generous proportion. This is to be contrasted with such
ravishing, more intimate numbers as the song given to Duparquet,
a sort of elderly Rodolphe out of *La Bohème*, who nostalgically
recalls his youth and last love. The *'Chanson de route'*, (*'Y a d'la
lune àu bord du toit qu'est ronde'*), is as brisk a marching song as
any Messager ever wrote. Another high-light of the score is the Act
II duet between Duparquet and Ciboulette. *'Nous avons fait un
beau voyage'*, they sing, describing the journey they've made and
echoing the famous line by the Renaissance poet du Bellay,
'Heureux qui, comme Ulysse, a fait un beau voyage.'

Jean Périer, the versatile singer who had been Debussy's first
Pelléas, took the rôle of Duparquet at the première in 1923.
Reynaldo, through shyness or indifference, had quietly gone out to
a cinema. Only on approaching the theatre as the audience came
out did he realize, with genuine astonishment, that *Ciboulette* had
been rapturously acclaimed.

The new operetta generally had excellent reviews. Some,
however, of the thorns among the roses were provided by André
Messager. Initially a friend, he had become a detractor of Reynaldo
whom he contemptuously dismissed as 'a singing-teacher for old
ladies in fashionable drawing-rooms'. A number of small incidents
combined to ignite his easily aroused anger. When he learned that
Reynaldo had been promoted to the rank of Officier in the Légion

d'Honneur his fury was such that his private comments remain unprintable. After writing the music for *Deburau* he had quarrelled with Sacha Guitry, himself not the easiest of colleagues. Sacha was already planning a 'comédie musicale' entitled *Mozart*, and when Messager refused his invitation to provide the music he turned to Reynaldo. Perhaps for the very reason that Messager had rejected the challenge, Reynaldo accepted it.

Mozart presents the boy composer on one of his visits to Paris. He is taken up by the Baron de Grimm (played by Sacha) and by Madame d'Epinay who sponsor his stay there. The piece is a slim tracery of eighteenth-century allusion gilded by Sacha's unerring wit and feathery dialogue. The master of theatre craft, an inspired creator of illusion, produced some lovely stage-pictures. 'Every theatre-goer has experienced moments of emotion, for the justification of which he must search his intelligence in vain,' wrote the drama critic James Agate. 'I have not forgotten, though it is twenty years ago, that people were seen to cry, and by "cry" I mean shed tears, when Music's heavenly child appeared at the top of the gilt staircase and descended it to kneel at the feet of Madame d'Epinay.'

Reynaldo, with admirable tact, blended Mozart themes and his own music in a web of enchantment. Extracts from an early violin sonata and the ballet *Les Petits Riens* are among the material he used. From time to time a quick reference to *Don Giovanni*, *Figaro* and the 'Paris' Symphony is slipped into the texture. It is all done with superb legerdemain. Yvonne Printemps, who played *en travesti* the child Mozart, had never been more beautiful. One of the most exquisite moments came when she sang the '*Air de la lettre*'. As the record she made of it shows, her immaculate diction and poignant voice conferred on this simple little air a true nobility. Yet we should remember that, great though her talent was, it depended on Reynaldo for the creative genius which gave it expression.

Some years later he was again involved with Sacha. *O mon bel inconnu* was a typical *jeu d'esprit* about a middle-aged shopkeeper who is bored to distraction by the tedious chatter of his wife and daughter. Where can he find a beautiful woman to solace him? He puts a box-number advertisement in a newspaper stating that a wealthy bachelor is looking for a soul-mate. Dozens of replies flow in. Among them are one from his wife and one from his daughter.

The adorable Arletty played the part of the wife in this new

'comédie musicale'. She was then at the height of her career. Born
Léonie Bathiat, she had turned herself into Arlette. This she
changed into 'Arletty', thinking it to be *chic anglais, up-to-date
English fashion'. The cast also included a young Simone Simon.
Reynaldo's music was good humoured and well bred. One of the
neatest numbers was the duet *Qu'est-ce qu'il faut pour être
heureux?'. You need two things, explains Félicie. First you need to
be young, then you need to be rich. Since, she tells her wealthy
suitor, I have youth and you have riches, we've all that's needed for
love. In another number, pert and jaunty with chromatic quirks,
the maid reflects on how difficult it is to keep everyone happy. The
piece is rounded off with a trio, *O mon bel inconnu*, in relaxed
waltz tempo.

The lighter stage was proving congenial to Reynaldo. In
between his more serious works — a rather diffuse piano concerto
and the operas *Nausicaa* and *Le Marchand de Venise* — he wrote
other operettas. With the fashionable playwrights Maurice
Donnay and Henri Duvernois he composed *Une Revue*, a series of
historical tableaux through which the figures of Balzac and Corot
vaguely flitted. Later, he incorporated a good deal of this music in
the operetta *Malvina*. This was a patriotic evocation of the
eighteen-thirties, and without trying hard for too obvious effects
Reynaldo's music expressed a subtle delight and pride in the
quality of being French. It was, though, a difficult time in his
private life. A *mignon* whom he idolized had just deserted him. His
collaborators found him agitated and depressed.

Le Temps d'aimer was an outright 'musical comedy' in the
new style that had become popular since the end of the war. It even
began with a 'who's for tennis' ensemble and later went on to a
fox-trot — the sort of thing Ravel pastiched in *L'Enfant et les
sortilèges* — and a Charleston which was rather less than
accomplished. These are partly atoned for by a restful *berceuse*
and by a 'Fable' which recalls the Verlaine setting, *'L'heure
exquise'*. Much more characteristic is *Brummell*, for which
Reynaldo provided music as svelte and polished as his dandy hero.

The same may not be said of his lyricist Rip, a bald and
repellent character who hated men and women and succeeded in
quarrelling with everyone. He wrote the words of countless revues,
most of them biting and sardonic. The actor Michel Simon, who
played in one of his sketches, was so horrified by the cruel lines Rip
gave him that he refused to speak them. Rip treated him to some of

the sharp invective in which he specialised. The burly Simon clambered down from the stage to deal with him. Rip took to his heels and was never seen again, not even at the first night. Soon afterwards he died of alcoholism — a condition which may help to explain his misanthropy.

Reynaldo never had another triumph like *Ciboulette*, though *Brummell* contains a variety of delights. Lady Eversharp's riding song, *'Le prince royal par tradition Aime l'équitation'*, is pointfully scored, as is the number where she expresses her satisfaction at being described as 'the Madame de Sévigné of England'. Ever since Baudelaire and Barbey d'Aurevilly discovered Brummell, there has been an intellectual sympathy with the theory of dandyism in France. The operetta should, by rights, have attracted large audiences, especially for such numbers as the *'Chanson pastorale'* in which Brummell speaks of his elegant distaste for the countryside. But if the individual lyrics were good, the piece as a whole was badly put together and did not run long.

During the inter-war years Reynaldo's output was astonishing. Besides composing operas, operettas, chamber works and incidental music for the stage, he gave many lectures, conducted at festivals, and published books on the art of singing. Another of his publications was a memoir of Sarah Bernhardt whom he had known well and admired with the same extravagant enthusiasm which contemporary patrons of kitsch reserve for Marlene Dietrich. For a long period he was regular music critic on several papers including *Le Figaro*. As he grew older this feverish activity served as compensation for the loneliness he increasingly felt. Again and again the young men he took under his wing deceived him and left him. His youthful good looks began to fade. He started wearing a wig. It looked, alas, a shade too obvious. A certain bitterness crept into his tone. He could rely for steadfast affection only on his loyal maid. She had been his father's servant and was said to be the originator of remarks which Proust put into the mouth of the cook Françoise in *À la recherche du temps perdu*. Most of all, he had the love of his dog. In tribute to Voltaire, his favourite writer, he named the animal Zadig. When it died he adopted a successor which he baptized, as was only fitting, Candide.

'Petit maître', 'drawing-room composer' — these were some of the dismissive epithets applied to him. He grew weary of the constant belittlement, of the denigrating rumours which once, for

example, suggested that 'L'Ile du Rêve had only been accepted at the Opéra-Comique because the twenty-three year old composer paid a bribe of twenty thousand francs. He was, more than usually, the target of malice. Envy surrounded his grand social life, hatred denied him credit for his artistry. To one of his persistent critics he wrote:

> I have been composing music since the age of eight. I have lived in it *all my life*, like a fish in water . . . I'm not keen on pedants and always try to avoid imitating certain of my colleagues who, having begun to study music at the age of thirty, pontificate about it with majesty when they are thirty-five! But I often smile at their assurance . . . . The day you construct, without advice or help from anyone, a four-act opera and it is criticized, you will realize the disproportion that exists between the work you have done and the remarks of those who talk about it . . . .

If by the term *'petit maître'* is signified an artist who chooses a given field and works it industriously within set limits, then Reynaldo qualifies for the description. Sometimes, like other composers mentioned in this book, he wished it could have been otherwise. The temptation to make a Browningesque attempt on the grand manner was an inviting one. He wisely resisted. Inside the boundaries he accepted he was able to achieve an individual perfection with his songs, with rare inspirations like *Le Bal de Béatrice d'Este*, and with an operetta that is among the best of its kind.

When France capitulated to the German aggressor in 1940 Reynaldo left Paris for Toulon, a favourite spot of his. From there he went on to Cannes and directed an opera season. In Paris the German authorities had just banned a revival of *Ciboulette*. As the son of a Jewish father he was obliged to go through a degrading search for certificates and documents that would prove his 'Aryan' quality. No sooner had he satisfied his tormentors than the tax collector was pursuing him. Born and brought up amid wealth and comfort, Reynaldo had no conception of how to handle money. Cheques and banks and shares were to him as Sybilline mysteries. His income fluctuated abruptly and depended on an irregular flow of royalties, conductor's fees and payments for journalism. Tax demands always arrived at the worst possible moment. It was no good explaining that even if the Germans had not forbidden performances of *Ciboulette* and the income it produced, he would still have been unable to pay since they had also, through a refinement of sadism peculiar to their mentality, frozen his Paris bank account at the same time.

What else could he do but work? He completed a third string quartet and a concerto, and began to write a new musical comedy entitled *Le Oui des Jeunes Filles*. He travelled throughout the south, conducting festivals and concerts. In leisure moments he found Sacha Guitry's *Le Roman d'un tricheur* a welcome diversion. As he sat by his hotel window overlooking the bay at Monte Carlo, an English submarine fired a torpedo at a German mine-layer nearby. The missile shattered the balcony outside. Fragments of steel, glass and brick hurtled upon and around him. In Paris, at the same time, he was denounced as a Jew and his flat was sealed up, despite the proofs of 'Aryanism' so laboriously collected.

The war ended. With his faithful maid, his friend the singer Guy Ferrant, two dogs and a mass of luggage he journeyed back to the capital. The nightmare was over. Though the tax gatherers continued to harass, new honours came Reynaldo's way. In 1945 he was elected to the Académie des Beaux Arts. Dressed in the hallowed green uniform and cocked hat of the Academician, bearing the ornamental sword which his friends had subscribed for him, the seventy year old composer joined the distinguished company to which had belonged his heroes Gounod, Massenet and Saint-Saëns. It must have been a satisfying moment.

Soon afterwards he was appointed director of the Paris Opéra. His reign, though short, was a creditable one and included some worthy revivals. Occasionally he found himself nodding off to sleep over his desk. Sudden lapses of memory began to hold up his work. Surgeons discovered a tumour of the brain. It had been caused, thought his doctors, by the Monte Carlo bombardment. He died on 28 January 1947.

To the end he retained a keen Parisian wit. Though his brown eyes were faded and the olive skin was shrivelled and haggard, he still accepted dinner invitations and meticulous courtesy. It was getting late on one such evening. Reynaldo looked at his watch and murmured to his neighbour, a man who, like the other guests, was notorious for his sharp tongue: 'I really must be off. I hope they won't notice I've gone.'

I'm sure they will, came the reply. 'What will they say about you when you're no longer here? But never mind. I'll defend you.'

'In that case,' answered Reynaldo with a grim smile, 'I'll stay!'

ii

The boobs of Tirésias

On 11th November 1918 an Armistice put an end to the dreary
years of war. The street of Paris filled with exultant crowds. Two
days later, in Offenbach's old theatre of the Bouffes-Parisiens, a
new operetta called *Phi-Phi* was introduced. No one thought it
would be very successful, least of all the impresario who produced
it. He had begun to have doubts about what had seemed at first to
be the shrewd idea of exploiting the current vogue for one-steps
and fox-trots. In the event, though slow to catch on, *Phi-Phi* ran
for several years and made the fortunes of its composer, author,
producer and publisher. It also, with its new approach, signalled
the end of traditional French operetta and inaugurated the age of
musical comedy.*

The time was six hundred years BC, and the hero the famous
Greek sculptor Phidias, nicknamed 'Phi-Phi'. To complete his new
group representing 'Love' he has engaged as models a handsome
young man and a beautiful young girl. His eye for her beauty is
more than professional and she infatuates him. Madame Phidias,
his long-suffering wife, yields to the wooing of the young man. The
eternal triangle thus becomes a square and, eventually, a
pentagon, since the statesman Pericles falls in love with Phi-Phi's
mistress also. At the end of the operetta husband, wife, lover,
mistress and protector line up to sing:

> *Nous formons le quintette,*
> *Que dans toute opérette,*
> *D'Audran ou de Planquette*
> *On verra s'embrasser . . .*

The mention of Audran and Planquette is not the only
reference to *Phi-Phi's* predecessors. In her song about the
importance of good clothes and make-up to a woman, Aspasie the
mistress, whether deliberately or not, recalls a number in
Offenbach's *La Vie Parisienne* which celebrates the Parisienne
dressed up to kill with *'Sa robe qui fait frou frou frou frou, Ses
petits pieds font toc toc toc'*. Another song good-naturedly parodies

---

*The London Pavilion version in 1922 featured Evelyn Laye, Stanley Lupino and Jay
Laurier.

the aria from Massenet's *Manon, 'Je suis encor tout étourdie'*.

The libretto, in which the ubiquitous Albert Willemetz had a hand, contains good jokes and clever rhymes. In this 'Greek' setting the characters often meet people in the rue du Panthéon, the Odéon and the rue d'Athènes. They refer to silent screen heroines of the time, Pearl White and Mabel Normand, and even *'le fameux'* Douglas Fairbank' (sic). All this gives *Phi-Phi* a period charm, together with the aid of dialogue which, in its day, was not a little daring, but which now has an amusing coyness. When Madame Phi-Phi prays to the gods to bring back her wandering husband, she bewails the fact that a pretty girl always produces in him a certain effect *'difficile à nommer d'un mot plus explicite'*. This *'Prière'*, incidentally, is quite a moving episode and is accompanied by a plummy tune for strings à la Massenet.

The music has a breezy and syncopated style. The ballet is provided by the rhythms of a soft-shoe shuffle. The *'Danse Grecque'* turns out to be a 'Java' in disguise. Always at hand is a chrous of models who pose for Monsieur Phi-Phi's statues — though they get none of the glory since one of them models the back of Diana, another the arms of the Venus de Milo, while a third remarks:

> *Moi, je le dis avec fierté,*
> *Oui pour le postérieur je pose —*
> *Et je suis fièr' que cette chose*
> *Passe à la posterité.*

The composer was a Swiss, Henri Christiné, who, a schoolmaster by profession, fell in love with a café-concert singer and moved to Nice where he started writing songs for music-hall stars. One of his big hits was *'Viens poupoule'* which, readers of Proust may remember, the ambiguous 'Charlie Morel' was to sing in *À la recherche*. *Phi-Phi* started Christiné on a successful stage career. He followed it with many other musical comedies including *Dédé* which gave Maurice Chevalier his big chance. He also wrote the famous song *'La Petite Tonkinoise'* for Harry Fragson.

Born in Belgium and raised in England by his brewer father, one Mr Pot, Fragson quickly changed his name and became a well-known Anglo-French entertainer at the piano. Madame Christiné, by now rather plump and saddened at her husband's infidelities, fell in love with Harry. Mr Pot senior, insane and alcoholic as well, suddenly reappeared and murdered his son. Madame Christiné, deserted by her husband for a twenty-year-old girl, saw that her last chance of happiness was gone and committed suicide. Years later, in 1941, it was Chrstiné's turn to die of sorrow: the woman for whose sake he broke up his marriage had left him.

Phi-Phi was borne to success on the wave of enthusiasm for dancing that swept through Paris during the nineteen-twenties. Establishments known as *'dancings'* sprang up everywhere. Here brilliantined young men and shingled young women traced the steps of the Shimmy, the Charleston, the Boston and the Java to the ceaseless moan of *'un jazz-band'*, refreshing themselves in between with *'un cocktail'* or *'un Bosom caresser'*. Hispano-Suizas and lordly Bugattis flashed along the roads to such newly modish resorts as Deauville.

Amid all this frenzy, hectic and chromium-plated, the last operettas of Messager and Hahn symbolized the golden sunset of a genre that had prospered for some ninety years and was now about to pass away. One composer alone, the prolific Claude Terrasse, kept up something of the old tradition. He was tall, heavily bearded and very thin. As a student at the Ecole Niedermeyer he liked to play on the organ quadrilles improvised from themes by Bach.

Terrasse wrote over twenty operettas. *Les Travaux d'Hercule* was a faint echo of *La Belle Hélène* and represented the labours of a Hercules confined to the boudoir. *Le Sire de Vergy*, making use of traditional songs, took its plot from the old medieval tale of the knight who murdered his wife's lover, cut out the heart, and served it up, cooked, on a dish. The grimness of the anecdote was entirely dissipated by facetious talk about chastity belts and by a cowardly lover called Le Sire de Coucy, (*couci-couça*, meaning 'so-so'). *Chonchette* contained a delightful whistling song and the expertise of Max Dearly as a broken-down old actor trying to seduce the daughter of a washerwoman. For the *'Valse du beau linge'* he contrived a number wherein, after pirouetting through laundry hung out to dry, he seized from the line a voluminous nightshirt, invited it to dance, and whirled it around with him as his partner in a vigorous waltz.

The American invasion began modestly in 1903 with *La Belle de New York* and reached full force in the nineteen-twenties. *No No Nanette*, *Mississippi* (*Showboat*) and *Rose-Marie* dominated theatre posters. Viennese operetta gained strength. *La Veuve joyeuse*, otherwise *The Merry Widow*, spawned imitations and, the final compliment, as many parodies. There were an *Un-Merry*

Widow, a *Silky Widow*, a *Chilly Widow*, a *Merry Widower*, and even, to vary the tone, a *Merry Virgin*.

Publishers' catalogues teemed with paso dobles, tangoes and fox-trots. *'Hallelujah. Ce fox est la folie de New York,'* announced one of them. 'Yet another success from America!' jubilated its rival. *'4 Shimmies Américains en vogue,'* promised a third. The new number, 'Shimmy Doll', was enticingly described as a *'Shimmy très entraînant'*. One's curiosity at finding the title 'Kama Sutra' is disappointed on reading further that it is only *'Un Fox-Trot très mélodieux'*.

A few composers remained faithful to the old-style operetta. Charles Cuvillier, who wrote a dozen or so stage works, had little success in his native country and only found recognition in Germany and England with *The Lilac Domino*. Georges van Parys, often in collaboration with Philippe Parès, rejuvenated old formulas, often with charming effect.

For the most part, though, 'musical comedy' reigned. The theme of naked women was popular, as in *L'école des femmes nues*, *Au pays des femmes nues*, *Réséda veut poser nue*, and in the abrupt command *Déshabillez-vous!* A master of this sub-cult was Raoul Moretti, whose *Trois jeunes filles nues* ran for a long time and included the young Jean Sablon in a minor rôle. Moretti was an adept at utilizing jazz rhythms and a virtuoso of the one-step and the 'slow-fox'. The level of wit in *Trois jeunes filles nues* — or rather the absence of it — is shown by the scene where Lotte climbs up a tree to pick cherries. The postman, the errand-boy and the gardener arrive. She calls down to them. On looking up they perceive she has forgotten to put on her knickers:

> *Mais saperlotte*
> *Cett' petit' Lotte*
> *N'a pas mis son pantalon.*

Knickers, garters and appendix scars are favourite topics throughout. The finale of Act II features *'Les Girls'*, who sing: 'San Francisco, New York And Chicago Becaus' *Y* lov' you Very well thank you you magic city *vingt cinq* ball's fifty New York And Santiago New York Colorado Whisky and cocktail Tell me Daily Mail . . . .'

The works of Maurice Yvain are not quite so terrible as Moretti's. He played in Monte Carlo night clubs and wrote songs for Maurice Chevalier and Mistinguett. His *Ta Bouche* made a

virtue of necessity by using the small orchestra and limited settings
which post-war economies demanded. He was able to absorb trans-
atlantic rhythms and, to a certain extent, gallicize them. 'Mouth'
being a novel change of key-word from 'naked', he followed up *Ta
Bouche* with *Pas sur la bouche* and *Bouche à bouche*. *Là-Haut*
gave Maurice Chevalier a sung fox-trot which continued the
propaganda campaign started by Offenbach in *La Vie Parisienne*:
'*Le premier, le seul, le vrai Paradis c'est Paris!*'

Joseph Szulc (be not afraid: his name is pronounced 'Schultz')
brought a Viennese strain to the Franco-American mish-mash.
Szulc's father had been conductor at the Warsaw Opera house and
had celebrated his silver wedding by playing, with the aid of his
half-dozen sons, Beethoven's *Septet*. Joseph came to Paris and wrote
the monosyllabic *Flup* which had a popular tango. The ageless and
versatile Jean Périer, who had been Debussy's Pelléas, appeared in
his *Quand on est trois* which the composer himself accompanied in
a tiny theatre at an even tinier piano. *Sidonie-Pacha* featured a
genuine cavalry charge with Spahis galloping on horses right up to
the footlights. Better still, *Le Coffre-fort vivant* showed a cruiser
leaving harbour and parachutists floating down onto the stage.

This line in spectacular showmanship was developed by
Francis Lopez, often in that huge Théâtre du Châtelet, a combination of Drury Lane and the Palladium, where Szulc had paraded
his show-stoppers. Lopez, in his youth, wanted to take up a career
more profitable than composition. He discovered a knack for
writing songs and was persuaded to compose a full-length work. *La
Belle de Cadiz* was an instant success and enjoyed fifteen hundred
performances. It opened the way for a series of entertainments,
gaudily dressed and flashily mounted, which starred Louis
Mariano and Tino Rossi, the latter florid and substantial of
waistline but adored by ladies of a certain age who crowded the
Saturday-night audiences on their trips up from the provinces.

By the end of the twenties and into the thirties titles had
grown wilder and wilder. *Minnie Moustache* was answered with
Yes. The Little Zap vied with *Knock-Out*. *You-You* and *Baby
paper* were succeeded by *Les Bootleggers*, *Mam'zelle Boy-Scout*
and *Billy-Bill*. With some relief one sees *White Horse Inn* emerging
from *L'Auberge du Cheval Blanc* and *Le Chant du désert* from
The Desert Song. The essence of all these works has been cleverly
distilled once and for all in the piece by Sandy Wilson that is known in
France, quite simply and without the definite article, as *Boy-Friend*.

One last musician from those giddy years should be mentioned. He was a Turk, Paul Misraki of Istanbul, who studied music in Paris under the famous teacher and composer Charles Koechlin. (The venerable Koechlin himself had written a *Seven Stars Symphony* as a tribute to Douglas Fairbanks, Greta Garbo and others, as well as *Danses pour Ginger* in praise of Ginger Rogers.) Misraki played in Ray Ventura's orchestra and wrote theatre works and film music. None of these will be remembered so vividly as a song he composed in 1936 which has come to epitomise the mood of France immediately before the war of 1939 — calm, careless, and sublimely indifferent to the ominous events that were building up. A marquise away from home telephones her butler James to find out how things are in her absence. Everything's quite all right, he replies imperturbably, except for a small trifle: one of her horses has just died. How? In a fire that burned down the stable, comes his bland reply, though apart from that everything's fine. Except, of course, that the fire has also destroyed the ancestral home. But how, James, did the fire begin? Well, the marquis, learning that he'd been ruined, committed suicide and overturned the candles that set fire to the mansion which burned the stable and killed the horse. But apart from these small incidents, '*Tout va très bien, Madame la Marquise.*' More than *Aux Bouffes on pouffe*, more than *Ta femme nous trompe*, those few verses capture the whole mood of an epoch.

In the nineteenth century, as we have seen, composers of more ambitious works often dallied with operetta. Saint-Saëns, Chabrier and Delibes all tried their hand at it. Our own period has been no different. Ravel composed *L'Heure espagnole* which, though technically an operetta, has a genius that transcends the form and is really outside the scope of this book. The more humble Gabriel Pierné committed a *Fragonard*. Like his heavier music, it is today ignored in favour of the bustling little piece called 'The entry of the fauns'. Henri Sauguet, prolific and whimsical, is no stranger to operetta. The surprising thing is that even the austere Albert Roussel has composed one.

The numbers of 'Les Six' could naturally be expected to involve themselves with operetta. This group of young composers in the nineteen-twenties had Jean Cocteau as theorist and Erik Satie as mentor. Since one of their aims was to de-mystify music, to bring it down into the streets, operetta was bound to attract them. Erik Sate had written a *Coco Chéri* which appeared briefly at Monte

Carlo in 1913. The eccentric hermit sometimes quoted in his piano pieces a snatch here and there from pop songs and operettas. More straightforwardly, his protégés, Darius Milhaud, Georges Auric and Germaine Tailleferre produced works for the stage that belonged to the medium. One of the most successful of their colleagues was Arthur Honegger. No one ever became rich through writing symphonies, and when the librettist Albert Willemetz invited Honegger to set a version of Pierre Louÿs's rather daring novel *Les aventures du roi Pausole*, the composer, for reasons that did not exclude money, fell in with the idea.

To the surprise of many *Les aventures du roi Pausole* entertained large audiences at the Bouffes-Parisiens toward the end of 1930. Simone Simon, Suzy Delair and Edwige Feuillère were among the beauties who surrounded the amorous King Pausole. The music was simple, direct, and showed an excellent grasp of the idiom with a touch of Massenet. The master of the oratorio and the symphonic poem could write in a lighter style without sacrificing any of his artistic ideals. The chorus *'Vive le roi Pausole'* was in effect a miniature cantata. A septet which featured the 'seven differing counsels' was ingenious and fluent, while the *'Air de la Blanche Aline'* had a silvery innocence. The king made his *'Sortie américaine'* to a blues rhythm. *Le roi Pausole*, though it contained no catchy tune for the audience to hum the morning after, has since been revived with happy results.

In 1937 Honegger took the same path with Jacques Ibert as his collaborator on *Les petites Cardinal*, an adaptation of Ludovic Halévy's witty novel about a dancer at the Opéra and her ambitious mother. Embellished with amiable parodies of Gounod and Rossini, the operetta proved a little too difficult for a cast not very well up in the techniques of modern music.

It was, however, Francis Poulenc, Honegger's fellow-member of 'Les Six', who wrote the operetta to end all operettas. Poulenc's music is an inimitable mixture of buffoonery and deep feeling. He will change at a moment's notice from clown to melancholy pierrot. And then, a split second after the mood has established itself, he will turn again to farce. Playboy, mystic, spoilt child, he is all these things singly and together. He had loved French operetta since boyhood, revelled in Offenbach, Lecocq and Messager, and prized the very idiocies of the *genre*. In *Les Mamelles de Tirésias* he wrote a valedictory piece that laughs at the convention with the tenderness of one who is really in love with it. The Opéra-Comique production in 1947 had decor and costumes by Erté, the suave magician of high camp.

'We see too few pregnant women about nowadays,' remarked the poet Guillaume Apollinaire at the opening of a tongue-in-cheek magazine article. Later, when he wrote the two-act 'surrealist' joke he called *Les Mamelles de Tirésias* (or 'The tits of Tirésias'), he amplified the idea into a boisterous farrago that took part of its title from the man-woman Tiresias of Greek legend. The other reference is to a gag Apollinaire had always wanted to exploit. How amusing it would be, he thought, if a woman on stage suddenly opened her blouse and released two large bosoms that floated heavenwards. His recipe for sublime nonsense also included a husband who stays at home and gives birth to forty thousand children a day.

In Poulenc's version all the little flounces and mannerisms of operetta are affectionately guyed. The heroine's twin charms take flight to the rhythm of a sonorous waltz. The comic characters Lacouf and Presto dance a polka that sums up all the polkas Offenbach and Métra ever wrote. Quick shreds of café-concert tunes and Twenties musical comedy are mingled with reminiscences of Chabrier and Lecocq. Once Poulenc even incorporates a whole phrase out of Messager's *La Basoche*. Yet he always, through some mysterious alchemy, fuses these elements into something personal, something that is instantly unique and recognizable.

Behind *Les Mamelles de Tirésias* you may discern the shade of the *Grand Duchess of Gérolstein*. Somewhere in the shadow lurks General Boom. The ghosts of La Périchole and of Véronique and, yes, of Ciboulette flit dimly by. For in this tribute to a dear dead genre the admiring Poulence, child-like but sophisticated, had written its epitaph and created its apotheosis.

Select Bibliography

Bruyas, Florian. *L'Histoire de l'opérette en France, 1855-1965*, (Emmanuel Vitte, Lyon, 1974)

Bruyr, José. *L'opérette* (Presses Universitaires de France, 1962)

Cucuel, Georges. *Les créateurs de l'opéra-comique français*, (Félix Alcan, 1914).

Drinkrow, John. *The Vintage Operetta Book* (Osprey, 1972)

Dussane, Béatrix. *Dieux des planches* (Flammarion, 1964)

Gheusi, P-B. *Cinquante ans de Paris* (Plon, 1939)

Harding, James. *Sacha Guitry, The Last Boulevardier* (Methuen, 1968)

— —, *The Ox on the Roof* (Macdonald, 1972)

Histoire du théâtre lyrique en France, 3 vols Poste National Radio-Paris (1937-1939)

Hughes, Gervase. *Composers of Operetta* (Macmillan, 1962)

Jacques-Charles. *Caf' Conc'* (Flammarion, 1966)

Lubbock, Mark, and Ewen, David. *Light Opera* (Putnam, 1963)

Maréchal, Henri. *Paris; Souvenirs d'un musicien.* (Hachette, 1907)

Pougin, Arthur. *Figures d'opéra-comique* (Tresse, 1875)

Rohinzinski, L. (Ed). *Cinquante ans de musique française de 1874 à 1925*, vol 1 (Editions musicales de la Librairie de France, 1925)

Soubies, Albert, and Malherbe, Charles. *Histoire de l'Opéra-Comique. La Seconde Salle Favart, 1840-1860* (Harpon/Flammarion, 1892)

Willemetz, Albert. *Dans mon rétroviseur* (La Table Ronde, 1967)

Wolff, Stéphane. *Un demi-siècle d'Opéra-Comique* (1900-1950) (André Bonne, 1953)

Wolff, Stéphane. *L'Opéra au Palais Garnier (1875-1962)* (L'Entr'acte, 1962)

Individual Composers:

ADAM, ADOLPHE

Adam, Adolphe, *Souvenirs d'un musicien* (Michel Lévy, 1857)

— —. *Derniers souvenirs d'un musicien* (Michel Lévy, 1859)

Halévy, F. *Souvenirs et portraits* (Michel Lévy, 1861)

Pougin, Arthur, *Adolphe Adam* (Charpentier, 1877)

HAHN, REYNALDO

Gavoty, Bernard, *Reynaldo Hahn, le musicien de la Belle Epoque* (Buchet/Chastel, 1976)

Hahn, Reynaldo, *Notes. (Journal d'un musicien)* (Plon, 1933)

— —. *L'oreille au guet* (Gallimard, 1937)

— —. *Thèmes variés* (J. B. Janin, 1946)

— —. *Du chant* (Gallimard, 1920/1957)

Proust, Marcel (Ed. P. Kolb). *Lettres à Reynaldo Hahn*, (Gallimard, 1956)

HERVÉ

Schneider, Louis. *Les Maîtres de l'Opérette française, Hervé, Charles Lecocq* (Librairie Académique Perrin, 1924)

LECOCQ, CHARLES

Musica, 'Lecocq', Numéro spécial, No 119 (August, 1918)

Schneider, Louis. *Les Maîtres de l'Opérette française, Hervé, Charles Lecocq* (Librairie Académique Perrin, 1924)

MESSAGER, ANDRÉ

Augé-Laribé, Michel, *Messager — musicien de théâtre* (La Colombe, 1951)

Boschot, Adolphe, *Portraits de musiciens*, vol 1 (Plon, 1947)

Busser, Henri. *De Pelléas aux Indes Galantes* (Arthème Fayard, 1955)

Février, Henri, *André Messager, mon maître, mon ami* (Amiot-Dumont, 1948)

Lalo, Pierre, *De Rameau à Ravel* (Albin Michel, 1947)

Musica, 'Messager', Numéro spécial, No. 72, September, 1908

Samazeuilh, Gustave. *Musiciens de mon temps* (Renaissance du Livre, 1947)

OFFENBACH, JACQUES

Adam, Adolphe. *Souvenirs d'un musicien* (Michel Lévy, 1857)

Bekker, Paul. *Offenbach* (Verlag von Marquardt & Co, 1909)

Brancour, René. *Offenbach* (Félix Alcan, 1929)

Brindejont-Offenbach, Jacques. *Offenbach mon grand-père* Plon, 1940)

Decaux, Alain. *Offenbach* (Pierre Amiot, 1958)

Henseler, Anton. *Jakob Offenbach* (Max Hesses Verlag, 1930)

Kracauer, S. *Offenbach and the Paris of His Time* (Constable, 1937)

Kristeller, Hans. *Jakob Offenbach* (Adalbert Schutz Verlag, 1931)

Lyon, Raymond, and Saguer, Louis. *Les Contes d'Hoffman* (Mellottée, 1948)

Offenbach, Jacques, *Histoire d'une valse*, (No publisher mentioned, c 1872)

— —. Preface to: *Les soirées parisiennes par un monsieur de l'orchestre* (Arnold Mortier, Dentu, 1875)

— —. *Offenbach en Amérique. Notes d'un musicien en voyage* (Paris, 1877)

Rouff, Marcel, and Casewitz, Thérèse. *Hortense Schneider*, (Tallandier, 1931)

Schneider, Louis. *Offenbach* (Librairie Académique Perrin, 1923)

Sitwell, Sir Sacheverell. *La Vie Parisienne* (Faber and Faber, 1937)

Zola, Emile. *Nana* (Charpentier, 1880)

INDEX

Adam, Adolphe Charles, composer, 1803-
1856, 9, 11-14, 15-17, 18, 20, 22, 23,
25, 43, 101-2, 137-138
   Le Brasseur de Preston, 22
   Le Chalet, 13-14
   The Dark Diamond, 12
   Faust, 12
   The First Campaign, 12
   Giselle, 12, 17, 138
   Les Pantins de Violette, 17, 18
   Le Postillon de Longjumeau, 14
   Richard en Palestine, 17
   Si j'étais roi, 14
   Le Toréador, 14, 17, 18
Aimée, Marie, singer, 71
d'Antigny, Blanche, grande horizontale,
32, 33
Apollinaire, Guillaume, (Wilhelm Apolli-
naris de Kostrowitsky), poet, 1880-
1918, 173
   Les Mamelles de Tirésias, 173
Arletty (Léonie Bathiat), actress, b 1898,
161-162
Auber, Daniel François Esprit, composer,
1782-1871, 9, 18, 19, 20, 21, 29, 79
   L'Erreur d'un moment, 18
Aubernon, Madame, hostess, 154
Audran, Edmond, composer, 1842-1901,
106-109, 166
   La Cigale et la Fourmi, 108, 109
   Le Grand Mogol, 107
   Miss Helyett, 108-109
   La Mascotte, 82, 107-108, 109
   Monsieur Lohengrin, 108
   Les Noces d'Olivette, 107, 109
   La Poupée, 109
   La Reine des Reines, 108
Auric, Georges, composer, b 1899, 143,
172

Bache, comedian, 50-51
Bacquero, Lino, fixer, 72

Barlow, Fred, composer, b 1881, 9
Baron, actor, 93
Beaumarchais, Pierre Augustin Caron
de, dramatist, 1732-1799, 142
   Le Mariage de Figaro, 142
Berlioz, Louis Hector, composer, 1803-
1869, 32, 77
   Les Troyens à Carthage, 32
Berners, Lord, composer, 1883-1950, 65
   Le Carrosse du Saint Sacrement, 65
Bernicat, Firmin, composer, 1843-1883,
121
   François les Bas-Bleus (with Messa-
ger), 121, 124
Beydts, Louis, composer, 1896-1953, 9
Bismarck, Prince Otto von, politician,
1815-1898, 34, 63, 67
Bizet, Georges (Alexandre César Léo-
pold), composer, 1838-1875, 17, 19,
35, 48, 79, 80, 119
   Carmen, 17, 119, 136
   Le Docteur Miracle, 48, 80
Boieldieu, François Adrien, composer,
1775-1834, 13, 20, 29
   La Dame Blanche, 13
Bouffar, Zulma, singer, 56-57, 61, 65,
68, 69, 88, 91, 92
Bovery, Jules, (Bovy), composer, 1808-
1868, 23
   Madame Mascarille, 23
Busnach, William, impresario and
librettist, 1832-1906, 81

Capus, Alfred, dramatist, 1858-1922, 142
   La Petite Fonctionnaire, 142
Carré, Albert, administrator and librettist,
127, 135
Carré, Michel, librettist, b 1865, 21
Chabrier, Alexis Emmanuel, composer,
1841-1894, 10, 90-91, 98-101, 128,
142, 171, 173
   Cocodette et Cocorico, 101

Une Education manquée, 100-101
España, 99
L'Etoile, 100
Fisch-ton-Kan, 100
Monsieur et Madame Orchestre, 101
"Quadrille" *(Tristan und Isolde)*, 99
Le Scalp!!!, 99
Vaucochard et fils 1er, 100
Cham, (Amédée de Noé), caricaturist, 1819-1879, 81
"Chant du départ" (Méhul), 74
Cherubini, Luigi, composer, 1760-1842, 39, 79
Chevalier, Maurice, singer, 1888-1973, 143, 167, 169, 170
Chivot, Henry, librettist, 82
Christiné, Henri Marius, 1867-1941, 167, 168
　　Dédé, 167
　　"La Petite Tonkinoise", 167
　　Phi-Phi, 166-167, 168
　　"Viens, poupoule", 167
Clapisson, Antoine Louis, composer, 1808-1866, 19-20, 119
　　La Fanchonnette, 19, 20
　　Gibby la Cornemuse, 19, 20
　　Le Pendu, 19
Clouet, Edith, (the first Mme Messager), 124, 129
Cocteau, Jean Maurice, poet, 1889-1963, 11, 90, 154, 158, 171
Crémieux, Hector, librettist, 50
Cuvillier, Charles, composer, 1877-1955, 169
　　The Lilac Domino, 169

Darty, Paulette, singer, d 1940, 108
Daudet, Alphonse, writer, 1840-1897, 154
Daudet, Léon, writer, 1868-1942, 155
Daudet, Lucien, dandy, 1879-1946, 155
Dearly, Max, actor, 1874-1942, 112-113, 168
Debussy, Claude-Achille, composer, 1862-1918, 95, 97, 100, 119, 126, 135, 141, 142, 156
　　Pelléas et Mélisande, 17, 135-136, 138, 141
　　Prélude à l'après-midi d'un faune, 158
Delair, Suzy (Suzanne Delaire), actress, b 1917, 172

Delibes, Léo (Clément Philibert), composer, 1836-1891, 53, 74, 101-104, 158, 171
　　Coppélia, 74, 101
　　La Cour du Roi Pétaud, 103
　　Deux Sous de charbon, 102
　　Les Deux Vieilles Gardes, 103
　　Les Eaux d'Ems, 103
　　Lakmé, 101, 158
　　L'Omelette à la Follembouche, 103
　　Le Roi l'a dit, 101
　　Six demoiselles à marier, 103
　　La Source, 103
　　Sylvia, 101
Dennery, Adolphe, dramatist, 1811-1899, 14-15
Diaghilev, Serge Pavlovitch de, impresario, 1872-1929, 101, 158
Donizetti, Gaetano, composer, 1797-1848, 29, 74, 100
　　La Fille du régiment, 74
Duparc, Marie Eugène Henri Fouques, composer, 1848-1933, 123
Duru, librettist, 82

Erté, artist and designer, 173
Eugénie, Empress, 1826-1920, 37, 48

Fauré, Gabriel Urbain, composer, 1845-1924, 95, 97, 122, 123, 124, 128, 147
Feuillère, Edwige (Caroline Cunati), actress, b 1907, 172
Flers, Robert de, dramatist, 1872-1927, 159, 160
Fragson, Harry, entertainer, (Victor Léon Philippe Pot), 1869-1913, 167-168
Franck, César Auguste Jean Guillaume Hubert, composer, 1822-1890, 128
　　Les Béatitudes, 128

Ganne, Louis, composer, 1862-1923, 113-114, 115, 127
　　Les Saltimbanques, 113-114
Gilbert, Sir William Schwenck, writer, 1836-1911, 66
　　The Pirates of Penzance, 66
Gounod, Charles François, composer, 1818-1893, 20, 21, 33, 35, 48, 75, 80, 88, 98, 106, 107, 128, 130, 155, 156, 165, 172
　　Faust, 21, 88, 98, 106, 136

Le Médecin malgré lui, 107
Mireille, 21
Granier, Jeanne, actress and singer, 87, 88, 89, 90, 93
Guiraud, Ernest, composer, 1837-1892, 76, 119
Gretna Green, 119
Madame Turlupin, 119
Guitry, Sacha, dramatist and actor, 1885-1957, 90, 113, 144-148, 154, 161, 165
L'Amour masqué, 146-147
Deburau, 147-148, 161
Mozart, 161-162
O mon bel inconnu, 161-162
Le Roman d'un tricheur, 165

Hading, Jane, singer, 93, 107
Hahn, Reynaldo, composer, 1875-1947, 9, 125, 136, 152-165, 168
Le Bal de Béatrice d'Este, 157, 164
Brummell, 162, 163
La Carmélite, 157
"Chansons grises", 155
Ciboulette, 159-160, 163, 164, 173
Le Dieu Bleu, 158
La Fête chez Thérèse, 157
L'Ile du rêve, 157, 164
Malvina, 162
Le Marchand de Venise, 158, 162
Miousic, 159
Mozart, 161
Nausicaa, 158, 162
O mon bel inconnu, 161-162
Le Oui des jeunes filles, 165
Portraits de peintres, 156
Une Revue, 162
"Si mes vers avaient des ailes", 155
Le Temps d'aimer, 162
Halévy, Jacques Fromental, composer, 1799-1862, 9, 18-19, 20, 21, 40, 45, 48, 79, 80
L'Eclair, 19
La Juive, 19, 40
Halévy, Ludovic, writer, 1834-1908, 18, 45, 46, 47, 50, 55, 57, 58, 60, 62, 64, 65, 66, 71-72, 73, 88, 93
Hérold, Louis Joseph Ferdinand, composer, 1791-1833, 20
Hervé (Florimond Ronger), composer, 1825-1892, 9, 22-36, 38, 44, 48, 73, 94, 102, 106, 110

Agamemnon, 28
Aladdin the Second, 34
The Ashantee War, 34
Chilpéric, 31-32, 38
Don Quichotte et Sancho Pança, 22, 23, 25, 44
Fla-Fla, 35
Les Folies Dramatiques, 26-27
Mam'zelle Nitouche, 25, 35
L'Oeil crevé, 31
L'Ours et le Pacha, 24
Le Petit Faust, 32-33
Roméo et Mariette, 32
Le Trône d'Ecosse, 34
Les Troyens en Champagne, 32
Hoffmann, E T A, writer and composer, 1776-1822, 74
Honegger, Arthur, composer, 1892-1955, 10, 143, 172
Les Aventures du Roi Pausole, 172
Les Petites Cardinal, 172
Humbert, impresario, 83, 84

Jonas, Emile, composer, 1827-1905, 119
La Poularde de Caux, (with Clapisson), 119
Judic, Anna, (Anna Maria Louise Damiens), 1849-1911, 35, 68-69, 70, 72, 118-119

Koechlin, Charles, composer, 1867-1950, 171
Danses pour Ginger, 171
Seven Stars Symphony, 171
Kosma, Joseph, composer, 1905-1969, 9

La Fontaine, Jean de, poet, 1621-1695, 73, 95, 124
Lacôme d'Estaleux, Paul, composer, 1838-1920, 117-118
Jeanne, Jeannette et Jeanneton, 118
Ma Mie Rosette, 118
Mademoiselle Asmodée (with V. Roger), 117
Lecocq, Alexandre Charles, composer, 1832-1918, 9, 36, 71, 73, 78-96, 97, 100, 101, 103, 106, 107, 108, 109, 116, 125, 130, 159, 160, 172, 173
L'Amour et son carquois, 81-82
La Camargo, 92
Les Cent Vierges, 83-84

179

Le Coeur et la main, 94
Le Docteur Miracle, 48, 80
La Fille de Madame Angot, 71, 84-86, 87, 88, 95, 96, 106, 159
Fleur de Thé, 71, 82, 83, 95, 130
Giroflé-Girofla, 86-87, 94, 95, 100, 106
Le Grand Casimir, 93
Janot, 93-94
La Jolie Persane, 93
Le Jour et la nuit, 94
Kosiki, 88
La Marjolaine, 88
Miousic, 159
Le Myosotis, 81
Ondines au champagne, 80
Le petit Duc, 73, 88-89, 90, 92, 95, 106
La Petite Mademoiselle, 93, 95
Pompon, 88
La princesse des Canaries, 94
Roussotte, 94
Léonce, comedian, 81, 82, 103
Livry, Emma, dancer, 1842-1863, 54
Lopez, Francis (Francisco), composer, b 1916, 170
La Belle de Cadiz, 170
Loti, Pierre (Julien Viaud), novelist, 1850-1923, 129, 157
L'Ile du reve, 157
Madame Chrysanthème, 129-130
Louis-Napoléon, Emperor, (Napoléon III), 1808-1873, 16, 26, 27, 34, 37, 43, 50, 51, 55, 62, 63, 67, 68, 152
Louis-Philippe, king, 1773-1850, 11, 16, 43, 49
Louÿs, Pierre, novelist, 1870-1925, 172
Les Aventures du Roi Pausole, 172
Lully, Jean-Baptiste, composer, 1633-1687, 89

Madrazo, Coco de, (Frédéric), 158
Maeterlinck, Maurice, poet, 1862-1949, 135
Pelléas et Mélisande, 135
Maillart, Aimé, composer, 1817-1881, 15
Les Dragons de Villars, 15-16
Mallarme, Stéphane, poet, 1842-1898, 156
Malraux, André, writer, 1901-1976, 137, 138

Mariotte, Antoine, composer, 1875-1944, 120
Gargantua, 120
Salomé, 120
Massé, Victor (Félix Marie), composer, 1822-1884, 21-22, 102
Galathée, 21-22
Les Noces de Jeannette, 21
La Reine Topaze, 102
Massenet, Jules Emile Frédéric, composer, 1842-1912, 35, 105, 119, 136, 152-153, 154, 155, 156, 157, 165, 167, 172
Le Jongleur de Notre Dame, 136
Manon, 152, 167
Mathilde, Princess, hostess, 1820-1904, 152, 154
Meilhac, Henri, writer, 1835-1897, 35, 45, 57, 59, 60, 62, 65, 66, 71, 73, 8, 93
Mendès, Catulle, writer, 1841-1909, 125, 157
Mérimée, Prosper, writer, 1803-1870, 65
Le Carrosse du Saint-Sacrement 65
Mérode, Cléo de, grande horizontale, 153, 155
Messager, André Charles Prosper, composer, 1853-1929, 9, 10, 36, 95, 97-98, 106, 121-150, 157, 159, 160-161, 168, 172, 173
Amants éternels, 130
L'Amour masqué, 146-147
Une Aventure de la Guimard, 140
La Basoche, 127-128, 130, 144, 173
La Béarnaise, 124, 130
Le Chevalier d'Harmental, 131, 132
Coups de roulis, 144, 118
Cyprien, ôte ta main d'là, 141
Deburau, 147-148, 149, 161
Les Deux Pigeons, 124, 136
Les Dragons de l'Impératrice, 95, 140
La Fauvette du Temple, 124
Fortunio, 140, 150
François les bas-bleus, 124
Isoline, 125
Madame Chrysanthème, 98, 129-130, 131
Mirette, 130, 136
Miss Dollar, 130
Monsieur Beaucaire, 140-141
Passionnément, 143

La Petite Fonctionnaire, 142
Les P'tites Michu, 132-133
Véronique, 133-134, 140, 173
Messager, Madame — see (i) Clouet, Edith, (ii) Temple, Hope,
Meyerbeer, Giacomo, (Jakob Liebmann Beer), composer, 1791-1864, 20, 47, 64, 101, 102, 104
L'Africaine, 104
Les Huguenots, 47, 64
Le Prophète, 101
Milhaud, Darius, composer, 1892-1974, 101, 103, 172
Miolan-Carvalho, Marie Caroline Félix, singer, 1827-1895, 21, 98
Misraki, Paul, composer, b 1908, 171
"Tout va très bien, Madame la Marquise," 171
Missa, Edmond, composer, 1861-1910, 119
Dinorah, 119
Muguette, 119
Mistinguett, (Jeanne Bourgeoise), singer, 1873-1956, 113, 143, 169
Moinaux, Jules, writer, b 1815, ·102
Moretti, Raoul, composer, 1893-1954, 169
Trois jeunes filles nues, 169
Morny, duc de, politician, 1811-1865, 26, 27, 44, 47, 55
Mozart, Wolfgang Amadeus, composer, 1756-1791, 10, 14, 47, 74, 76, 136, 141, 142, 156, 161
Cosi fan tutte, 141
Don Giovanni, 136, 141
Figaro, 161
The Impresario, 47
"Paris" Symphony, 161
Les Petits Riens, 161
Musset, Alfred de, poet, 1810-1857, 54, 140
Le Chandelier, 54, 140

Nadar, (Félix Tournachon), photographer, 1820-1910, 53
Niedermeyer, Louis, composer and teacher, 1802-1861, 106, 108
Nijinsky, Vaslav Fomitch, dancer, 1890-1950, 158

Offenbach, Auguste Jacques (son), 1862-1883, 55-56, 76
Offenbach, Berthe (Madame Charles Comte), 1845-1927, 60
Offenbach, Herminie (wife, née de Alcain), 1826-1887, 41-42, 52, 53, 54, 55, 66, 76
Offenbach, Isaac (father,) 1779-1850, 38-39, 40
Offenbach, Jacques (Jakob), composer, 1819-1880, 9, 10, 13, 16-17, 35, 36, 38-77, 79, 80, 81, 82, 85, 87, 88, 90, 93, 95, 96, 97, 100, 102-103, 106, 110, 111, 114, 115, 116, 118, 119, 121, 134, 144, 151, 152, 157, 166, 169, 172, 173
L'Alcôve, 16, 43
Ba-Ta-Clan, 47
Barbe-Bleue, 60-61
Les Bavards, 56, 67, 82
La Belle Hélène, 57-58, 59-60, 62, 67, 73, 74, 76, 88
Les Bergers, 60
La Boulangère a des écus, 71, 72
Les Braconniers, 69
Les Brigands, 66, 93
La Chanson de Fortunio, 54-55, 140
Le Château à Toto, 65
Monsieur Choufleury, 55
Les Contes d'Hoffmann, 74-75, 76, 97, 119
La Créole, 72
Croquefer, 49
Les Deux Aveugles, 45, 46
La Diva, 65
La Fille du Tambour-Major, 73-74, 82
La Foire Saint-Laurent, 111
La Grande Duchesse de Gérolstein, 62-63, 64, 70, 73, 74, 76, 89, 103, 173
La Jolie Parfumeuse, 70, 87
Lischen et Fritzschen, 56
Madame l'Archiduc, 70
Madame Favart, 73
Maître Péronille, 73
Orphée aux enfers, 16, 49-50, 51, 54, 55, 57, 59, 60, 62, 66, 70, 71, 73, 76, 80
Oyayaye, 38, 44
Papillon, 54
La Périchole, 65, 76, 173

Pomme d'Api, 70
Robinson Crusoe, 64
Le Roi Carotte, 68, 69
La Romance de la Rose, 67
La Vie Parisienne, 61-62, 76, 95, 166, 179
Offenbach, Jules (brother), 1815-1880, 39, 40

Perier, Jean, singer, b 1869, 160, 170
Pessard, Emile (Louis Fortuné), composer, 1843-1917, 119-120
    L'Armée des vierges, 120
    Le Capitaine Fracasse, 120
    L'Epave, 120
Pierné, Gabriel (Henri Constant), composer, 1863-1937, 171
    Fragonard, 171
Planquette, Robert, composer, 1848-1903, 110-112, 127, 166
    Les Cloches de Corneville, 110-111
    Le Paradis de Mahomet, 112, 113
    Rip van Winkle, 111-112
Pougy, Liane de, grande horizontale, 153-154, 155
Poulenc, Francis, composer, 1899-1963, 10, 100, 126, 127, 143, 172-173
    Les Biches, 126
    Les Mamelles de Tirésias, 127, 172-173
Printemps, Yvonne (Wigniolle), actress and singer, 1894-1976, 146-147, 148, 149, 161
Proust, Marcel, writer, 1871-1922, 19, 155-156, 163, 167
    Jean Santeuil, 156
    Portraits de peintres, 156
    A la recherche du temps perdu, 156, 163, 167
Puccini, Giacomo, composer, 1858-1924, 130
    Madame Butterfly, 130
Pugno, Raoul, pianist and composer, 1852-1914, 120-121

Raimu (Jean Auguste César Muraire), actor, 1883-1946, 144
Rameau, Jean Philippe, composer, 1683-1764, 89, 95, 142
    Castor et Pollux, 95
Ravel, Joseph Maurice, composer, 1875-

1937, 126, 155, 162, 171
    L'Enfant et les sortilèges, 162
    L'Heure espagnole, 171
Richepin, Tiarko, composer, b 1884, 9
    Rapatipatoum, 9
Rip, writer, 162-163
Roger, Victor, composer, 1853-1903, 117
    La Dot de Brigitte (with Serpette), 117
    Joséphine vendue par ses soeurs, 117
Rossini, Gioacchino (Antonio), composer, 1792-1868, 20, 42, 43, 47, 48, 172
    Il Signor Bruschino, 47-48
Roussel, Albert, composer, 1869-1937, 124, 171

Sablon, Jean, singer, b 1906, 169
Saint-Saens, Charles Camille, composer, 1835-1921, 10, 17, 79, 90, 91, 97-98, 122-123, 124, 128, 130, 155, 156, 157, 165, 171
    Le Carnaval des animaux, 98
    Gabriella di Vergi, 98
    Les Odeurs de Paris, 98
    La Princesse Jaune, 97, 98, 130
    Phryné, 98
    Sonata for violin and piano in D minor, 156
Sardou, Victorien, dramatist, 1831-1908, 68, 69-70
    La Haine, 69-70
    Le Roi Carotte, 68, 69
Satie, Alfred Erik Leslie, composer, 1866-1925, 101, 108, 114, 119, 171, 172
    Chapitres tournés en tous sens, 112
    Coco chéri, 171-172
    "La Diva de l'Empire", 108
    "Je te veux", 108
    Parade, 114
Sauguet, Henri (Poupard), composer, b 1901, 114, 171
    Les Forains, 114
Schneider, Hortense, singer, 1833-1920, 46-47, 50, 58-59, 61, 63-64, 71, 87
Scotto, Vincent, composer, 1876-1952, 9
    Les Gangsters du Château d'If, 9
Scribe, Eugène, writer, 1791-1861, 13, 16
Serpette, Gaston, composer, 1846-1904, 116-117, 119
    Adam et Eve, 116
    Le Château de Tire-Larigot, 116
    La Demoiselle du Téléphone, 116

Fanfreluche, 116
Jeanne d'Arc, 116
Madame le Diable, 116
Shakespeare, 116
Shaw, George Bernard, dramatist, 1856-1950, 73
Silly, Léa, singer, 58-59
Simon, Michel, actor, 1895-1975, 162-163
Simon, Moïse, composer, 1888-1945, 9
Simon, Simone, actress, b 1911, 162
Strauss, Johann, composer, 1825-1899, 57
Sullivan, Sir Arthur, composer, 1842-1900, 97, 98
HMS Pinafore, 98
The Mikado, 97
The Pirates of Penzance, 66
Szulc, Joseph, composer, b 1875, 170
Le Coffre-fort vivant, 170
Flup, 170
Quand on est trois, 170
Sidonie-Pacha, 170

Taglioni, Marie, dancer, 1808-1884, 54
Tailleferre, Germaine, composer, b 1892, 172
Tautin, Lise, singer, 50
Temple, Hope (Dotie Davies), the second Madame Messager, 1859-1938, 130-131, 140
Terrasse, Claude, composer, 1867-1923, 106, 168
Chonchette, 168
Le Sire de Vergy, 168
Les Travaux d'Hercule, 168
Théo, Louise, singer, 70, 116, 118, 121
Thomas, Charles Louis Ambroise, composer, 1811-1896, 100, 116

Van Parys, Georges, composer, 1902-1971, 169
Varney, Louis, composer, 1844-1908, 9, 55, 114, 115, 116
Les Mousquetaires au couvent, 114, 115
Varney, Pierre (Joseph Alphonse), composer, 1811-1879, 55, 114, 115-116
Vasseur, Léon, composer, 1844-1917, 118-119
La Timbale d'argent, 118
Verlaine, Paul, poet, 1844-1896, 91, 95, 100, 155
Chanson d'automne, 155
Green, 95
L'heure exquise, 155, 162
Verne, Jules, writer, 1828-1905, 14, 72, 73
Around the World in Eighty Days, 14
Villemessant, Jean Hippolyte Auguste Carrier de, editor, 1812-1879, 44, 53

Wagner, Richard, composer, 1813-1883, 58, 72, 99, 122, 125, 128, 141
Parsifal, 139
Das Rheingold, 138
Tannhäuser, 58
Die Walküre, 126
Wales, Prince of, (later King Edward VII), 1841-1910, 32, 63, 157
Willemetz, Albert, writer, 1887-1964, 142-143, 144, 146, 149, 150, 167, 172
"Mon homme", 143
"Valentine", 143
Wilson, Sandy, (Alexander Galbraith), composer, b 1924, 170
Boy Friend, 170

Yvain, Maurice, composer, 1891-1965, 143, 169
Bouche à bouche, 170
Là-haut, 170
Pas sur la bouche, 170
Ta bouche, 169-170